Number One: The Texas A&M University Economics Series

Regulating Competition in Oil

*Government Intervention in the U.S.
Refining Industry, 1948–1975*

Regulating Competition in Oil

Government Intervention in the U.S.
Refining Industry, 1948-1975

by

E. Anthony Copp

Texas A&M University Press

COLLEGE STATION AND LONDON

Copyright © 1976 by E. Anthony Copp
All rights reserved

Library of Congress Cataloging in Publication Data

Copp, Emmanuel Anthony, 1945–
    Regulating Competition in oil.

    (Texas A&M University economics series; no. 1)
    Bibliography: p.
    Includes index.
    1. Petroleum industry and trade—United States. 2.
Petroleum refineries—United States. 3. Energy policy—
United States. 4. Industry and state—United States.
I. Title. II. Series: Texas. A&M University, College
Station. Texas A&M University economics series; no. 1.
HD9566.C68   338.4'7'665530973   76-19795
ISBN 0-89096-014-3

Manufactured in the United States of America
FIRST EDITION

To Linda, Tara, and Aurora

Contents

List of Tables

List of Illustrations

Acknowledgments

THIS work developed from my doctoral dissertation and through my experience while working as senior economist at the American Petroleum Institute and in my current position as manager, Petroleum Group, Salomon Brothers. The opinions expressed in this work are my own and do not in any way represent the position of the API or Salomon Brothers.

I regret that I am unable to list all of those who have assisted or influenced me in this work. I do wish to say a special word of appreciation, however, for the guidance and counsel of John Hodges, American Petroleum Institute; Henry Steele, University of Houston; John Garrett and Warren Davis, Gulf Oil Corporation; Tor Meloe, Texaco; and Ted Eck, Standard of Indiana. In particular I am indebted to Eirik Furubotn, M. L. Greenhut, and the late C. E. Ferguson, all of the Texas A&M University Department of Economics, and for periodic discussions on oil to my professional petroleum economist colleagues M. A. Adelman, Massachusetts Institute of Technology; Richard J. Gonzalez, private consultant; Edward Erickson, University of North Carolina; Robert Spann, V.M.I.; Phillip Verleger, Data Resources, Inc.; and Paul Frankel, Petroleum Economics, Ltd. Finally, I wish to thank Texas A&M University for the generous support it has accorded to me in this publication and in my graduate studies.

New York, N.Y.   E. ANTHONY COPP

Introduction

THE "energy crisis" of the 1970's is not a unique event in the energy history of the United States. The petroleum industry has experienced several almost cyclic periods of shortage in the past and has always managed to increase output. This current "energy crisis," however, differs from previous ones in that it has been associated with a world movement toward nationalism in oil-producing countries and a concurrent limitation in the ability of the U.S. petroleum industry to maintain commercial control over its foreign sources. The present crisis has revived interest not only in the industrial structure and performance of the U.S. petroleum industry but also in the changing structure and performance of the international industry.

Federal and state policy makers have closely watched the continuing dominance of major refining companies at the expense of a declining number of smaller, independent refining firms. Their preoccupation with monopolistic tendencies is not, of course, a recent one; it has characterized each previous period of energy shortage. Old policy prescriptions have included the deconcentration of refining, the limitation of refinery mergers, and the divestiture of vertically integrated operations from large refiners. The newer policies consist of cost equalization programs among refiners, output allocation schemes, price controls, and limitations on transfer pricing practices between the foreign affiliates and the domestic refining divisions of the major refiners. The kernel of these policy prescriptions is the intent to ensure industry competition by subsidizing the survival of small, independent refiners, producers, or marketers, thereby limiting the actual or potential monopolistic behavior of the majors.

The fact that the oil industry is virtually divided against itself —that is, the majors versus the independents—is a phenomenon with deep historical, legal, and organizational roots.[1] However, never before has a countervailing foreign economic force such as the Organization of Petroleum Exporting Countries (OPEC) been effective in narrowing the gap in the potential or actual market power of the majors and independents. Indeed, the assault on the majors' market power has gone through several stages, but the end result has been the irreversible and permanent entry of foreign and domestic governments into the energy business. The rules of the game that affect the allocation of energy resources are now strongly weighted by government planning. It is a theme of this book that the independents may not gain at the expense of the majors, but that more likely both majors and independents will yield actual or potential market power to government. For in fact, even though previous federal regulation was tailored to recognize the industry's major/independent division, the end result was most often to the detriment of one or both classes of firms and ultimately to final energy consumers. In response to the apparent monopolistic power of OPEC the U.S. government has chosen to try to dismantle what it perceives to be the bridge of economic power from OPEC through the major oil companies to the consumer. This punitive approach may actually lengthen the term of the present crisis and thus, as in the past, contribute to greater misallocation of energy resources.

Petroleum policies for the last quarter-century also have been justified on grounds of the need for national security or national defense. In particular, import quotas, state oil prorationing, natural gas price regulation, and tax advantages were uniformly justified on

---

[1] The confrontation of the majors with independents has occurred within each component of the petroleum industry. The independents in refining are not necessarily the same independent firms in marketing or production, but the confrontation is always with the same basic group of majors.

those grounds. The national security rationale, however, was never precisely defined or evaluated. The following chapters provide evidence that the national security justification was a catchall used to warrant what Stigler (1971) has called "acquired regulation," that is, regulation that was desired and actively sought by the petroleum industry. Whatever real merit there may have been for a national security justification was undermined by both industry and government; it took the actions of a major outside force—OPEC—to bring the policy weakness of both industry and government to light.

By combining national security and antimonopoly policy as inseparable parts of a national energy policy, the government imposed upon itself constraints which could only undermine its achievement of long-term energy goals. National security policy itself is an argument, in effect, to violate the normal rules of efficient allocation of resources. Defense policy cannot be completely ignored, but when the resultant misallocation results in unacceptably high costs, alternatives must be examined and weighed with great care. Antimonopoly policy may be viewed in the same light. There is unavoidably a cost to ensure national energy security. However, as will be seen in subsequent chapters, government energy policies adopted ostensibly to ensure both security and competition have been uncoordinated, have often conflicted, and have resulted in unacceptably high costs.

The desire of the industry's two segments to acquire advantageous federal regulation is most pronounced with respect to petroleum import policy, but that policy has boomeranged. The government's determination to ensure competition by guaranteeing the survival of small firms was revealed in the import regulations it imposed. However, the adverse impact of natural gas price regulation and the ineffective tax advantages, the state oil prorationing, the numerous exemptions granted under the import quota program, and the untimely regulation of refinery inputs, including crude oil, unfinished oils, and natural gas liquids, for environmental protection all tended to discourage the development of new domestic petroleum supplies while stimulating excessive demands for imported petroleum to meet equally excessive (and rapidly growing) consumer demands for petroleum products. The end result was the energy crisis of the 1970's.

Through the first half of the 1970's, the full cost of these failing energy policies could be measured by the apparent vulnerability of the United States to the dictates of foreign oil-producing nations. Crude oil shortages forced cutbacks in domestic industrial production and contributed to unemployment. Price controls and arbitrary product allocations were the policy tools that government was compelled to adopt. The blame for the apparent shortage of energy can be shared by Congress, the oil industry, each administration since 1948, and the consuming public. The mismanagement has been colossal.

In this study I shall primarily evaluate the influence of governmental energy policies on petroleum refining, particularly with respect to the misallocative effects that the premise of ensuring both national security and competition has had. Specifically, for the time period 1948–1975 the study will (1) show how certain federal and state policies have tended to influence industry growth and structure in petroleum refining; (2) delineate fundamental features of policy that affect entry into petroleum refining; (3) employ the "survival principle" in assessing changes in the size structure of the industry while testing, through an empirical model, the "permanent" versus the "transitory" factors that affect concentration in refining; (4) suggest an alternative national security rationale for federal and state energy policy divorced from any rationale for ensuring competition; (5) outline the reasons behind the failure of oil import policy, natural gas policy, and state prorationing policies since 1948 and show how they have contributed to the current energy crisis; (6) evaluate current administration policy efforts; (7) show the economic implications of OPEC's rise to world economic power and its impact on regulation of the oil industry; and (8) suggest solutions that should be considered in the development of a new national energy policy.

I shall also delineate the roles of the majors and the independents in effecting energy policy. I shall show how federal import regulations and later rules on price controls and output allocation tended to reinforce the permanent component of market power of the majors while forcing the majors to subsidize the survival of smaller refining firms. The history of the oil import control program will show how the government undermined its own importers' cartel through numerous exemptions and special privileges.

My study will also point out the fundamental false assumptions of federal energy policy from 1948 to the present: (1) that the United States had a cushion of spare refining capacity and spare productive capacity and that supply would always exceed demand; (2) that the long-term supply curve of foreign oil was perfectly elastic and that restrictions on foreign oil would increase national energy security; (3) that energy policies could be developed for specific petroleum raw materials and refined products and that consideration of the costs of crude oil and natural gas as joint products could be ignored; (4) that national energy security is enhanced by the ensured survival of small, independent petroleum firms; and (5) that regulation and planning could supplant the market system.

As noted, the period of this study is from 1948 through 1975. The earliest year, 1948, is unique because it was the first year since 1922 that oil imports exceeded oil exports and it was the first year that Middle East oil was imported into the United States in substantial quantities. A major fuel shortage was feared from the 1948/1949 winter. The energy crisis of the early 1970's in many ways paralleled that of 1948. In 1948 domestic production was not expected to rise, limited spare refining capacity existed, and imports—95 percent of which entered ports on the East Coast—were rising to supplement domestic requirements. The fact that "shortages" were indeed avoided was attributed only to the mild winter.

By early 1975 OPEC oil, particularly that from Saudi Arabia, Nigeria, and Venezuela, had accounted for over 40 percent of new imports. The U.S. government slowly began to realize that for the short term there were few substantive alternatives to using OPEC oil. Nevertheless, it persisted in attempting to sever the perceived linkages of joint economic behavior between OPEC and the oil companies. Demands that OPEC lower its price, punitive legislation against foreign operations of oil companies, and import levies were all part of the reactive government policy.

Since the turn of the century, major energy crises seem to have demonstrated a twenty-five-year cycle: the 1920's, 1948–1949, and the 1970's. The government role in the earlier crises was one of stimlating solutions with industry guidance and counsel. The present crisis initially, however, demonstrated less a policy of joint reassessment and more a policy of distrust of industry opinion. The oil business appeared to be one of permanent government direction and limited managerial flexibility. By the mid-1970's the range of solutions to the energy problem made it obvious that a mutually reinforcing planning effort would be required of both industry and government. Moreover, even though the possibility of a surplus of energy on the U.S. West Coast seemed imminent with the discovery of Alaskan oil and gas, the persistent long-term historical energy deficit east of the Rocky Mountains, and particularly on the East Coast, appeared to be worsening. In addition, there was alarming evidence that the economic costs of developing synthetic forms of oil and gas and other alternatives to OPEC oil were far greater than ever expected. Thus, it was likely that the energy problems of the early 1970's were but a prelude to a more serious energy crisis during the 1980's.

Regulating Competition in Oil

Government Intervention in the U.S.
Refining Industry, 1948–1975

1

Refining Industry Structure, Market Power, and the Government

TO appreciate the impact of government energy policies on refining, we must take an overview of the long-term evolution of refining in size, technical complexity, and industrial structure. In particular, this chapter examines (1) industry location and structure, (2) the adoption of "best-practice" refining techniques by majors and independents, (3) the long-term shift toward refineries of more efficient size, and (4) the components of market concentration in refining. Particular emphasis is given to the post-1948 period and to the importance of the international practice of classifying refining firms as majors and independents. The historical emphasis on these two groups in the industry resulted from the importance that U.S. government energy policy placed on ensuring the joint survival of both.

The definition of majors and independents is inevitably an arbitrary consideration. For purposes of this study the "top twenty" refining companies from 1948 to late 1975, ranked on the basis of operable refinery distillation capacity, will be considered the majors. Companies ranked below the top twenty are defined as independents. Use of the top twenty as the majors is based upon their dominance of U.S. refining and their dominance over vertically integrated operations that include crude oil and natural gas production and transportation. Majors are often characterized as being large companies vertically integrated into at least one segment of the petroleum industry other than refining; their vertical integration often crosses national boundaries. Independents are often characterized as smaller, generally domestic companies with little or no vertical integration.

A study by McLean and Haigh (1954) has shown that in the United States our top twenty major oil companies control about 40 percent of all the U.S. crude oil produced. Yet there are more than five thousand independent firms engaged in exploration for and production of crude oil in this country.[1] On the other hand, the majors have normally accounted for some 80 percent of total U.S. refining capacity. Although all of the majors are owners of domestic petroleum reserves, none of them are fully self-sufficient in providing inputs to their refineries or in providing oil products for their markets. Major companies have tended to build refinery capacity in excess of their crude-producing capability and have marketed products in excess of the quantities they manufacture. Most U.S. refiners, both majors and independents, purchase crude oil for their refineries.

Justification of the top twenty as majors is based also upon the historical market dominance, until OPEC's challenge, of the United States over worldwide crude oil and product prices and crude oil supply. Now that the OPEC countries have obtained control over supply, the concept of foreign oil production by a company has limited relevance. Because company production implies ownership and control, only oil available where oil property rights are under jurisdiction of the home country can now be considered as company production. Other sources of crude during this era of resource nationalism should be considered as uncontrolled sources. Today, the term *crude oil liftings*—crude oil that is contractually accessible and is lifted from foreign wells for company account, but that is not controlled by the company—is more appropriate than *company production,* and the substantial volumes of crude oil from OPEC are more appropriately referred to as OPEC liftings, not company Middle East production, Venezuelan production, or the like. Thus, as an indicator of the extent of vertical integration into domestic production and of the OPEC and non-OPEC liftings of selected major

[1] The composition of the "top twenty" varies over this period and due to mergers and acquisitions, this basic group was effectively twenty companies by 1975. The current membership of the Independent Petroleum Association of America is estimated to be slightly over five thousand firms. In 1948–1949, seven thousand companies were estimated to be engaged in the search for and production of crude oil.

petroleum companies in 1974, Table 1 shows that with the exception of Getty Oil, *none* of these companies was 100 percent self-sufficient, although some supplied more than 75 percent of their refinery requirements from company-owned sources.[2] The companies in Table 1 are ranked by company crude oil production in the United States as a percentage of domestic refining capacity.

In the United States, the refining industry consists of fewer than two hundred refiners, each producing a relatively homogeneous mix of products including motor gasoline, distillate fuels, and residual products. For each product, numerous firms compete aggressively for market shares. However, in the competition for crude oil only the largest refiners exert price leadership. Historically, the leaders posted prices at which they were willing to buy crude from domestic oil-producing fields. Smaller refiners normally followed the price leaders and offered a similar price. With the advent of price controls, however, separate prices were posted for "old" and "new" crude oil as defined by the Federal Energy Administration (FEA). Crude oil fields are linked by pipeline to only a few major refiners, and if the crude oil producer is not satisfied with the posted price, there are few effective alternatives available to him. He can seek more distant refiners, but he will incur costly transactions to conclude new agreements and build a new pipeline or connect into another pipeline.[3] In the short run, a crude producer can only deal with a few refiners in a classic oligopsonistic structure.[4]

This oligopsony provides the environment for effective market control over entry into refining. Consistent with the theory of limit

[2] Because few firms are self-sufficient in crude oil or products, and because of the spatial separation of refineries, intercompany exchange of crude, unfinished oils, and products has always been a standard practice. These competitive buyer/seller exchanges, or "arms-length" transactions, tend to generate a substantial degree of "effective competition" in petroleum refining.

[3] In the short run, the strength of the oligopsony of the majors, and in some cases large independents, over a given field is derived largely from their ownership and operation of intrastate crude oil pipelines (see de Chazeau and Kahn 1959).

[4] By "classic" I mean the closest proximity to the textbook example of a relatively organized oligopsonistic market in which crude buyers tend to follow the price leader. For different oil fields, unorganized oligopsony, in which a price change may not be followed by rivals and hence the original firm may have to back down, may result. This is a form of "kinked" oligopsony. (See, for example, Machlup 1952, pp. 126–132).

TABLE 1
Controlled and Uncontrolled Crude Oil Supply and Refining Capacity for Selected Major Refiners, 1974
(000 bbl./calendar day)

Major Company	United States			Foreign				Oil Production as Percentage of Refining Capacity		
	Net Oil Production	Refining Capacity	Refined Product Sales	OPEC Liftings	Non-OPEC Liftings	Refining Capacity	Refined Product Sales	U.S.	Foreign*	World† Total
Getty	300	219	254	126	3	50	26	137	48	112
Cities Service	213	268	349	2	8	—	—	79	4	80
Exxon	890	1,250	1,782	4,305‡	503	5,425	3,723	71	72	21
Texaco	705	1,058	1,338	3,442	161	2,153	2,108	67	112	27
Phillips	256	404	541	66	40	87	107	63	22	58
Continental	218	364	364	284	89	177	247	60	67	57
Gulf	476	861	861	2,122§	102	1,292	812	55	103	27
Union	270	487	449	69‖	25	8	66	55	19	60
Sun Oil	266	484	573	104	13	98	86	55	22	48
Marathon	174	318	280	196	7	70	69	55	52	52
Shell	586	1,127	1,060	—	—	—	—	52	—	52
Std. of Ind.	539	1,065	1,031	143	193	198	150	51	26	58

TABLE 1 (continued)

Major Company	United States			Foreign				Oil Production as Percentage of Refining Capacity		
	Net Oil Production	Refining Capacity	Refined Product Sales	OPEC Liftings	Non-OPEC Liftings	Refining Capacity	Refined Product Sales	U.S.	Foreign*	World† Total
ARCO	383	785	698	183	30	47	104	49	26	50
Std. of Calif.	413	952	1,006	3,195#	100	1,267	1,178	43	148	32
Mobil	363	950	928	1,882	112**	1,765	1,342	38	73	14
Amerada Hess	99	728	591	41	18	—	—	13	1	15
Std. of Ohio	30	388	333	—	—	—	—	8	6	8
Ashland	23	362	457	7	—	—	—	6	2	8

SOURCE: Annual oil company reports and statistical supplements, and Securities and Exchange Commission 10-K reports, 1974.

* Includes OPEC liftings and U.S. refining capacity.
† Does not include OPEC liftings.
‡ Includes 48.7 percent of special crude offtake.
§ Includes production from associate OPEC members.
‖ Union OPEC production is 100 percent offtake.
Includes crude oil under participation agreements of 54 percent or 1,671,000 bbl./day.
** From non-OPEC sources.

pricing in oligopoly,[5] major price leaders are theoretically in a position to set the posted price at a level that would not attract new entrants.[6] Before the 1970's, the higher the price of the produced crude, the greater the depletion allowance. Theoretically, the floor to the limit price was the cost of crude oil production, while the ceiling was the realization on refined products. Therefore, high crude prices could limit entry and provide an improved oil depletion allowance for vertically integrated firms (Karg 1970, Rooney 1970, Galal 1970). This condition substantially changed in the 1970's with the elimination of depletion allowance, the tremendous rise in domestic crude prices, and the price controls on crude.

Structure of the U.S. Petroleum Refining Industry

Refining activity in the United States is geographically delineated for statistical reporting by the Bureau of Mines' Petroleum Administration for Defense (PAD) districts. As shown in Figure 1, PAD Districts I–IV include all territory east of the Rocky Mountains. The Bureau of Mines further delineates the industry and collects data by refinery districts, as indicated in Figure 2. PAD District I includes the East Coast and Appalachian No. 1 refinery districts; PAD District II encompasses the Appalachian No. 2, Indiana, Minnesota, and Oklahoma groups; PAD District III consists of Texas, the Louisiana Gulf Coast, and the northern part of Louisiana, Arkansas, and New Mexico; and PAD District IV is the Rocky Mountain area. PAD District V includes the West Coast, Alaska, and Hawaii.

Table 2 shows the refinery capacity of each PAD district. About 70 percent of total U.S. distillation capacity and gasoline output capacity is located in PAD Districts II and III. The Texas and Louisiana Gulf Coast refinery districts have the greatest output, with 6,211,263 barrels per calendar day of crude oil distillation

---

[5] The theory of limit pricing was developed by Bain (1956), Lydall (1955) and Sylos-Labini (1962) and focuses on the role of entry barriers in oligopoly.

[6] The literature on price leadership distinguishes between "dominant" price leadership and "barometric" price leadership. The former is characterized in the works of Lanzillotti (1957) and Stigler (1947), and the latter has been developed by Markham (1951).

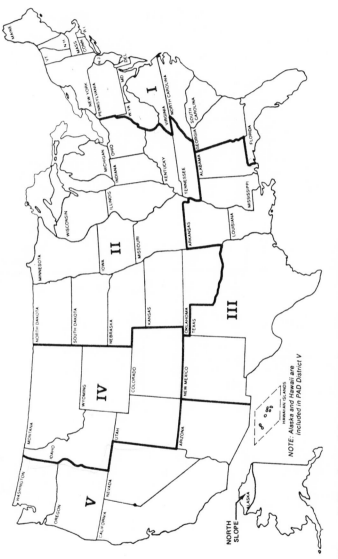

FIGURE 1. Petroleum Administration for Defense (PAD) Districts

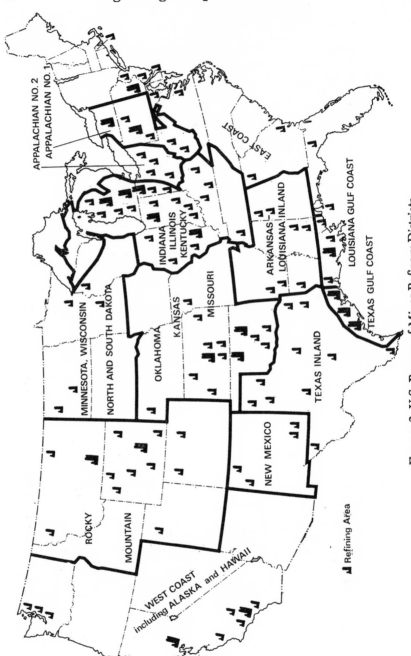

FIGURE 2. U.S. Bureau of Mines Refinery Districts

capacity, and some 2.8 million barrels per day of gasoline production capacity. This output constitutes over 40 percent of the nation's total distillation and gasoline production capacity. Many of the smaller plants are specialty operations for such products as lube oils and asphalt. Most of the asphalt plants are located in PAD Districts I and II. Recent asphalt production has ranged as high as 13 million barrels per year, and current U.S. asphalt capacity is slightly over 30,000 barrels daily.

TABLE 2

Distribution of Operating and Shutdown Refineries, Distillation Capacity, and Gasoline Output Capacity, January 1, 1975

PAD District	Number of Refineries		Distillation Capacity (bbl./calendar day)	Gasoline Output Capacity* (bbl./calendar day)
	Operating	Shutdown		
I	29	3	1,617,720	695,920
II	67	10	4,010,114	1,858,192
III	89	5	6,211,263	2,828,064
IV	29	6	548,331	241,356
V	48	4	2,309,322	1,191,815
Total	262	28	14,696,750	6,815,347

SOURCE: Bureau of Mines annual, 1975.
NOTE: Puerto Rican refineries are excluded. There were three operating refineries in Puerto Rico with 283,800 barrels per calendar day in distillation capacity as of January 1, 1975.
* Includes cracking, reforming, coking, and alkylation capacity.

The largest refineries are also located on the Gulf Coast. Table 3 indicates the number of refineries by size for the Texas-Louisiana Gulf and inland areas compared to the entire nation. Although almost one-half of the refineries, including asphalt plants, in the United States have capacities of less than 20,000 barrels per day, most of the total capacity is in larger plants located in coastal zones where access to economical transportation is most convenient. Low transportation costs resulting from the introduction in the early 1960's of large tanker transports have attracted refineries to deep-water ports accessible to the large crude oil tankers, and the cost-saving transports have induced an increase in the size of refineries, since a refinery must have sufficient capacity to be able to receive these large tankers.[7] Assuming that a refinery would not normally take more than a ten-day supply of crude oil in one shipment, it will have to have a capacity of 140,000 barrels per day to be able to receive a vessel of 200,000 deadweight tons. A smaller refinery to be supplied by such a transport would have to compare the additional cost of storage versus the lower transport costs and would have to consider long-term plans for future expansion. Exceptions to this principle occur when companies control a network of refineries or use crude oil pipelines from deep-water terminals so that more than one refinery can share the cargo, which, of course, is general practice.

TABLE 3

Refineries, by Sizes, in the United States and
the Texas-Louisiana District, 1975

Refinery Size Class (bbl./day)	United States	Texas-Louisiana	
		Gulf	Inland
100–20,000	114	8	20
20,001–40,000	39	4	4
40,001–60,000	31	2	2
60,001–80,000	16	4	2
80,001–100,000	18	5	1
100,001–120,000	8	2	0
120,001–140,000	9	2	0
140,001–160,000	2	0	0
160,001–200,000	10	2	0
200,001–300,000	8	4	0
300,001+	7	6	0
Total	262	39	29

SOURCE: Bureau of Mines annual, 1975.
NOTE: Puerto Rican refineries are excluded.

During the early years of petroleum refining, firms tended to locate their plants near proved reserves of crude oil. The discovery,

[7] The advantage of new transport technology and its impact on world agglomeration of refining has been developed by Frankel and Newton (1963, pp. 23–36).

often overnight, of major crude oil fields led to the rapid location of small batch distillation stills. In the absence of conservation laws, the "law of capture" dictated rapid field production. The law of capture was basically a system of oil property rights stating that the owner of land who produced oil from a well on his land was recognized as having produced or "captured" it, even though part of it was drained from his neighbor's property (Lovejoy and Homan 1967). Many drillers sank wells to offset oil capture by their neighbors. This crowding also led to an agglomeration of refining plants near field discoveries. The East Texas field, discovered in the early 1930's, was once the location of more than 150 "refineries," which often amounted to no more than simple batch distillation units. As production from such fields declined, the "refineries" would shut down permanently or be dismantled for future use. The advent of oil conservation laws and prorationing helped eliminate the wasteful location of these plants at major crude oil discovery sites.

By January 1, 1975, according to the U.S. Bureau of Mines (annual, 1975) there were 136 companies with 262 operating refineries (28 shut down) in the United States. They represented a total operable crude distillation capacity of more than 14.6 million barrels per day. By contrast, there were 15 companies operating 38 refineries in Canada, with a crude distillation capacity of more than 2.0 million barrels per day. In the United States in the 1975 calendar year the largest twenty refiners controlled over 80 percent of operable distillation capacity. The number of operating refineries in the United States has declined from a high of 461 at the beginning of 1940 to 262 in 1975, although total operating distillation capacity has increased. In 1948 there were 215 refiners; in 1975 there were 136. Integration of several processes into a single plant was one of the major innovations in refining over the twenty-five-year study period. It was common practice for major refining companies to close down a number of smaller, obsolete plants while building a single larger refinery.

In the United States, shipments of refined products to other districts are dominated by PAD District III. Table 4 shows interdistrict trade in refined products and foreign imports for 1974 (latest data available). The table also demonstrates the product supply dominance of District III and the virtual reliance of District

I on District III for interdistrict shipments and imports. PAD District III is a net exporter of refined products to *all* the other PAD districts, but its central product shipment zone is essentially its own internal market and those of Districts I and II. As Table 4 depicts, there is a relative interregional trade balance between PAD Districts I and II. Districts III, IV, and V are virtually self-sufficient in the production of refined products. The discovery and development of Alaskan crude oil have made PAD District V the only significant U.S. energy surplus area, and as its crude is produced in 1978, its potential for exporting to PAD Districts I–IV may ease their condition of energy deficit.

PAD District I has the greatest demand for refined products from both U.S. and foreign regions. Indeed, the energy deficit of District I has historically been the overriding concern of federal energy policy. That district provides less than 25 percent of its product demand from local refineries, which use imported crude oil and unfinished oils for their input. It imports more than 90 percent of its residual fuel oil requirements, as does the Canadian East Coast. Outside of PAD District I, individual refinery regions have relied upon negligible amounts of interdistrict and foreign supplies to meet intradistrict product demand.

Technically, it is irrelevant to discuss the "average" refinery, because rated engineering capacity differs for each refinery in terms of the type of input that can be used and the relative yields of jointly produced products.[8] For example, refineries are equipped to handle a limited API gravity range of crude oils and an even more limited allowable contaminant range within each gravity range. In addition, depending on the quality of the input and the refinery process, the product yield from a barrel of crude can be technically increased or decreased within certain limits. The greatest demand for refined products is for use in transportation, and the price in cents per gallon is generally greatest for gasoline. Therefore, re-

---

[8] The problem of capacity measurement for petroleum refineries has recently been studied by Griffin (1972). He defines industry capacity as the minimum of the short-run average cost function. The refinery industry defines capacity in terms of its rated "stream" or "calendar day" basic distillation capacity. Levels of operable capacity are defined in terms of inputs to refineries as a percentage of total operable distillation capacity. See also Division of Statistics and Economics, American Petroleum Institute (weekly).

TABLE 4
U.S. Refined Product Interdistrict Shipment, Imports, and Domestic Demand, 1974
(000 bbl./calendar day)

From PAD District	(1) To PAD District					(2) Total Inter-district Shipments	(3) Total Imports by District	(4) Total Domestic Demand by District	(5) Total Percent-age of District Demand from (2)	(6) Total Percent-age of District Demand from (3)
	I	II	III	IV	V					
I	—	164	—	—	—	164	2,046	6,172	44	33
II	66	—	80	8	—	154	85	4,501	19	2
III	2,637	649	—	29	73	3,388	115	3,278	3	4
IV	—	25	10	—	66	101	16	469	12	3
V	3	—	—	20	—	23	139	2,192	6	6
Total	2,706	838	90	57	139	3,830	2,401	16,612		

SOURCE: Data compiled from U.S. Bureau of Mines, *Crude Petroleum, Petroleum Products, and Natural Gas Liquids*, Mineral Industry Surveys, 1974.

fineries have been designed to convert the greatest proportion of a barrel of crude oil into motor gasoline. Throughout most of the 1950's and 1960's, most of the advances in refining technology went toward the goal of increasing the proportion of gasoline produced, thus reducing the "heavier ends," or residual output, from a barrel of crude.[9]

Although refinery yields tend to vary at any given point during the year, the technical heterogeneity of products for all refinery districts is substantial. In general, however, motor gasoline and distillate fuel oil now account for two-thirds of all refinery yields. Less than 10 percent of the refinery yields of PAD Districts I–IV are for residual fuel oil. In contrast, in 1948 average yields contained a larger percentage of residuals than of the lighter distillates. These figures indicate the technological shift toward increasing domestic yields of gasoline and distillate. Not unexpectedly, the greatest portion of imports of refined products from 1948 to 1975 has been residual fuel oil.

The typical refinery process can be viewed as two fundamental and continuous operations: distillation and conversion. The conversion units exist solely to alter the product mix yielded by the basic distillation units. These complex conversion units account for the greatest proportion of fixed costs at refineries, and they require relatively little labor for their operation. There is virtually no substitution between labor and installed process units. Figure 3 is a typical flow chart of a petroleum refining operation. (Technical definitions of refinery processes and terms are given in the Glossary.)

The average life of a large oil refinery is between twenty-five and thirty years, with about five years of salvage value. The life of a small refinery may be from fifteen to twenty years. Refinery life also depends on whether the refinery is designed to process "sweet" (low-sulfur) crudes or "sour" (high-sulfur) crudes, with sweet refineries (and those sour refineries built with corrosion-resistant materials) having a longer life.

---

[9] For some refiners the yields on gasoline have remained relatively unchanged, which suggests that refiners have attempted to supply the rising demand for middle distillate without fundamentally influencing the levels of gasoline yields. This provides an alternative interpretation of innovation diffusion by refiners.

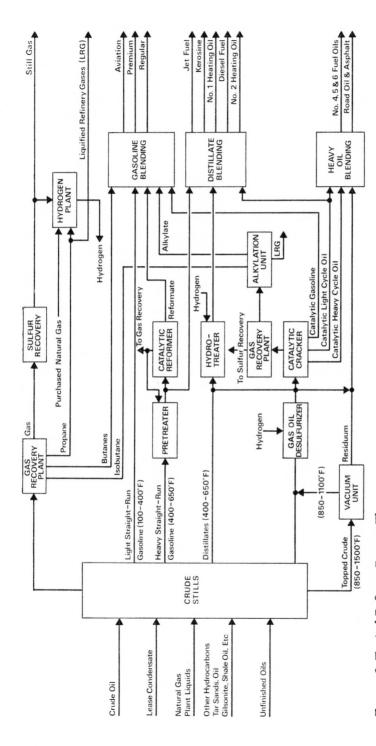

FIGURE 3. Typical Refinery Process Flow

Refining Process Development, 1900–1948

Petroleum refining techniques in use today are the outgrowth of a series of dramatic changes which began about 1900. At that time two important inventions transformed the demand pattern for petroleum products. As Enos (1962, p. 1) writes:

> At the beginning of the twentieth century the introduction of two new products, the electric light and the automobile, exerted a profound effect on the petroleum industry. By replacing the kerosene lamp as the main source of artificial illumination the electric light reduced the demand for kerosene, until then the industry's most profitable product. By replacing the horse as the main mode of transportation, the automobile greatly increased the demand for gasoline, previously of little value. The petroleum industry responded by shifting its attention from kerosene to gasoline, developing in the process new refining techniques and new methods of distribution.

Only a limited amount of redistillation was performed by the typical refinery of 1910. Before then the distillation process was not even continuous. By 1915 Burton stills, the first cracking units, were in operation, their patents controlled by Standard Oil Company of Indiana. The Burton process yielded 35 percent more gasoline per barrel of crude oil than did the older vertical stills. Thermal cracking beyond initial distillation was a timely innovation. The supply of natural gasoline from crude oil was declining, and casinghead gasoline was not considered to be a substantive alternative. Products from basic or "straight-run" distillation no longer met required market standards. With the increasing demand for greater volumes and better grades of gasoline, refiners expanded exploration for new supplies of crude oil and intensified research efforts to develop new refining techniques which would provide the "best practices" for yielding a larger fraction of gasoline.

Before the introduction of commercial cracking processes, refining could be characterized as an activity with joint products in fixed proportions. According to economic theory, when the prices in the demand schedules for two products produced in fixed proportions are highly inelastic, under competition one product will bear the major burden of the cost of the joint process and the other will command only a low price. The former product is considered the primary product, and the latter is the "by-product." As Enos noted, before the turn of the century the primary product of refineries was kerosine. Gasoline and residual fuel oil were products with low unit values, and gasoline was often dumped into local streams, where that practice was permitted. Refiners often blended kerosine with gasoline; indeed, it became necessary to regulate the flash point of kerosine because of that practice. The advent of the automobile changed the entire picture. Gasoline became the main product, and kerosine the by-product. In 1904 the price per gallon of gasoline and kerosine was relatively the same, but by 1913 the price of gasoline was twice that of kerosine. Kerosine, in fact, was being blended with gasoline.

When the cracking process was first introduced in 1913, it ended "straight-run" fractional distillation refineries, and hence the fixed-proportions nature of refining, and heralded the beginning of joint supply in variable proportions. The refiner, using cracking processes, could subject the middle distillates—kerosine and oil—to high pressures and temperatures and convert them to gasoline, residual oil, and refinery gas. Thus, the proportions of the products could be varied at will. Later improvements in cracking processes allowed the conversion not only of middle distillates but also of residual fuel oil into gasoline. The basic motivation of the developers of the Burton process, however, was the desire to economize on the use of crude oil:

> The supply of crude oil in the Midwest had been adequate for the local refinery until about 1905, but production was declining and the refiners recognized that there was little likelihood that the trend would be reversed. As the demand for products from crude oil increased, Midwest refiners had to import crude oil from other regions. Midwest refiners had the greatest inducement to reduce their consumption of crude oil. The means utilized in the Burton Process was a reduction in raw materials inputs. [Enos 1962, p. 238]

Between 1910 and 1930 numerous processes were introduced which allowed the finer separation of products, thus providing for the continuous cracking of both light and heavy charge stocks. During the period from 1930 to the outbreak of World War II thermal reforming and visbreaking were introduced. Tetraethyl lead was sometimes added to gasoline to increase its octane rating. Also during this period catalytic cracking ("cat cracking") units were introduced. By 1940 the advantages of cat cracking were clearly recognized: lower costs, higher yield, and improved quality of gasoline.

Although World War II interrupted the adoption of cat cracking units by most refineries, several large fluid cat cracking units were constructed during the war; after the war many additional refineries hastened to adopt the process. Most of these early process innovations were pioneered by major refiners, but quite often the initial adopters were independent refiners. Leading innovators were Jersey Standard (now Exxon), Sun Oil, Standard of Indiana, and Atlantic Refining (now Atlantic Richfield).

In summary, the technical history of refinery expansion in the United States before 1948 has consisted of a gradual expansion of basic distillation capacity and the rapid adoption and expansion of new technical processes that maximized the yields of high-value products. Technical innovations were biased toward improving gasoline yields for each barrel of crude oil processed. Firms that failed to adopt the "best practice" in their refineries were most often the firms that failed to survive in refining. Nonetheless (as we shall see later) this natural tendency for the refiners who incurred high costs to either adopt new technology or leave the industry was arrested in part by federal policy on petroleum imports—a policy that tended to extend the economic life of the refinery plants that followed old practices.

Refining Process Innovation and Expansion after World War II

The period after 1948 was one of rapid innovation and diffusion of new refining techniques, which generally necessitated the scrapping of older plants with their older processes and more costly investments. Economic theory suggests a standard criterion for adopting an innovation: adoption should occur if the average variable cost for older plants is greater than the average total cost of operating with the new technology (Fellner 1958). This criterion has been shown by Salter (1969) and Swan (1970) to be equally relevant for competitive firms as well as for a monopolistic or oligopolistic price leader. Salter viewed innovation as a continuous process of factor substitution, such as a modern process replacing an outmoded process. However, the timing of the adoption of innovations based on this criterion was altered by a special external force.

Following World War II, and in the interest of national security, the government deliberately encouraged, through subsidy and tax advantages, the growth of domestic refining capacity. That growth is shown in Figure 4. The PAD encouraged the creation of a "cushion" of excess refining capacity through two basic policies: granting accelerated amortization on new plant facilities, and liberally permitting access to construction material under the Controlled Materials Plan. More than 150 refineries were modernized under these programs. More than half of the new or "grass-roots" refineries constructed in the early 1950's ranged in capacity from 2,500 barrels per day to 30,000 barrels per day. Thus, government support was influential in allowing many small refiners to replace outmoded plants with newer processes. This influence explains the general trends in the balance of processes used by majors and independents before the period of import restrictions in the late 1950's. The majors and independents have generally kept pace with each other in process expansion.

Since 1948 the major innovations in refining have been the introduction of catalysts to improve the quality of refined products together with a general phasing out of thermal refining and the introduction of alternative conversion processes. New catalysts for cracking and reforming were actively being developed early in this period, and by the early 1950's commercial applications of cat cracking and reforming, coking, and vacuum distillation were initiated. In addition to these innovations, refiners began to develop complementary organizational innovations by "combination processing" and "process balance." To increase processing productivity, refiners learned to combine or interlock sequentially various processes, thereby gaining greater output flexibility and greater efficiency in processing and reprocessing crude fractions to meet the higher quality standards. The new technology allowed more intensive processing of each barrel of crude. In line with Salter's factor substitution theory of innovation, refiners improved the efficiency of conversion operations by interlocking the processes. Indeed, the advent of the modern petrochemical plant is a spinoff of this interlocking.

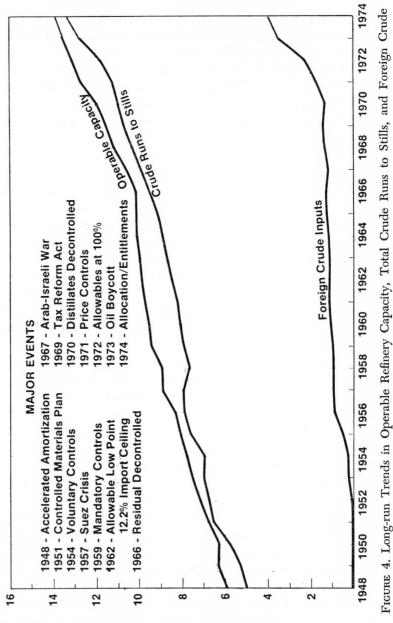

FIGURE 4. Long-run Trends in Operable Refinery Capacity, Total Crude Runs to Stills, and Foreign Crude Inputs, 1948–1974

In 1952 it was widely believed that it would be impossible to build a completely modern refinery, since some of the designs would be at least partially obsolete before the refinery was in operation. For example, after the Korean War the Defense Department decided to sell its alkylation units, which were primarily used for the production of aviation gasoline. Private refiners did not have such units and showed little interest in purchasing Defense Department units since they doubted their postwar usefulness. In this case it was the perception of alkylation as a nearly obsolescent technology that caused the hesitancy among refiners. All the surplus units were eventually purchased, however, when private refiners realized the value of alkylate production to upgrade motor gasoline.

Postwar expansion of refining capacity was thus aimed at modernization, and this trend was apparent in both medium and small refineries. Tables 5 and 6 compare process expansion and balance for majors and independents for selected years from 1948 to 1974. The reduction in thermal operations and the increase in catalytic and hydrotreating processes was apparently in balance for both classes of refiners. What is noticeable is that from 1956 onward—the era of voluntary and mandatory import controls—the apparent decline of thermal operations in the process balance was actually much faster for independents than for majors. Thermal cracking units were less efficient and were incapaple of yielding the improved qualities of gasoline that came to dominate the U.S. market. Yet it appears that the majors with access to greater quantities of low-cost foreign crude maintained thermal capacity much longer. This fact refutes some of the testimony given before congressional committees that criticized the inefficiency of the independents and argued against allowing such firms to share in import license rights.

The tables also reveal that for some processes, like catalytic reforming, the independents tended to lead initially in the addition of cat reforming to their process balance but were eventually surpassed by the majors. The majors, however, were clearly dominant in hydrotreating, which by 1972 had become a dominant process. The gradual decline in thermal cracking operations began in 1947, and new thermal operations in the early 1950's consisted almost entirely of coking units used for improving asphalts and specialty products. The ratio of thermal operations (cracking, reforming, visbreaking) to

TABLE 5
Process Expansion by Major Refiners in Selected Years, 1948–1974

	1948	1952	1956	1960	1964	1968	1972	1974
Number of companies	20	20	20	20	20	20	20	20
Number of refineries	132	132	126	125	124	119	124	127
Crude capacity (000 bbl./day)	4,514	5,907	7,312	8,301	7,531	9,641	11,582	11,098
Thermal capacity	—	1,824	1,973	1,642	1,355	1,357	1,333	1,176
Percentage on crude	—	30.8	26.9	19.7	17.9	14.0	11.5	10.6
Cat cracking	1,228	1,592	2,103	2,772	3,267	3,526	3,932	4,146
Percentage on crude	27.2	26.9	28.7	33.3	43.3	36.5	33.9	37.3
Cat reforming	—	—	722	1,521	1,957	1,982	2,785	2,694
Percentage on crude	—	—	9.8	18.3	25.9	20.5	24.0	24.3
Hydrotreating	—	—	369	1,733	2,247	3,507	4,564	5,541
Percentage on crude	—	—	5.0	20.8	29.8	36.3	39.4	49.9
Alkylation	—	—	218	316	404	543	639	701
Percentage on crude	—	—	2.9	3.8	5.3	5.6	5.5	6.3
Polymerization	—	—	96	114	99	85	—	—
Percentage on crude	—	—	1.3	1.3	1.3	0.8	—	—
Coking	—	—	116	15	17	20	37	37
Percentage on crude	—	—	2.1	0.1	1.2	0.2	0.3	0.3

Source: Data compiled from Bureau of Mines annual, 1948–1974.

TABLE 6
Process Expansion by Independent Refiners in Selected Years, 1948–1974

	1948	1952	1956	1960	1964	1968	1972	1974
Number of companies	195	166	143	138	126	125	124	116
Number of refineries	224	195	168	169	164	150	129	130
Crude capacity (000 bbl./day)	1,456	1,405	1,646	2,060	3,194	2,017	2,127	3,747
Thermal capacity	—	412	383	388	365	290	198	309
Percentage on crude	—	29.3	23.2	18.8	11.4	14.3	9.3	8.2
Cat cracking	325	377	534	565	720	833	643	1,457
Percentage on crude	22.3	26.8	32.4	27.4	22.5	41.2	30.2	38.9
Cat reforming	—	—	204	392	461	403	384	768
Percentage on crude	—	—	12.4	19.0	14.4	19.9	18.0	20.5
Hydrotreating	—	—	64	209	502	556	535	1,333
Percentage on crude	—	—	3.9	10.1	15.7	27.5	25.1	35.6
Alkylation	—	—	36	92	100	10	131	167
Percentage on crude	—	—	2.1	4.4	3.1	0.5	6.1	4.5
Polymerization	—	—	45	34	35	13	—	—
Percentage on crude	—	—	2.7	1.6	1.0	0.6	—	—
Coking	—	—	30	1	4	8	4	6
Percentage on crude	—	—	1.8	0.04	0.1	0.39	0.2	0.2

SOURCE: Data compiled from Bureau of Mines annual, 1948–1974.

total crude distillation capacity dropped from about 40 percent after World War II to less than 30 percent by 1954.

The continued addition of catalytic capacity allowed the conversion of successively greater fractions of crude each year. It also led to a reduction in yields of residual fuels. The early postwar adoption of catalytic reforming was characterized by the building of many small units, with an average size of about 3,400 barrels per day, by independent refiners. By 1954 major oil companies began to adopt cat reforming essentially to upgrade straight-run naphthas and to raise octane levels of motor gasoline. It is noteworthy that most of the refinery units permanently shut down from 1950 to 1954 were owned by major refiners and that virtually all of that obsolete capacity had been used for thermal cracking.

Before the imposition of import controls, small refiners were industry leaders in developing high-octane gasoline and other quality products. Even in 1955, when octane requirements were temporarily stable, the competition for increased production forced small firms to develop new gasoline additives designed to alleviate octane requirements by suppressing the effects of preignition. But many independent plants failed to adopt the new combination processing. These plants included a large number of small "skimming" or "topping" plants that could produce a full line of products. Most of them were specialty plants making asphalt, lubricants (lubes), heavy fuel, jet fuel, and so on. Only about one-fifth of them were operated by majors, with the remaining eighty run by smaller refiners. Thus, the gradual lag on the part of small refiners to adopt cat cracking is attributable to their resistance to adapt to the economies of combination processing.

Hydrogen treating, used to desulfurize and otherwise improve petroleum fractions from wax to naphtha and to upgrade various middle distillates, was introduced in 1957. One attraction of this process was that the planning and construction of hydrotreating units normally took less than a year. However, by 1957 it was apparent that even new cracking and reforming operations would not satisfy the expanding octane requirements for regular, premium, super-premium, and aviation grades of gasoline. Hence, alkylation, isomerization, and related operations were expanded. The increased demand for jet fuels also affected gasoline yields. More than three-fourths of jet fuel output was supplied from gasoline, which was used as a blending material to produce kerosine. Without this new demand for jet fuel, gasoline yields from the daily level of refinery inputs would have been greater. By the late 1950's the process make-up of all nontopping refineries was essentially designed to minimize yields of residual fuel oil. Consequently, it was not surprising that when the clamor for import controls began, inland refiners—where the incentive to reduce yields was greatest (that is, where distillate fuels commanded higher prices)—favored decontrol of residual fuel oil. East Coast and Gulf Coast refiners, in areas where the incentive to reduce yields was less, favored some controls on residual fuel oil.

The introduction and adoption of new processes altered the refiners' costs in two fundamental ways. First, the development of continuous operations changed the method of refining from production in fixed proportions to production in variable proportions. Second, distillation costs became a relatively smaller fraction of the total capital requirements of refining. Overall operating costs actually increased. Unlike the situation before World War II, few, if any, products from primary distillation were suitable for the specifications of the growing market. Distilled products were either further refined or were blended with other products obtained in additional processing. This novel condition for refiners directly influenced the special treatment of "unfinished oils" in the Mandatory Oil Import Control Program (see chapter 2).

Imports of crude oil and products continued to increase during the 1950's and had an impact on refinery yields. Most of the increases in product imports by 1958 displaced crude oil at refineries, since most of the increases were in products lighter than residual fuel oil. But these imports did not displace equal volumes of domestic products, because part of the product imports (almost half in 1958) came in as unfinished oils which required further processing. Indeed, this program of importing unfinished oils also accounted for part of the shift in product yields. Percentage of yields is obtained by dividing product output by the total amount of crude plus the unfinished oil products that are rerun. Before 1958 most imports of unfinished oils were topped crude for asphalt, with a portion of the total finding its way into the heavy fuel group. There was a definite shift in that year, however: imports of topped crude continued, but the big growth in imports of unfinished oil was in products closer to gasoline. The calculated yield of gasoline averaged 45.5 percent of the total of crude and unfinished oils processed during the year. This yield was an all-time record, with the previous closest being the 45 percent reported for 1939.

Evolution of Refining Process Technology, 1960–1969

By the beginning of the 1960's, government policy encouraged the expansion of excess refining capacity, which reduced the incentive to develop new process technology. Because of this excess capacity, few refiners maintained an operating capacity of more than 85 percent of their maximum. Although this "cushion" of refining capacity satisfied the concern of policy makers for national defense, it had the counterproductive effect of delaying the introduction of new processes. The general feeling throughout the industry was that only small improvements were necessary in existing processes and techniques. Economical refinery operation, with the integration of process units, was the primary thrust, and it was aimed at intensive efforts to "debottleneck" existing refining capacity. With refineries operating at an average of less than 85 percent of total capacity, and with the competition from imports, existing processes were expected to meet the rising octane requirements for premium and regular gasoline.

This focus on existing processes led to the reevaluation of the substitution capability of processes. For example, the role of hydrotreating changed from that of catalytic reforming of feedstock to a more diversified one. It, as well as alkylation, became increasingly important in meeting motor octane ratings. Such intraprocess emphasis also led to a further reduction in yields of residuals as prices of these products, in the period 1960–1965, reached the lowest levels on record. The ineffectiveness of import restrictions tended to weaken domestic product prices and induce the location of new heavy oil refineries in the Caribbean. This period of depressed price levels also led to the permanent shutting down of smaller, outmoded refineries and to investment in capacity solely to gain the economic benefits associated with large, modern units. On the West Coast (PAD District V), which was normally oriented toward residual production, the competition from the natural gas that was rapidly being introduced with the growth of interstate pipelines contributed to a drop in demand for heating oils. Thus, this period on the West Coast was characterized by the rapid introduction of greater capacity for lighter fuels and the increase of residual oil reducing processes for both majors and independents.

By early 1963 federal concern for air and water pollution control was increasing. Planning for process expansion had to consider emission controls at plants as well as the potential emissions of the motor gasolines and fuel oils produced. Indeed, by 1966 federal pollution control legislation, plus thirty-five new water conservation laws in nineteen states, began to have an inevitable impact on expenditures for refinery process growth. For example, in 1966 refiners had a total intake of about 3.6 billion gallons of water per day, primarily for cooling. The new laws required additional treatment of the water before its discharge. The initial reaction of refiners was to switch to air cooling.

Most of the domestic crude oil consumed at U.S. refineries was sweet, and most of the refineries in the United States had been engineered to process sweet crudes. Although hydrotreating was useful in processing high-sulfur crudes, technical knowledge of desulfurization was limited, and known processes were quite costly. The net effect was to put a premium on sweet crudes, both domestic and imported. By the late 1960's the technical limitations of desulfurization forced the widespread practice of blending sweet with sour inputs.

Trends of the early 1960's were also characterized by the growing importance of condensate and natural gas liquids and the continued reduction in yields of residual fuel oils. In keeping with the increased use of natural gas, condensate and gas liquids tended to displace increasing amounts of raw crude as refinery inputs. In turn, residual oil became a charge stock in the sense that it also replaced some crude oil. Therefore, it is not entirely surprising that residual imports were completely decontrolled by 1966, nor is it surprising that import controls on crude oil were set at 12.2 percent of U.S. production of *both* crude oil and natural gas liquids. The incentive to use gas liquids was reinforced by the fact that state prorationing laws did not apply to them.

By 1964 hydrocracking had gained wide acceptance as a replacement for cat cracking, which showed a decline for the first time in twenty-five years. The need to upgrade residual fuels into more profitable products was responsible for the accelerated growth of hydrocracking; it made its greatest initial growth in PAD District V. California crude oils are generally medium- to high-sulfur oils and are largely asphaltic. Thus, with the introduction of natural gas into California markets, some of the new hydrocracking units were located there. In some of those units residual fuel oil could be charged directly to the hydrocracker without going through such intermediate steps as coking or propane deasphalting.

Although decontrol of residual fuel oil imports in 1966 also encouraged expansion of hydrocracking, it was the introduction in the same year of improved cracking catalysts that assured this process its place as the refiner's principal gasoline-producing tool. One basic contribution was from zeolitic catalysts that increased yields of gasoline while using lower recycle ratios, that is, converting a higher percentage of the feedstock to gasoline on its first pass through the reactor. Other catalytic crackers using different processes (such as the fluid type) increased gasoline yields with higher recycle ratios.

The initial appearance of sulfur content standards for products in 1967 and the push for a lead-free gasoline placed new emphasis on hydroprocessing capacity, particularly hydrorefining. In addition, reforming, isomerization, and alkylation became the primary processes from which the higher pool octanes necessary in unleaded gasoline could be achieved.

By 1971 and 1972 process expansion was relatively insignificant, because a cumulative number of uncertainties plagued investment decisions. Lead removal schedules were continually being revised by the Environmental Protection Agency, and uncertainty about oil import changes reduced refiners' incentives to build new capacity, as did the growing shortage of domestic low-sulfur crude oils. Many of the large low-sulfur crude fields in the United States were declining in daily average production. Many refiners, both on the Gulf Coast and inland, were for the first time forced to use foreign sweet crudes, the high cost of which led to intensive efforts to develop a less costly desulfurization process.

In summary, since 1948 refining has been characterized by the evolution of new and costlier technologies, with the competitive elimination of older processes, and the gradual increase in the size of refineries. In many cases, the introduction of new, competitive technological advances required the simultaneous development of larger distillation plants. However, few empirical studies have been attempted to evaluate the organizational efficiency of the refining industry in terms of resource use. In particular, identification of the most efficient size of plant and, moreso, the most efficient balance between the most effective technological process and distillation capacity could provide an evolving benchmark useful for examining the efficiency of the majors and the independents.

This general overview of process expansion has been concerned mainly with the influence of demand for improved qualities and greater volumes of motor gasoline. The equally important influence of government policy will be examined in depth in a later chapter, but policy is so inextricably involved in technological advances, supply, demand, price, and the very survival of petroleum companies that it will pop up time and time again throughout this and succeeding chapters. Government intervention in stimulating the expansion of distillation and conversion under the guise of national security nevertheless was a major factor in the limited expansion of the early 1960's.

Competition and Concentration in Refining

Ensuring the survival of the small, independent refiner has been one of the two fundamental rationales of government oil policy. Because it is so closely related to oil import policy, as previously mentioned, a separate chapter will deal with its development and its interaction with other federal and state oil policies. Nevertheless, this survival rationale of government policy was, presumably, meant to ensure competition in refining. The question whether, in the absence of government supports, competition would have increased, decreased, or remained unchanged was never addressed by policy makers. The small independents, of course, claimed to represent the last vestiges of competition in refining, thus implying anticompetitive behavior by the majors.

According to the structuralist theory of industrial organization, monopolistic or collusive oligopolistic behavior can be expected in

industries where entry is limited by artificial barriers (Stigler 1968).
Bain (1956) has argued that the "condition of entry" refers to the
extent to which, in the long run, established firms can elevate their
selling price above the minimum average costs of production and
distribution (that is, those costs associated with operation at optimal
scales) without encouraging potential entrants to enter the industry.
With this disadvantage potential entrants could not make satisfactory profits at such prices—or at the even lower prices that could be
expected after their new outputs were added to market supply. Bain
concludes: "The highest selling price that established sellers in an
industry can persistently charge without attracting new entry may
be referred to as the 'maximum entry-forestalling price.' Then the
condition of entry is measured numerically as the percentage by
which the maximum entry-forestalling price exceeds the minimum
attainable average costs of established firms" (pp. 192–193). Bain
and others have also classified the "immediate" condition of entry
into an industry in terms of degrees of disadvantage to potential entrants and degrees of advantage to established firms.

This method of determining the condition of entry has come to
be known as the theory of limit pricing.[10] Mathematically, it can be
described in the following way. Assume that established firms can
maintain a price P_o above the long-run competitive level P_c without
attracting new entry. If E is the value of the condition of entry, then
$E = (P_o - P_c)/P_o$.
The lower the value of E, the easier the entry. When $E = 0, P_o = P_c$.
Firms can either choose a price higher than P_o and have new entrants appear, or they can take note of E and select a price for P_o
that will exclude new entry and sacrifice short-run profits for long-
run gains. The theory of limit pricing suggests the latter as best
policy. On the pre-entry demand curve, firms will select the highest
entry-barring price, P_e.[11] Note that this theory of limit pricing is as

[10] The theory has tended to focus on the short-run consequences of *potential* entry. The argument presented here is in static terms. Recently, Kamien and
Swartz (1972) have focused on the probabilistic approach to potential entry.

[11] The profit maximization problem for a monopolist to limit entry is to:

(1) maximize: $\pi = P_e Q - C(Q)$

(2) subject to: $P_e \leq \overline{P}$,

where P_e is price, $P_e = P(Q)$, $P_e' < 0$, Q is output and $C(Q)$ is cost, and $\overline{P}$ is
the price at which entry can reasonably be anticipated;

important from the standpoint of price as from the standpoint of control over market output, that is, concentration.

Entry cannot be effectively impeded, for example, if outside, factors have a strong influence on the firm's pricing practice. Neither will it be effectively impeded if technology is rapidly changing and there are no patent barriers to the adoption of new technology; here, potential entrants will have cost advantages over established firms using older, higher-cost technology. In refining, the latter undoubtedly has been the case, especially during the 1950's when introduction of new processes was quite rapid. In addition, if entrants find they can enter on a scale lower than the minimum efficient scale (MES), the value of the condition of entry will also be reduced. (The MES is a measure of the size of a plant or process that is increasing in relative importance compared to other plants or processes, whose sizes are declining in relative importance. Although the MES is difficult to measure precisely, several statistical approaches are available and are developed later in this chapter.) Double entry barriers are created, however, if attaining the current MES requires major capital outlays and high-cost financing. This barrier effect is reinforced if achieving the MES requires a larger market share. Also, because of the unique relationship of vertical integration into crude oil production and the competitive effective size of crude oil refining, the ability to maintain a high crude oil price to nonintegrated entrants may also effectively impede entry into refining. In the last case, P_e will be a price that is less than the entry-inducing $\overline{P}$ for refined products but that is high enough to support a high posted field price for crude petroleum. With this strategy, established integrated refiners can block entry, and even stymie expansion, by smaller competitors, but if the market share required to achieve the MES by a firm with a single plant is small, then this strategy of joint price limitation may not impede entry. The advantages of optimal size may offset the disadvantages of nonintegration.

The general condition of entry supposedly will have constant

---

(3) $P_e = MC/[1 - 1/\eta\,(1 - \lambda/Q)]$,
where λ is the Lagrange multiplier and reflects the shadow price of the constraint.

values only if potential entrants are all equally disadvantaged and if the economies of large-scale firms are unimportant. In petroleum refining, economies of scale are important as factors influencing entry; however, a sizable amount of suboptimal capacity in the industry suggests that economies of scale have not been an effective barrier to entry. Entry of firms at less than the MES suggests that potential entrants into petroleum refining have not been disadvantaged. The existence of differential advantages that violate normal considerations of economic efficiency must explain why newcomers continue to enter. Political privilege provides one example of such an advantage. Another example derives from the fact, which Bain and others failed to note, that the established firms' lack of complete, quality information on the maximum entry forestalling price is sufficient to attract entrants. Imperfect information regarding the costs to be incurred by potential entrants can result in setting prices lower than the entry foreclosing level of the least disadvantaged potential entrant. Furthermore, as Greenhut (1970) and Isard (1972) have shown, separation of refineries from their final markets can provide interstices for smaller firms in the marketing areas of the established refiners. Surely some of the entry into refining by smaller, independent firms has been at locations distant from the market areas dominated by established firms.

Harrod (1952), Hicks (1954), Kaldor (1952), and Hahn (1955) have argued that since established firms are differentiated in size, quality, and managerial efficiency, any particular firm at a given moment is faced with close and distant rivals in terms of similarity of product, convenience of location, customer services, access to comparable quality inputs, and so on. In turn, entry of a new rival typically will not have equal (or negligible) impact on *all* existing firms, but will have greater effect on one or several firms already in the industry and less impact on the others. Thus, the 1968 entry of Getty Oil into refining on the U.S. East Coast had more impact on refiners marketing in PAD Districts I–IV than on those in PAD District V or in Canada.

Harrod (1952) and others have argued that an established firm would recognize the possible entry of a close rival and would attempt to forestall it or take its possibility into account when selecting plant size. Because the production rates before and after a rival's entry will differ, plant size cannot be optimal for both periods; in fact, it will not be optimally chosen for *either* production rate alone. There may actually be a range of optimal production. Nevertheless, this analysis leads to the conclusion that capacity after a competitor's entry may be excessive. This rationale differs from that posed by Chamberlin (1951), who argues that a firm in monopolistic or imperfect competition would operate a productive facility at a lower rate than that at which average cost achieves its minimum. According to Chamberlin, economic profits will attract rivals to the point that profit is eliminated. The existence of excess capacity with simultaneous low or no profits will make an industry unattractive to potential entrants. Indeed, such a condition could lead to consolidation efforts by established firms and exit from the industry by firms which cannot survive with plants operating at less than the MES.

Artificially induced expansion of plant operations at less than the MES and increases in excess capacity can be caused by government intervention. As previous sections indicated, government tax support contributed to the rapid buildup of refining capacity during the 1950's. This support inevitably undermined the effect of any limit pricing behavior by major firms. Nevertheless, the normal market reaction to excess capacity was the accelerated shutdown of less competitive plants and the eventual exit from the industry of firms with higher-cost, less efficient operations. To survive under conditions of rising excess capacity, both large and small firms may seek alternative ways to reduce costs, or at least to prevent other established firms from gaining any additional advantage. For example, firms may seek increased regulation of industry that will accomplish what market activity has failed to provide.

Stigler (1971) has argued that government involvement is based on a theory of supply of and demand for regulation. To survive, firms may demand that the government provide cash subsidies, restrict entry, suppress the growth of substitute or complementary industries, or control prices. Stigler argues that as an industry becomes increasingly regulated, more and more small firms will have a correspondingly increasing amount of influence, a greater amount of influence than they would have in an unregulated industry. This characteristic is particularly true when a specialized domestic resource such as crude oil is necessary for industry operation. In the case of refining, the government contributed to stimulating a costly amount of excess capacity and, when the survival of a small fraction of the industry was threatened, responded by providing the smaller segment with special subsidies and other regulatory privileges couched within oil import policy and later within the framework of the Federal Energy Administration's allocation and entitlements program (see chapter 2).

To examine these entry restraining or inducing propositions, we first evaluate exit from and entry into the industry and the extent of suboptimal capacity in the industry and then evaluate the changes in market power in refining over time.

THE RECORD OF EXIT AND ENTRY IN REFINING

Entry is defined as (1) new firms in refining, and (2) "shutdown" entrants who actually shut down their plants and then reenter by making those plants operable at a later date. Exits consist of (1) permanent exits from refining—those who permanently abandon or close their refineries; (2) transitory exits—firms that shut down their facilities temporarily and reenter at a later date; and (3) mergers and acquisitions—firms which leave the industry as distinct business entities and merge with other firms. We define changes in the industry's operable refining capacity by the following:

$$NRCAP_t = RCAP_t - RCAP_{t-1} \qquad (1)$$

and

$$NRCAP_t = RCAP_t + E_{t-1} - X_{t-1} + K_t \qquad (2)$$

where $NRCAP_t$ = net change in operable industry capacity

$RCAP_t$ = total operable capacity at time t

$RCAP_{t-1}$ = total operable capacity at time $t-1$

E_{t-1} = entry capacity from the previous time period

X_{t-1} = exit capacity from the previous time period

K_t = internal capacity expansion

The record of the components of expansion in total refinery capacity is provided in Table 7. From 1948 to 1975 there were a total of 220 entrants, including 179 new entrants and 41 shutdown entrants. The cumulative capacity of the new entrants accounted for only 1.6 million barrels daily. Most of the new entrants were small to medium-sized firms. New entry was split fairly evenly between the periods 1948–1960 and 1961–1975, with 88 and 91, respectively. Shutdown entrants were insignificant, particularly after 1961. Notable exceptions were 1974 and 1975, when, during the advent of the refiner cost equalization program, shutdown entrants were the highest of the entire postwar period. All of them were smaller refiners.

Total exits over the period accounted for 304 firms and some 4.1 million barrels of operable capacity. The number of permanent and transitory exits was greatest between 1961 and 1975. Merger and acquisition, in terms of the number of firms involved, was also split fairly evenly between the 1948–1960 and 1961–1975 periods. However, of the eighty-three mergers and acquisitions, accounting for over 2.3 million barrels of operable capacity, most of the merger activity occurred between 1961 and 1975. Internal expansion of existing firms, however, constituted the majority of net industry expansion, accounting for over 10.7 million barrels per calendar day for the total period. Internal expansion includes new "grass-roots" refineries of established firms as well as on-site expansions.

It is consistent with limit pricing theory that most of the entry into refining occurred during a period of falling real prices of crude oil in the 1950's. Because this period was also one of rapid technical advance, cost advantages for new entrants may also have been a factor. Later, the entry-restraining impact of the increase in real crude oil prices in 1974 appears to have been offset by the FEA's crude oil entitlements or "cost equalization" program. Nevertheless, most exits from the industry occurred during the 1950's. The great majority of these exiting plants, however, were obsolete topping or thermal processing plants that were often too small to be economical. The small capacity accounted for by exits from 1948 to 1958 totaled less than one million barrels. From 1958 onward—the period of oil import quotas which, paradoxically, were designed to guarantee the survival of independent refiners—the volume of capacity of exiting plants increased significantly. The vast majority of these exits consisted of mergers and acquisitions among small refiners operating older, smaller plants. The FEA entitlements and alloca-

TABLE 7

Components of Net Changes in Growth of Operable Refinery Capacity, 1948–1975

Year	Total Entry		New Entry		Shutdown Entry		Total Exits	
	No.	Capacity	No.	Capacity	No.	Capacity	No.	Capacity
1948	—	—	—	—	—	—	—	—
1949	6	27,100	6	27,100	—	—	20	77,295
1950	11	21,250	8	12,450	3	8,800	24	185,500
1951	14	39,700	7	10,900	7	28,800	15	97,255
1952	12	26,710	9	21,400	3	5,310	11	19,300
1953	4	9,950	4	9,950	—	—	15	87,537
1954	6	27,000	5	26,000	1	1,000	13	44,840
1955	6	26,750	5	26,000	1	750	11	148,350
1956	13	104,300	12	99,800	1	4,500	12	88,050
1957	11	75,634	11	75,634	—	—	11	102,300
1958	4	35,800	4	35,800	—	—	7	46,300
1959	14	104,950	11	94,150	3	10,800	13	100,700
1960	8	92,302	6	79,802	2	12,500	10	158,850
Subtotal	109	591,446	88	518,986	21	72,460	162	1,156,277

TABLE 7 (continued)

Year	Total Entry		New Entry		Shutdown Entry		Total Exits	
	No.	Capacity	No.	Capacity	No.	Capacity	No.	Capacity
1961	5	23,830	5	23,830	—	—	11	104,100
1962	4	9,700	4	9,700	—	—	3	62,000
1963	8	82,000	8	82,000	—	—	15	184,800
1964	4	104,840	4	104,840	—	—	7	36,400
1965	7	129,950	7	129,950	—	—	15	97,019
1966	4	407,600	3	406,700	1	900	7	624,540
1967	6	93,000	5	68,000	1	25,000	7	108,900
1968	12	277,950	12	277,950	—	—	9	493,100
1969	5	70,100	5	70,100	—	—	10	849,000
1970	7	48,200	7	48,200	—	—	3	9,700
1971	5	43,800	5	43,800	—	—	10	102,210
1972	7	180,400	7	180,400	—	—	7	105,200
1973	6	35,500	5	34,500	1	1,000	2	1,900
1974	17	157,450	8	54,450	9	103,000	24	180,350
1975	14	299,130	6	90,890	8	208,240	12	60,050
Subtotal	111	1,963,450	91	1,625,310	20	338,140	142	3,019,269
Total	220	2,554,896	179	2,144,296	41	410,600	304	4,175,546

TABLE 7 (continued)

Year	Permanent Exits		Transitory Exits (Shutdowns)		Mergers and Acquisitions		Internal Expansion	Total Change in Industry Capacity	Total Industry Capacity
	No.	Capacity	No.	Capacity	No.	Capacity			
1948	—	—	—	—	—	—	—	—	5,825,566
1949	8	24,860	7	10,235	5	42,200	455,134	+404,939	6,230,505
1950	7	21,650	14	106,650	3	57,200	156,743	−7,507	6,222,998
1951	3	4,600	4	11,855	8	80,800	536,372	+478,817	6,701,815
1952	5	9,200	3	4,500	3	5,600	452,141	+459,551	7,161,366
1953	4	11,200	7	11,637	4	64,700	397,922	+320,335	7,481,701
1954	5	15,560	5	4,780	3	24,500	318,242	+300,402	7,782,103
1955	4	15,850	5	31,500	2	101,000	411,651	+287,051	8,069,154
1956	9	68,050	1	5,000	2	15,000	295,397	+311,647	8,380,801
1957	4	37,900	4	18,000	3	46,400	454,706	+428,040	8,808,841
1958	2	17,000	4	12,800	1	16,500	141,566	+131,066	8,939,907
1959	7	52,400	3	17,000	3	31,300	506,584	+510,834	9,450,741
1960	5	80,100	3	3,250	2	75,500	159,136	+92,588	9,543,329
Subtotal	63	358,370	60	237,207	39	560,700	4,285,594	3,717,763	

TABLE 7 (continued)

Year	Permanent Exits		Transitory Exits (Shutdowns)		Mergers and Acquisitions		Internal Expansion	Total Change in Industry Capacity	Total Industry Capacity
	No.	Capacity	No.	Capacity	No.	Capacity			
1961	4	21,100	—	—	7	83,000	166,666	+86,396	9,629,725
1962	1	5,000	—	—	2	57,000	216,323	+164,023	9,793,748
1963	5	32,800	3	12,000	7	140,000	123,843	+21,043	9,814,791
1964	3	19,400	2	4,400	2	12,600	179,933	+248,373	10,063,164
1965	8	14,775	5	56,244	2	26,000	212,716	+245,647	10,308,811
1966	4	414,040	2	15,000	1	195,500	227,288	+10,348	10,319,159
1967	2	30,000	2	5,900	3	73,000	261,988	+246,088	10,565,247
1968	5	236,800	1	3,000	3	253,300	975,397	+760,247	11,325,494
1969	3	52,750	5	24,250	2	772,000	1,182,035	+403,135	11,728,629
1970	1	3,500	1	5,000	1	1,200	268,064	+306,564	12,035,193
1971	2	11,500	5	16,400	3	74,310	834,265	+775,855	12,811,048
1972	3	96,000	4	9,200	—	—	367,370	+442,570	13,253,618
1973	0	—	2	1,900	0	—	425,053	+458,653	13,712,271
1974	8	62,500	8	56,200	8	61,650	480,395	+740,845	14,453,116
1975	4	19,500	5	27,800	3	12,750	507,594	+527,434	14,980,550
Subtotal	53	1,019,665	45	237,294	44	1,762,310	6,428,930	5,437,221	
Total	116	1,378,035	105	474,501	83	2,323,010	10,714,524	9,154,984	

SOURCE: Data compiled from Bureau of Mines annual, 1948–1975.

tion program of the 1970's may well have been responsible for further extending the economic life of high-cost, uneconomic refineries.

MARKET STRUCTURE AND THE EXTENT OF SUBOPTIMAL CAPACITY

In refining, suboptimal capacity is that fraction of industry output produced by a fringe of small plants which are declining in relative importance, basically because of technical disadvantages associated with operating at less than the MES. To estimate the MES, the "survivor principle" developed by Stigler and later applied by Weiss (1964) and Saving (1961) is used. The fundamental postulate of the survivor principle is that competition between different sizes of plants sifts out the more efficient enterprises. Stigler argued that if a particular size of plant increased in relative importance, then that size had advantages of scale over smaller or larger plants whose size classes were declining in relative importance. Stigler attributes the technique to Mill and Marshall. For example, Marshall (1920, p. 597) states: "For as a general rule the law of substitution—which is nothing more than a special and limited application of the law of survival of the fittest—tends to make one method of industrial organization supplant another when it offers a direct and immediate service at a lower price."

The measure of the optimum size of a survivor is consequently a measure of comparative efficiency. It serves as one basis for evaluating how efficiently an industrial organization uses available resources. As an increasing cost industry, firms in refining are under continuous pressure to allocate resources efficiently for a given state of technology. With technical improvement, efficient firms will tend to gradually adopt the "best-practice" technology in their effort to increase output and survive in their markets. To measure the optimum size for a survivor, plants in the refining industry are first classified by size. The share of operable refinery distillation capacity of each size class is calculated over a period of time. Only operating capacity is considered; shutdown capacity is eliminated. If the share of a given class falls, it is relatively inefficient; in general, the more rapidly the share falls, the more inefficient is the size class. Of course, changes in the market shares held by plants in various size classes may result from those influences, other than scale economies, which dictate how efficiently the refining industry uses its resources. The shift in relative importance of plants of various size classes could be attributable to the oligopsonistic power of integrated refiners in crude oil markets. On the other hand, policies of the federal government could also influence the shifts, or even subsidize inefficient firms, to such a point that there would be little incentive to shift plants toward more efficient sizes. The effect of oligopsony would tend to encourage expansion toward the MES, while public policy intervention in the form of special privileges for small firms could delay the normal expansion toward the MES over time.

In applying the survivor technique to petroleum refining, one measures plant size by operating capacity expressed as a percentage of the industry total. Capacity is an acceptable measure of plant size since refining is an industry in which production is on a continuous daily basis, and an increase in production trends also implies a similar increase in capacity. In addition, production data are not uniformly reported by every major and independent refiner from 1948 to 1974. Separate estimates of the firm and plant MES have been made for majors and independents, although a more relevant MES statistic would relate to the individual plant or refinery. Note also that although the multiplant firm may be expected to build MES refineries, insufficient data to identify multiplant organizations prohibit an examination of further economies which may result. For the same reason, capacity which was either shut down or under construction has also been excluded from these estimates. The results are limited to the period ending with 1972 price controls.

Initially, without company or regional classification, Table 8 shows the trend toward the optimal size of firm for selected years. The table clearly shows that firms controlling less than 1 percent of the operable capacity of the industry have shown a marked decline. Firms controlling between 1 percent and 5 percent of industry capacity have remained relatively stable, while firms controlling between 5 percent and 10 percent have clearly increased their share. Since 1948, firms with less than 0.1 percent of capacity have either lost their shares of the industry or have moved to a higher size classification. Note that firms in the 0.75 percent and under classifications experienced solid declines from 1948 to 1956, but between

TABLE 8

Distribution of Operable Refining Capacity by Relative Size of Company,
Total United States

Company Size (as percentage of operable industry capacity)	Percentage of Operable Industry Capacity							Number of Companies with Operable Capacity as of Jan. 1						
	1948	1952	1956	1960	1964	1968	1972	1948	1952	1956	1960	1964	1968	1972
Under 0.1	5.39	4.21	3.83	2.96	3.00	2.28	2.20	131	114	97	85	78	68	61
0.1–0.2	3.87	3.68	3.00	3.23	2.10	2.31	2.77	28	26	20	22	14	17	20
0.2–0.3	4.21	2.09	1.43	2.13	2.38	1.64	2.21	17	8	6	9	9	7	9
0.3–0.4	3.42	1.59	2.68	3.09	2.47	3.13	1.34	10	5	8	9	7	9	4
0.4–0.5	1.73	1.84	2.08	2.24	1.79	1.31	0.87	4	4	5	5	4	3	2
0.5–0.75	4.10	4.71	4.40	3.36	1.24	3.10	4.41	7	3	7	6	2	5	7
0.75–1.0	0	1.63	0	0	1.86	4.17	2.47	0	2	0	0	2	5	3
1.0–2.5	11.98	12.25	11.25	16.21	22.28	13.26	13.00	7	7	7	9	13	8	6
2.5–5	14.32	16.70	14.14	16.11	12.90	17.57	12.86	4	5	5	5	4	5	4
5–10	39.78	40.26	46.49	50.66	49.98	51.22	57.87	6	6	7	7	7	7	8
10–15	11.20	11.02	10.69	0	0	0	0	1	1	1	0	0	0	0
Total	100	100	100	100	100	100	100	215	186	163	157	140	134	125

SOURCE: Copp 1974b.

1956 and 1968 their shares declined less rapidly and in some cases actually increased.

PLANT-LEVEL MES FOR MAJORS AND INDEPENDENTS

For the United States it is appropriate to distinguish two refinery markets—PAD Districts I–IV and PAD District V. Results limited to operations in PAD Districts I–IV indicate a pattern similar to that of the national total. The decline in relative shares is more pronounced for firms controlling less than 0.75 percent of capacity. Firms whose shares are between 0.75 percent and 5 percent have shown the greatest growth. The trend of smaller size classes toward sharp declines from 1948 to 1956, however, is sharply reversed for the period from 1960 to 1968. Moreover, when the additional classifications of major and independent are introduced for PAD Districts I–IV only, we find that the greatest significant change over the twenty-five-year period has occurred between major firms in size classes 0.75 percent to 1 percent. The independents, as expected, demonstrated a tendency to expand toward larger size classes. A more desirable statistical indicator of the MES would be the most efficient balance of conversion processes for all refiners.[12]

Because the interpretation of the MES for a firm is ambiguous

---

[12] A comparison by process is available in Copp 1974b. The processes chosen for comparison include thermal cracking, thermal reforming, hydrocracking, catalytic cracking, and catalytic reforming. The rather extensive computations for these processes show the gradual elimination of thermal reforming by both majors and independents. Thermal cracking also has been phased down by both classes of firms. Independents tended to have a relatively greater amount of thermal cracking capacity in their plants of minimum efficient size. High levels of suboptimal capacity of independents are apparently related to relatively high levels of thermal cracking capacity.

Thermal processes were less efficient in converting a barrel of crude into higher-value products. Current "best-practice" techniques to produce gasoline and distillates are those which use hydrogen treating in cracking and those which employ catalytic processes in cracking and reforming. Catalytic processing has been quite adaptive to both large and small size classes of distillation capacity. The most notable exceptions were the smallest size classes of independents in PAD Districts I–IV. PAD District V data show that even for smaller size classes of majors, cat cracking is not a dominant process. None of the independents in District V had any cat cracking capacity. The opposite was true for cat reforming in District V as well as in Districts I–IV. No unique pattern for hydrocrack-

and can be misleading, the appropriate unit for MES estimates is the plant, particularly individual plants owned by majors and independents by PAD districts. We can detect whether both majors and independents tend to adjust their plant scales toward technically optimal or efficient levels. Table 9 for majors in PAD Districts I–IV indicates that since 1948 the bulk of their refining capacity has expanded toward plant sizes that accounted for 0.4 percent to 5.0 percent of industry capacity. Their MES appears to lie in the size classes accounting for between 0.4 percent and 1.0 percent of operable industry capacity. Thus, some other explanation must be found for the survival capability of plants that are below minimum efficient size. The distribution for independents in PAD Districts I–IV in Table 10 shows that independents have also shifted away from smaller plants, but not to the extent required for minimum efficient size. Indeed, for the size class 0.1 percent to 0.2 percent the number of plants declined in the period 1948–1956 and then *increased* in 1960–1968. A similar reversal occurred for the size distribution 0.3–0.4 percent.

PAD District V results for majors showed that the minimum efficient plant capacity was in the 1.0 percent size class. Relatively greater capacity is contained in the 1.5 percent to 6.0 percent size classes. Very few plants are in size classes above that range. Independent refiners, however, are few in PAD District V. About two-thirds of their 3.58 percent of PAD District V industry capacity in 1972 was in size classes 0.4 percent to 0.75 percent. All plants of independents were below the MES for majors' plants.

These plant data for PAD Districts I–IV and District V can be plotted to show the long-run MES curves for majors and independents (see Figure 5). The date of the reversals of MES trends for both independents and majors at about 1960 suggests that nontechnical advantages may have allowed the survival or extended life of otherwise technically obsolete plant sizes. Because the cost of raw petroleum inputs represents almost 85 percent of refinery operating cost, factors affecting the supply of crude oil to both major and in-

---

ing by size classes is apparent. It is clear, however, that hydrocracking was more rapidly adopted by majors than by independents, even though the process was readily adaptive to both small and large refineries.

TABLE 9
Distribution of Operable Refining Capacity by Relative Size of Plant, Majors, Districts I-IV

Company Size (as percentage of operable industry capacity)	Percentage of Operable Industry Capacity							Number of Plants with Operable Capacity as of Jan. 1						
	1948	1952	1956	1960	1964	1968	1972	1948	1952	1956	1960	1964	1968	1972
Under 0.1	0.97	1.07	0.63	0.61	0.50	0.55	0.45	16	18	11	9	7	9	6
0.1–0.2	2.82	3.01	2.65	2.36	2.34	0.89	0.79	19	21	19	15	15	6	5
0.2–0.3	3.85	2.83	2.17	2.13	1.64	2.06	1.67	16	11	9	9	7	9	7
0.3–0.4	2.64	1.69	3.10	2.14	2.14	2.87	2.89	8	5	9	6	6	8	8
0.4–0.5	3.96	5.48	5.38	5.46	6.61	7.74	5.76	9	12	12	12	15	17	13
0.5–0.75	9.23	5.53	10.04	10.88	9.94	7.55	6.16	14	9	16	18	17	12	10
0.75–1	5.78	11.52	7.54	10.61	10.53	11.52	10.16	7	13	9	12	12	13	12
1–1.5	8.38	9.87	10.36	7.30	9.64	9.73	17.13	7	8	9	6	8	8	14
1.5–2.5	14.01	18.82	15.89	20.88	21.08	15.91	16.08	7	9	8	11	11	9	8
2.5–4	14.47	9.54	21.40	15.84	12.85	17.76	21.79	5	3	7	5	4	6	7
4–5	12.49	12.37	4.46	4.52	4.31	4.36	—	3	3	1	1	1	1	—
5–6	—	—	—	—	—	—	—	0	0	0	0	0	0	—
Total	78.61	81.74	83.63	82.73	81.58	80.95	82.86	111	112	110	104	103	98	90

Source: Copp 1974b.

TABLE 10

Distribution of Operable Refining Capacity by Relative Size of Plant, Independents,
Districts I–IV

Company Size (as percentage of operable industry capacity)	Percentage of Operable Industry Capacity							Number of Plants with Operable Capacity as of Jan. 1						
	1948	1952	1956	1960	1964	1968	1972	1948	1952	1956	1960	1964	1968	1972
Under 0.1	5.26	5.04	3.87	3.36	3.01	2.68	2.45	123	119	96	91	84	79	69
0.1–0.2	5.32	4.04	2.30	3.53	2.79	2.79	2.10	39	27	17	23	20	20	15
0.2–0.3	2.50	0.76	3.22	2.99	3.53	3.30	3.38	10	3	14	12	14	13	14
0.3–0.4	2.74	2.81	2.50	1.78	2.77	2.74	2.04	8	8	7	5	8	8	6
0.4–0.5	2.67	1.91	1.42	2.70	1.36	1.74	1.22	6	4	3	6	3	4	3
0.5–0.75	2.90	3.71	2.31	2.91	3.08	3.79	3.50	5	6	4	5	5	6	6
0.75–1	—	—	0.75	—	0.85	0.83	2.44	—	—	1	—	1	1	3
1–1.5	—	—	—	—	1.04	1.17	—	—	—	—	—	1	1	—
Totals	21.39	18.27	16.37	17.27	18.43	19.04	17.13	191	167	142	142	136	126	116

SOURCE: Copp 1974b.

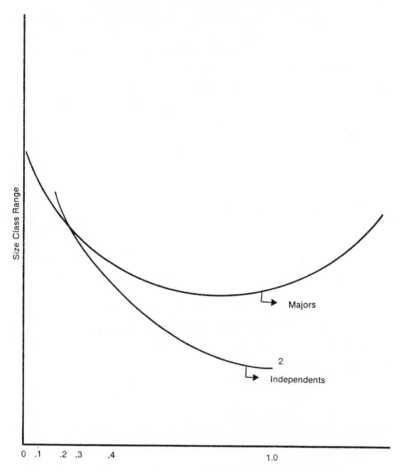

FIGURE 5. Illustrative MES Curves for Major and Independent Plants, PAD Districts I–IV

dependent refiners over time may provide the explanation for these trends.

Nevertheless, the existence of a substantial number of plants of suboptimal capacity that have survived in competition with the more efficient plants, particularly among independent firms, remains to be explained. Small firms may survive and expand because of other advantages that outweigh the technological disadvantages. These advantages can include monopsonistic positions in relatively distant crude oil fields that are not large enough to attract larger refiners. For some refiners such is undoubtedly the case. However, since most independents and smaller majors tend to be attracted to similar classes of fields, these monopsonistic refiners inevitably come under the oligopsonistic "umbrella" maintained by the price leaders. If the independents become vertically integrated into crude production, this integration could explain their survival capability. Most independent refiners, however, are either not integrated into production or else hold very small crude oil supplies relative to their refinery needs. Thus, some other factors affecting the cost of crude supply must provide the explanation. For the independent refiners, these factors have been favorable periodic tax treatment (that is, the Accelerated Amortization Plan) and, more important, our nation's oil import policy and recent price control and product allocation policy.

This section has shown that, in terms of a range of minimum efficient sizes, there appears to be substantial suboptimal or less than minimally efficient capacity among plants operated by independents. For conversion processes there appears to be no set pattern of deviation from the MES. Scale requirements of advanced technical processes do not seem to have created any real disadvantages. In failing to adopt the optimal distillation conversion mix, particularly with respect to the most efficient distillation size of plant relative to conversion processes, the smaller independents have survived with uneconomic costs of operation. Failure to expand toward the MES appears to be correlated with the relatively greater use of older refining techniques. That is, the higher cost of operating at less than minimally efficient capacity has precluded the relatively more intensive use of downstream "best-practice" techniques.

Results of this section indicate that refining industry resources have been misallocated because of the substantial fraction of suboptimal capacity. The explanation for the higher social cost of production by plants of less than MES is explainable by government petroleum policy, often justified on the dual grounds of national security and the need to ensure survival of the small, independent refiner. By attempting to ensure competition in refining, the government has encouraged the otherwise uneconomical survival of small firms. Indeed, it has been this concern for the gradual "disappearance" of small, independent refiners that has led Congress and the Federal Trade Commission (FTC) to periodic investigation of the major refiners. Their pervasive theme has been that competition in the petroleum industry contributes in a positive way to national security. It appears that in the absence of such a mixed-monopoly energy policy, industry resources might have been better aimed toward achieving the MES.

Estimating Market Power in Refining

Investigations of the market power of the majors during each energy crisis have most often employed the static average concentration ratios. For a single time period, the ratio of output, say of the top eight firms, divided by the total output of the industry was used as the measure of concentration (CR) for the top eight firms. A recent FTC complaint cites "increasing concentration" by the top eight major refiners. In 1972 and 1973 a major effort was made in Congress to remedy this situation. The Industrial Reorganization Act of 1972 (S.R. 1167), introduced by Senator Phillip Hart, authorized the breaking up of firms in industries in which four firms account for 50 percent or more of total output or sales. This proposed bill replaced the Concentrated Industries Act of 1971 (S.R. 2614), which called for a "critical concentration ratio" of 70 percent. The difficulty with such ratios is that while they are easy to compute, the economic meaning of their measurements is still ambiguous (Biesiot 1970).

Economists disagree on the purpose of concentration measures. Stigler (1968, p. 30) states that the ultimate purpose of measures of industry concentration is the comparative analysis of the concentration of different industries or of the same industries at different times. He also argues that the next most important purpose of any concentration measure should be to predict the extent of the departure of rate of return or price from the long-run competitive level. However, does a concentration ratio of 0.50 percent imply more competitive profits compared to a ratio of 0.70 percent? The fact that no concise answer is provided by the static concentration ratio suggests its limitations.

A static measure by itself cannot indicate monopoly power. Static measures can only indicate a probability that monopolistic practices might be expected to exist, and even this conclusion is subject to numerous qualifications. A large number of industry behavior patterns are compatible with a concentration index. The same ratio can exist for several different shapes in concentration curves. A further objection to concentration ratios as descriptions of market structure or indications of market power is that high ratios may exist although there is considerable instability in the market shares of individual firms. The ability of leading firms to maintain their relative positions is more important as a measure of the intensity of competition than is the extent of concentration at a single point in time. This objection applies just as well to legislation implicating monopoly based on a critical concentration ratio. A more acceptable market power indicator might be a comparative average concentration ratio tested over five to ten years, depending on the activity. The three-year period suggested by Senator Hart's bill is too short to account for random influences on the positions of the companies holding market shares. A longer-term ratio would indicate "turnover," or exit and entry into the top four or eight positions in a particular activity, and relate this transitory phenomenon to the permanent aspects of concentration. A similar objection is applicable to all summarily time-restricted measures which fail to recognize that an indicator of reduced or increased competition can be valid only in terms of estimates over a period of time.

The theoretical foundation for concentration ratios is that competition increases as the number of firms in a market or industry increases. Fama and Laffer (1972) and others have recently demonstrated, however, that even under the theoretical market assumptions of perfect competition, the number of firms is not critical to a competitive market. They conclude: "When there are at least two non-colluding firms in an industry, there is no clear-cut relationship between the number of firms and the degree of competition. The absence of perfect competition . . . must arise from such things as indivisibilities, factor immobility, non-maximizing behavior by factors, monopolistic access by individual firms to production techniques, and lack of information concerning the returns earned by given factors in different uses" (p. 670).

Furthermore, when consideration is given to the geographic extent of market areas for each firm, the use and even the theoretical justification for aggregate average concentration ratios break down. Not all firms in the top four, eight, or twenty in an industry compete in all market areas. Thus, the spatial separation of sales competition can effectively eliminate a national concentration ratio as a useful tool in deriving any measure of market control. This effect of spacing on competitive pricing is not normally considered in the economic theory of firm and market organization. The economic theory of perfect competition implicitly assumes that all buyers and sellers are located at a single point. When buyers and sellers are considered to be dispersed, an unavoidable functional relationship between price and distance appears: the elasticity of consumer demand at a relevant price may well change as the sales radius of a firm expands. In terms of S.R. 1167, regional application of the critical-concentration-ratio test would require an arbitrary definition of the extent of the market. The monopoly power implied by a regional ratio would therefore be arbitrarily designed into the test instead of observed from market forces.

Moreover, consideration of the spatial separation of refiners would more accurately reveal the impact on variable market power resulting from the joint economic influence of ownership of regional refineries plus crude oil and oil product pipelines. Pipeline control can reinforce the power provided through refining dominance. How- ever, as Cookenboo (1955) has ably pointed out, there is no meaningful measure of concentration for crude oil pipelines. The relationship of barrels per day carried in lines owned by majors to the total number of barrels carried might appear to be an appropriate measure, but since the same oil is carried by two connecting lines, much of it would be counted twice, and thus the concentration would be overstated. The use of barrel-miles instead of barrels is more appropriate, but on a national basis, or that of a large region such as PAD Districts I–IV, it can cause erroneous conclusions. Thus, only the percentage of pipeline capacity from a given producing area or import center to a given refining center that is owned by the top four or eight companies would be a more appropriate statistic. Even this regional statistic, however, would not solve the problem of the spatial market areas of the major and independent refiners and, consequently, the problem of the meaningfulness of aggregate concentration ratios for refiners.

Finally, measures of regional concentration become ambiguous; because of the difficulty of defining homogeneous market areas for a group of firms, the meaning of regional monopoly power inferred from a summary measure remains imprecise. Adelman has argued that economists should concern themselves only with the implications of fewness of firms instead of studying the entire industry.[13] However, in order to evaluate potential entry and the probability of the existence of monopoly power, it is necessary to have a knowledge of changes in intraindustry structure over a period of time.

For example, examine the average concentration ratio (ACR) and marginal concentration ratio (MCR) in petroleum refining for the top four, eight, twenty and thirty firms for the continental United States, PAD Districts I–IV and PAD District V, from 1948 to 1974, as shown in Tables 11–12. The static ACR is the percentage of total industry refining accounted for by the top four firms, the top eight firms, and so on. The marginal ratio, such as MCR_8, is the difference between ACR's of the eight firms and the four firms and is the share of refining accounted for by firms ranked fifth, sixth, seventh, and eighth in refining. Looking at the ratios for individual years, one can conclude that concentration is relatively low in refining compared to other industries. However, each ACR is merely a single point on a concentration curve. If two such curves intersect, say at the eight-firm level, one cannot state that the industry was more concentrated at that particular period. The successive differences in the ACR's from the MCR's suggested by Miller (1967) for PAD Districts I–IV and District V also show relatively little change over time.

As discussed above, turnover is one potential indicator of competitive activity. At best one can measure the turnover through what

---

[13] Summary measures account for the distribution of all firms in an industry. These include the Herfindahl-Hirschman Index, the Rosenbluth Index, the entropy index, and the Comprehensive Concentration Index (CCI). (See Herfindahl 1950; Rosenbluth 1955; Hart 1971; and Horvath 1970.)

TABLE 11
Average and Marginal Refining Concentration Ratios, Districts I–IV

	ACR_4	ACR_8	ACR_{20}	ACR_{30}	MCR_8	MCR_{20}	MCR_{30}
1948	.3786	.5959	.7860	.8391	.2173	.1901	.0531
1952	.3776	.5931	.8173	.8807	.2155	.2242	.0634
1956	.3693	.5908	.8363	.8932	.2215	.2455	.0569
1960	.3522	.5595	.8273	.8848	.2073	.2678	.0575
1964	.3348	.5402	.8157	.8963	.2054	.2755	.0701
1968	.3441	.5449	.8094	.8922	.2008	.2645	.0828
1972	.3374	.5573	.8286	.9100	.2199	.2713	.0814
1974	.3122	.5370	.8117	.8952	.2248	.2747	.0835

Source: Data compiled from Bureau of Mines annual, 1948–1974.

TABLE 12
Average and Marginal Refining Concentration Ratios, District V

	ACR_4	ACR_8	ACR_{20}	ACR_{30}	MCR_8	MCR_{20}	MCR_{30}
1948	.6180	.8704	.9603	.9904	.2523	.0899	.0300
1952	.6234	.8813	.9643	.9922	.2579	.0830	.0279
1956	.6672	.9140	.9855	1	.2467	.0715	.0144
1960	.6238	.9049	.9851	1	.2811	.0801	.0148
1964	.6164	.8876	.9888	1	.2711	.1012	.0111
1968	.6035	.8645	.9811	1	.2609	.1165	.0188
1972	.5760	.8164	.9642	.9990	.2403	.1478	.0357
1974	.4395	.7879	.9699	1	.3484	.1820	.0300

Source: Data compiled from Bureau of Mines annual, 1948–1974.

could be called an "identical firm" concentration ratio. A concentration ratio can stay constant over the years, thus failing to measure the intense competition among firms which manifests itself in a constant shakeup in their rank order. To examine turnover, the top four, eight, and twenty firms in 1948 are first identified; then the shares of industry output of these same firms are examined in each succeeding year. This is the identical firm ratio. The difference between it and the orthodox concentration ratio is an indicator of displacement through turnover. In an earlier work I have estimated the identical firm displacement indices for average and marginal concentration ratios (Copp 1974*b*). That study showed that only until

1964 does any significant change occur in the rankings among the top eight. Rankings among the top twenty however, have shown changes in every period; similar results occurred for the top thirty.

One difficulty in interpreting static concentration measures is that raised by mergers and acquisitions. Other things being equal, mergers always increase concentration ratios. It does not follow that they always decrease competition. For example, a merger of smaller firms may improve their competitive position with larger rival firms.

A concentration ratio itself cannot indicate the degree of monopoly power in refining. The monopoly power of major refining firms ultimately depends upon their ability to inhibit the entry and the growth of competitive firms, large or small. Static measures in themselves do not isolate or account for any random or temporary influences that can affect the time lag of entry and exit. The time element is important because if entry is a threat in a reasonably short period of time, the large firms might find it best to forego short-term monopoly profits in order to forestall that entry. The fact that they seldom do so reflects the inability of large firms to maintain their market shares over a short period of time, and it could be evidence that these firms either have no monopoly power or that any monopolistic power they may have is only for the short run. Conversely, the ability of large firms to maintain their market shares over a long period of time would indicate their ability to foreclose their own and other markets to smaller firms and potential entrants. However, no exhaustive tests have been made of the integration of static and dynamic measures.

Permanent and Transitory Concentration in Refining

One approach, conceptualized by Grossack (1972) but still untested, attempts to measure the degree of monopoly by the ability of firms to foreclose new entry, as reflected in their permanent component of market shares. Based on the concepts of Friedman and Kuznets (1954) in their work on income distributions, market shares of firms in an industry can be conceived of as two sets of components, one permanent and the other transitory. The permanent component is that portion of the market shares that firms are able to maintain over a period of time. This permanent component derives from advantages that can be thought of as being relatively impregnable. Such advantages could result from the control of scarce, specialized resources, access to favorable trade connections, and the like.

In developing this measure of the permanent component of market shares, the Herfindahl Index is used. This index (also employed by Stigler in his test of oligopoly concentration) is useful in that it takes into account the complete size distribution of firms. It also incorporates both of the two static size structural features that are probably most relevant to the ability of the larger firms to enhance price with a minimum of market loss: the smallness of the number of firms, and the variation among the sizes of the firms. The index is defined as follows:

$$H = \sum_{i=1}^{n} X_i{}^2, \tag{3}$$

where X is the market share of the ith firm expressed as a ratio and n is the number of firms in the industry.[14] The limit of the Herfindahl Index is 1 (the case of pure monopoly).

The notions of "permanent" and "transitory" imply a reference to different periods of time. Thus, some determinants of a particular firm's advantages are permanent if they operate in, say, two or more years, while they are transitory if they operate in only one year. To isolate these components, a base period and a reference period must be used. In addition, such a measure can shed light on whether any losses of shares by the large firms have been to other large firms or to small firms and new entrants to the industry.

First, designate X_{i_0} as the ith firm's observed market share in year O, the base year, and let X_{i_t} be the same firm's observed market share in year t, the reference year. A firm in the industry that produces in only one of these years can be assigned a market share of zero in the other year so that n, the number of firms, will be the same in both years. In addition, designate X_{i_0} and X_{i_t} as deviations of the ith firm's shares from the mean market shares in the two

---

[14] If X_i is the deviation of the ith firm's share from the mean, Adelman has shown that equation (3) can be expressed as

$$H = \sum_i X_i{}^2 + 1/n.$$

Thus, the Herfindahl Index increases either with greater variation in the $\sum X_i{}^2$ of the firms (the summed term) or with a smaller number of firms.

years. Because of the way exits and entries are handled, the mean market shares will be the same for both years. The firm's observed deviation from this mean can be conceived of as consisting of two parts, a transitory and a permanent component, in each of the years. Just as Friedman and Kuznets assumed permanent consumption, we can assume that permanent advantages have the same absolute impact on the permanent components of every firm's market shares in both years. The implication is that permanent advantages have a constant impact. In addition, variability in observed market shares from one year to the next is entirely due to transitory advantages.

Based on the equality assumption, the patterns for PAD Districts I–IV and for PAD District V, using 1960 as the base year, are shown in Figures 6(a) and 6(b), respectively. The abscissas denote the reference years with respect to the base year, while the ordinates measure H_{op}. Points on the graph represent the permanent Herfindahl Index for year O for a particular reference year. The H_{op} for year O, with year O as the reference year, is H_o, the observed Herfindahl Index. The results of Figure 6(a) indicate that transitory advantages were relatively unimportant in influencing market shares before 1960. After 1960 they became influential, but not enough to eliminate the strong permanent component. This finding is consistent with the ability of large firms to inhibit the entry and the growth of smaller firms. The panel also suggests that there were some disadvantages of size relative to the base period for larger firms. These disadvantages appear to have been insignificant. Results for PAD District V indicate that no fluctuations from the permanent component of concentration occurred before 1960, and that only after 1960 did transitory factors have an impact.

The turning point for both PAD Districts I–IV and District V was after 1956, which was about the time of the beginning of the Mandatory Oil Import Control Program, the initiation of price control on natural gas, and the start of the active role of state conservation agencies. The evidence presented here seems to indicate that in the post-1960 period, disadvantages of size, as reflected in the increasing role of smaller-scale firms, were insignificant. Thus, transitory advantages appeared to arrest the rising trend toward greater economies of scale. This evidence is consistent with the hypothesis

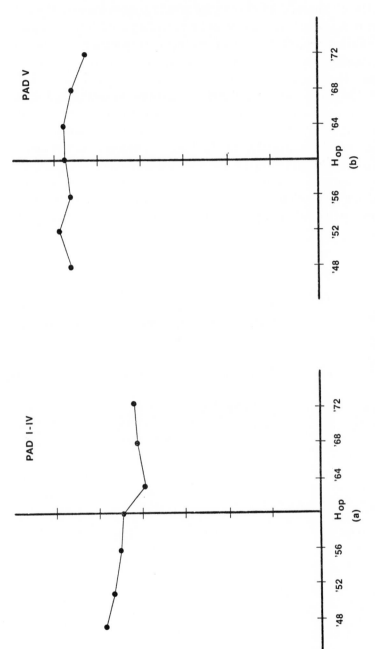

FIGURE 6. Patterns of the Permanent Component of Refining Concentration, with 1960 as the Base Year

that the oil import control program served only to increase the cost of refined products to consumers by providing a subsidy to smaller, less efficient refiners. The high permanent component shown here is also consistent with the data of Table 7, which showed that the influence of mergers and acquisitions since 1948, and particularly since 1960, may have stimulated the addition to established firms' relatively permanent power. Capacity absorbed in mergers and acquisitions is almost double that accounted for by new entry.

It will be instructive to see how government import policy tended to aid and support the independent refiners against the major companies while indirectly tending to speed up the independents' extinction and to reinforce higher domestic crude oil prices that constituted a major barrier to entry by newcomers to refining.

2

Economic History of Public Policy
toward Refining

SINCE the turn of the century the oil policies of the United States
have ranged from free trade in oil through mandatory quotas, tariffs,
price controls on natural gas, and support for state prorationing to
the conscientious effort to develop foreign oil resources. The history
of U.S. oil policy, the cornerstone of U.S. energy policy, can be
roughly divided into five phases: from 1900 to 1932, from 1932 to
1939, from 1939 to 1954, from 1954 to 1973, and finally the era com-
mencing with the abolition of import quotas in 1973. The last phase
continued through 1975, and it saw the evolution of new administrative energy planning bureaucracies and price controls on crude oil
and refined products. Generally, the history of U.S. import policy
has been characterized by periodic restrictionism weighted alter-
nately in favor of major and independent oil companies.

The Free Trade Era to 1932

Throughout most of the first quarter of this century, the United
States was a net exporter of oil. Before World War I only small volumes of oil were imported, and they were of little consequence to
the total national oil supply. Pre–World War I policy was dominated
by domestic antitrust activity against Standard Oil of New Jersey
(Burns 1958). Until the early 1930's, oil was on the list of free imports. The situation had begun to change by the end of World War
I: total export and domestic demand exceeded domestic production
after 1918, and increased imports from Mexico became necessary to

fill the supply-demand deficit (Raciti 1958). From 1920 to 1922 the United States became a net importer of petroleum for the first time, and there was widespread belief that the nation was on the verge of exhausting its stock of oil resources. A U.S. Geological Survey study concluded that the United States had only a ten years' supply of oil remaining (Congress, Senate, 1945, pp. 299–301). In addition, oil output from sources dominated by the United States in Mexico and Rumania was declining.

The dependence on oil by the growing industrial economy of the United States, as well as the major importance foreseen for oil in any major military conflict, influenced government policy to actively assist domestic oil companies in obtaining access to foreign concessions and production. Concurrently, Great Britain also followed this form of "oil mercantilism," that is, the use of state power to increase control over new world oil reserves. This policy largely induced development of Venezuelan, Iraqi, and Iranian oil resources by firms dominated by the United States and Britain (Hartshorn 1967).

Three basic features characterized U.S. oil policy during the pre-1932 phase: (1) the lack of restriction on the importation of crude oil, (2) the need for foreign crude oil to supplement indigenous production, and (3) the active encouragement by the federal government of both major and independent domestic oil companies to explore and develop foreign crude oil reserves. The unprecedented growth in demand for oil during and following the war, coinciding with the oil shortage scare, was a major factor influencing government interest in foreign oil. By the mid-1920's imports had reached 300,000 barrels per day. Fear of imminent exhaustion of domestic resources of oil, considered vital to national security, encouraged a free-trade policy in oil imports.

Fear of oil shortages, however, began to wane late in the twenties, and with it waned active government support for U.S. oil interests abroad. Significant new oil fields in Oklahoma, Texas, and California ended the shortage anxiety. Control of excess domestic supply, along with the advent of the protectionist sentiment of the early thirties, began to dominate the attention of policy makers. By 1929 independent domestic producers formed the Independent Petroleum Association of America (IPAA) to lobby for the restriction of crude oil imports and to institute the imposition of excise taxes on imports.[1] Two companies during this period, Gulf and Standard of New Jersey (now Exxon), were the major oil importers. Pressure on them to voluntarily restrict imports was part of the overall government policy to conserve and efficiently use domestic resources.

However, two real price effects served to reduce the flow of imports into the United States. The domestic price of oil, reacting to the huge stocks of newly discovered reserves, declined from $1.88 per barrel in 1926 to $1.17 per barrel in 1928. Prices fell sharply into the 1930's. Increased imports could have worsened this decline. On the other hand, the tariff on imports was high. It accounted for more than 30 percent of the price of crude oil and more than 40 percent of the price of heavy crude products. These effects are representative of the second phase of U.S. oil policy.

The Early Protectionist Era, 1932–1939

The federal government's policy toward oil imports during the early 1930's was largely an outgrowth of its interests and participation in the oil conservation programs of producing states, which were imposed to cope with the problem of excess crude supply. The domestic wellhead price of oil dropped to $0.65 per barrel in 1931, and a record low of $0.25 per barrel for Mid-Continent oil with a gravity of API 36° was the price in mid-1933 (McClean and Haigh 1954, chap. 4; API 1970, pp. 47, 375).

The National Industrial Recovery Act of 1933 (NIRA) had a special petroleum code that allowed the president to restrict imports, and quantitative import controls were imposed that year. Imports were restricted to amounts not to exceed those of the last six months of 1932 (Lichtblau 1964, p. 105). These restrictions were removed in 1935 when NIRA was declared unconstitutional; nevertheless, the Revenue Act of 1932, strongly supported by IPAA on the grounds that it maintained a strong domestic oil-producing ca-

[1] At a conference called by the federal government in June, 1929, to discuss conservation, a controversy developed between the majors and the independents over imports. The latter wanted no curtailment of domestic production as long as some of the majors brought in any imports they pleased. The independents, determined to shut out imports, left the conference to form the IPAA (Kemnitzer 1938; Manes 1961).

pability, was symbolic of the strong protectionist attitude during the thirties.

Liberalization of Trade Barriers, 1939–1954

The Reciprocal Trade Agreement of 1934 was the foundation of the trend toward more liberalized trade from 1939 onward. In 1939 a bilateral trade agreement with Venezuela reduced tariffs on oil imports from that country in return for concessions on a number of U.S. export commodities. A similar agreement was later made with Mexico, although it was rescinded in 1950. Both treaties were initiated under the most-favored-nation clause of the 1934 act.

The advent of World War II greatly increased the volume of imported oil—92 percent from 1939 to 1945. Following the war, the government encouraged the development of foreign resources and again expanded oil imports. The reasoning again was that reduced domestic resources required access to the vast stocks of foreign oil. "Principles of economic cooperation" were introduced to reduce the trade barriers between the United States and Canada, while a revision of the trade agreement with Venezuela lowered oil import tariffs (FTC 1952; Department of State 1950).

In 1952 the Paley commission, the blue-ribbon Presidential Commission on Materials Policy charged with evaluating the nation's resources, advised that: "In view of its future needs and limited resources, this nation should welcome crude oil imports, not place obstacles in their way. Tariffs on crude oil imports should therefore be held down, reduced, or eliminated, within the limits imposed by national security considerations" (Office of the President, Materials Policy Commission, 1952, p. 109).

Following World War II imports increased at an average of 15 percent annually, and by 1954 they totaled 1.1 million barrels per day. Indeed, in 1948 the United States became a net importer of oil for the first time since 1922. The liberalization of imports was forced by the increased postwar demand for crude oil and products; widespread shortages of heating oils occurred. Importers were asked by the federal government to step up imports, and export controls were implemented in 1949. The rapid rise in imports by 1950 again caused considerable concern to independent petroleum producers and coal producers. Largely through the House Select Committee on Small Business, these factions began to demand a switch in government policy toward increased import limitations.

By 1954 the principle that imports should be related in some way to domestic production came to be accepted by both independent and major producers. The slogan of the period was that imports should "supplement, not supplant" domestic supply. National energy security meant a *healthy* domestic producing industry and *excess* refining capacity (Congress, House, Select Committee on Small Business, 1950). The notion of a "peril point" as the foundation of the national security argument became popular. The peril point was the amount of imports as a percentage of domestic production beyond which great damage would be done to the domestic industry and, thereby, to the national energy security. National security was the important reason cited by independents for favoring some restriction on imports.

At no time was national energy security specifically defined. It was clear that the underlying concern of the independents was the dramatic fall in wellhead prices that reduced the value of their proved reserves. The existence of vast amounts of idle productive capacity in the early fifties, along with the availability of cheaper oil imports, lay at the heart of the argument for a viable domestic industry.

In 1949, however, the newly formed National Petroleum Council (NPC), an advisory body to the Secretary of the Interior, issued a formal energy statement, *A National Oil Policy for the United States* (NPC 1949). This report argued for the development of both domestic and foreign oil and provided the seed of what was to become the basic assumption of future government policies—that it was in the national security interest of the United States to have a surplus cushion of spare crude oil productive capacity and excess refining capacity. Imports in excess of economic requirements were seen as retarding the domestic exploration and development of new oil fields. The NPC argued that a target level of one million barrels per day in excess of current demand should be maintained "in the interest of national security and national defense." Selected firms among the majors, members of the famous "Seven Sisters," favored more intensive development of imports. However, the independents argued through the IPAA that imports, plus the states' practices of setting allowables, were damaging to the health of the domestic petroleum industry.

An aggressive campaign began against imports in 1949 and 1950. Actually, in adjusting to meet an unexpectedly rapid postwar demand for petroleum, refiners were unable to meet all demands for heating oils in the winter of 1947/1948. Severe shortages developed in many parts of the country. Importers were requested by the government to increase imports, and controls on exports went into effect. The momentum of that winter's fuel shortage carried over into 1948, 1949, and 1950. The IPAA demanded that the House Select Committee on Small Business, headed by Eugene J. Keogh, investigate the rapid increase in imports. The impact of the Korean War, however, and the closing of the Iranian oil fields temporarily assuaged the fears of independent producers (Congress, House, Select Committee on Small Business, 1950). Nevertheless, the Keogh committee hearings constituted a major victory by the independents for their future import demands. The majors accepted the principle of import restrictions and the concept that imports should not exceed a level considered reasonable relative to domestic production.[2] Indeed, major importers had a substantial interest in domestic production of crude oil and hence had strong economic reasons for not dumping more foreign oil on the American market. The big question was: What amount of imports was reasonable? When the total number of importers were few, a consensus was feasible. However, as their numbers grew it became evident that even a voluntary program of import control would be destined for failure. In fact, it was the increase in the number of newcomers that forced the imposition of a mandatory program.

It is surprising that the use of increased tariffs, as opposed to voluntary quotas, was never seriously considered in 1950. The Keogh committee found no reason to believe that a "duty as high as $1.05 a barrel, *or any other amount*, would limit the importation of *any* quantity of oil, a certain quantity of oil or all oil imports" (Congress, House, Select Committee on Small Business, 1950, p. 142,

---

[2] Meloe (1966, p. 46) argues that the Keogh committee used the NPC statement on national oil policy as a lever to pry from each of the major importers a reaffirmation of the principle of import limitation.

italics mine). This statement is extreme, and from the equivalence theorem on tariffs and quotas it would seem to be false,[3] yet the businessman's rationale behind the statement was that tariffs were considered a negligible element of the cost of imported oil. Tariffs were almost 20 percent of the average wellhead crude price in the late 1930's, but they had declined to less than 10 percent by 1942 and less than 3 percent by 1958.

The government's policy of reducing postwar trade barriers effectively eliminated the political possibility of an increased tariff. By early 1950 Venezuela accounted for more than 70 percent of total imports, and a supplemental trade agreement with Venezuela was signed in 1952 (Peterson 1959; Congress, House, 1953). In the congressional battle over this agreement the IPAA argued the peril-point concept of tariffs to protect domestic producers against excessive imports. And as Meloe (1966) noted, the U.S. Tariff Commission was required under the peril-point provision of the 1948 Trade Agreement's Extension Act to determine the level of tariffs below which harm could come to the domestic industry. Instead, the executive office established a peril point lower than that considered minimal by the IPAA. Tariffs were $\frac{1}{8}$ cent per gallon on crude petroleum under a gravity of API 25° and $\frac{1}{4}$ cent per gallon on crude petroleum with a gravity greater than API 25° (Congress, House, 1953). Even then, crudes of higher gravity could be commingled with those of lower gravity so that deliveries would have a gravity of API 24.9°. In addition, special regulations by the Venezuelan government on computing royalty tax payments allowed deductions for U.S. import taxes, which also eliminated any real effective protection from the tariff.[4]

In addition to the ineffective tariffs, another government influence on increased imports was the exemption of the petroleum industry from the "Buy American" Act (Raciti 1958, p. 65), under which the federal government was to give preference to domestic

---

[3] The equivalence theorem proposes that under a restrictive set of conditions a tariff can be set that will provide for the same amount of imports that is allowed under a quota (Bhagwati 1969).

[4] As cited by Manes (1961, p. 61), the Venezuelan government declared that "Royalty payments made by each company . . . shall be subject to deduction for U.S. import taxes."

industry when making purchases for public use. A directive by the General Services Administration in 1954 exempted petroleum from the provisions of this act, further encouraging foreign imports at a time when domestic production was reduced through lower allowables.

During this 1948–1954 period two other key factors influenced the focus on cheap foreign oil: state prorationing and precentage depletion. All of the thirty-two producing states in the United States had petroleum conservation regulation statutes.[5] The federal government cooperated by sanctioning the limited cooperation of the producing states under the Interstate Compact to Conserve Oil and Gas (IOCC); by assisting regulatory agencies in establishing statewide production restrictions through their monthly forecasts of oil demand in each state; by outlawing interstate shipments of oil produced in violation of state regulations (otherwise coming under the Connally "Hot Oil" Act of 1935); and by subjecting operations on federal lands to the production restrictions and drilling and operating practices of the states on which these lands lay, or of the contiguous states, such as Texas and Louisiana, in the case of offshore areas (McDonald 1971, pp. 29–30).

Although all thirty-two states had conservation statutes, the conservation regulations of only a few major producing states were more significant than those of all other states put together. For example, Texas, Louisiana, and California alone accounted for over 70 percent of total U.S. production from 1949 to 1951; ten years later, the relative shares of Texas and California had declined, but Louisiana's relative share had almost doubled. These three states still accounted for three-fourths of the nation's oil output.

McDonald (1971) delineates three kinds of petroleum production control exercised by states: (1) well density control, (2) maximum efficient recovery (MER) control, and (3) market demand prorationing. Restriction of well density on the basis of statewide uniform rules is practiced in Illinois, Pennsylvania, Indiana, Ohio, Kentucky, and West Virginia. By regulating well density, or spacing, so that fewer wells tap a reservoir, lower production from the reservoir results. A major stimulus to this form of regulation came from

[5] Several nonproducing states also had conservation statutes. These included Georgia, Idaho, Iowa, North Carolina, Oregon, and Washington.

the federal government during World War II when the agency controlling field regulation, the Petroleum Administration for War (PAW), adopted a basic requirement of 40-acre spacing for oil wells and 640-acre spacing for gas wells. Before this regulation, typical spacing requirements had been 10 to 20 acres for each oil well and 40 to 160 acres for each gas well (McDonald 1971, p. 41). The second form of control is limitation of the output of each reservoir to its maximum rate of production consistent with no significant loss of ultimate recovery. The reservoir maximum rate of production for long-run productive efficiency is popularly labeled the MER.[6] States employing this practice include California (where it is voluntary), Alaska, Colorado, and Wyoming.

The third form of production control is restriction of area output to market demand. This is the dominant form of production control and is employed by Texas, Louisiana, Oklahoma, Kansas, and New Mexico. Under market demand prorationing, the state regulatory authority determines monthly the planned purchases of oil in the state, or market demand, and allocates this total among reservoirs and wells in proportion to their basic allowables. The states' major oil purchasers, the refiners, then indicate those volumes they will require for the month. In addition to these refiners' "nominations," the state commissions, such as the Texas Railroad Commission, have the U.S. Bureau of Mines' monthly consumption forecast and data on inventories. Thus, the federal government provides information for the states' production control decisions. Price offered for crude oil is not mentioned in purchasers' nominations. When the basic state production, or allowable, is determined by the state regulatory commissions, it is adjusted for expected changes in inventory and corrected for estimated underproduction of allowables from wells that are temporarily shut down. The basic state allowable is the sum of exempt and non-exempt oil volumes, which include (1) the exempt volumes, that is, maximum production of fields or wells assigned special allowables or permitted to produce at capacity, such as water-flood secondary recovery fields, discovery wells, statutory marginal wells, and stripper wells; (2) the MER's in fields subject to MER restriction; and (3) the top allowables specified for

[6] For an excellent discussion of the MER technique, see Zimmerman (1957).

wells in fields subject to a statewide depth acreage schedule such as the Texas Yardstick (McDonald 1971, p. 160). The production total of all exempt wells is subtracted from the total allowable estimated by the state regulatory commission to match market demand. The remainder is allocated to nonexempt fields and wells in proportion to their respective basic maximum allowables. In Texas, Louisiana, and Oklahoma, allocation to nonexempt fields is accomplished by means of a market demand factor, which is a decimal fraction representing the ratio of the total nonexempt share of allowed production to the total nonexempt basic allowable; the factor is then multiplied by each well's basic allowable to compute its actual allowable for the effective period.

How significant were exemptions from market demand restrictions? In Louisiana, exempt wells in 1963 accounted for 20 percent of total crude production. However, exempt wells accounted for 43 percent of total crude production in Texas, 58 percent in Oklahoma, 47 percent in New Mexico, and 61 percent in Kansas (Office of Oil and Gas 1965, p. 26). Indeed, a good portion of the regulatory activity of the Texas Railroad Commission was devoted to evaluating exemptions from regulation. Regulatory exceptions have characterized the work of every governmental energy agency from the state commissions to the FEA.

The top producing states under conservation regulation have accounted for almost three-fourths of the total national production of crude oil, and almost half of this amount was not subject to the alleged price stabilizing effect of state prorationing. Indeed, the price stabilization efforts of state regulatory commissions from 1952 to 1958, carried out by decreased allowables (or increased shutdown days), were indirectly designed to offset the price-depressing threat of rising imports. Yet the IPAA members who were clamoring for import restriction had a clear economic incentive because the output from their exempt, higher-cost properties was threatened by foreign supply. Nonexempt wells possessed a more unfavorable status, since reduced allowable days of production as well as competition from foreign oil were a double threat to their economic operation.

Because integrated major companies owned a greater proportion of nonexempt wells compared to the independents (and vice-

versa with regard to exempt wells), their dissatisfaction with the
rising number of shutdown days could have been lessened by a
more than corresponding rise in price. The reasoning was twofold:
the present value of the reservoirs could increase, and a higher crude
oil price could be made an effective barrier to potential entrants
into refining. However, with the lower level of nonexempt production, the effects of state prorationing cutbacks were offset. The increase in imports along with continued full production from nonexempt wells effectively tended to depress wellhead prices of crude
oil. Because state budgets relied on the existence of high crude
prices, state commissions began arguing for import restrictions as
an adjunct to conservation. In early 1953 the Texas Railroad Commission set up a reporting system under which all importers with
production in Texas were required to report their projected imports
several months in advance (Meloe 1966, p. 53). The long-run objective of the states was to stabilize prices and, they hoped, to prevent
continuing overcapacity within their borders. However, the incentive provided by exempt status and unique provisions of federal tax
laws tended to stimulate development drilling, at the expense of
wildcat drilling, and to generate substantial excess capacity.

The inverse relationship of Texas allowable days and imports
into PAD Districts I–IV from 1951 to 1959 was ample proof to the
IPAA that the villain was foreign oil (see Figure 7). Nominal crude
prices across the country tended to stabilize throughout this period,
noticeably after 1958. From 1958 the real price of crude declined
(Manes 1961).

With stable or declining crude oil real prices, what economic
incentive existed to expand productive capacity? The answer lies in
operations of the integrated firm and the favorable tax provisions
for depletion that applied to the exploration, development, and production of crude oil. It seems almost irrational that producers would
continue to add to their productive capacity while the real price of
their output was declining. However, since 1926 each oil operator
was allowed to deduct a maximum of 27.5 percent of the gross receipts from sales of crude oil and natural gas for depletion, provided
that the deduction was not greater than half of his net taxable income (McDonald 1963). Thus, the greater the price of crude oil and
natural gas under conditions of inelastic demand (normally pre-

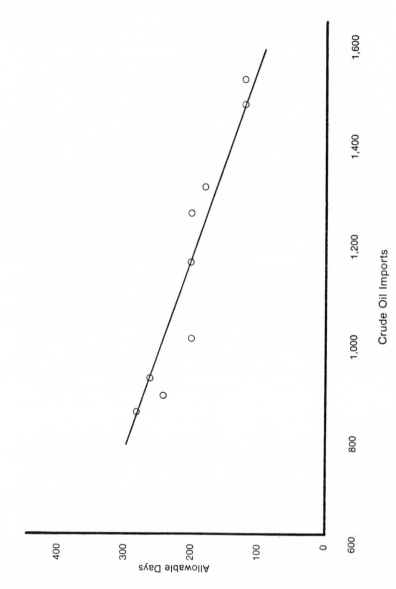

FIGURE 7. The Relationship between Allowable Days and Oil Imports, 1948–1959

sumed to exist for crude), the greater the allowed deduction. If a company was vertically integrated, high profitability in production could help subsidize losses in refining or marketing; indeed, since 1948 the backward integration of smaller and larger refiners is actually a story of survival (McClean and Haigh 1954). Depletion allowance was trimmed to 22.5 percent in 1969 and was eliminated on most oil and gas production in 1975.

Nevertheless, the more relevant factor that influenced excess capacity was favorable tax treatment for intangible development well costs. The majority of proved reserves of oil and gas added since World War II have been developed under the API reserves definition of "extensions and revisions," resulting primarily from development drilling, as opposed to "discoveries," which can be attributed to wildcatters.[7] Development wells and proved reserves were by far the most dominant factor in contributing to the excess U.S. productive capacity that increased through 1959. Development wells consistently accounted for almost three-fourths of the total number of wells drilled and for a slightly higher average number of additions to proved reserves. Firms could charge all intangible development costs to expenses, thus creating a relative advantage for development drilling over wildcat drilling.[8]

[7] The API explanation of extensions and revisions is as follows: The ultimate size of newly discovered fields, or newly discovered reservoirs in old fields, is normally determined by drilling in years subsequent to discovery. Wells drilled in subsequent years usually add to the proved area of previously discovered reservoirs, thereby serving to increase estimates of proved reserves. The reserves credited to a reservoir because of enlargement of its proved area are classified as "extensions."

Both development drilling and production history add to the basic geological and engineering knowledge of a petroleum reservoir and provide the basis for more accurate estimates of proved reserves in years following discovery. Changes in earlier estimates, either upward or downward, resulting from new information (except for an increase in proved acreage) are classified as "revisions." Revisions for a given year also include (1) increases in proved reserves associated with the installation of improved recovery techniques, and (2) an amount which corrects the effect on proved reserves of the difference between estimated production for the previous year and actual production for that year.

[8] The essential difference, for investment purposes, between exploratory, wildcat wells and development wells is the degree of risk and uncertainty of the success of the venture. As Megill (1971) notes, intangible drilling costs—that is, those without salvage value—usually account for 70 percent of the total cost

Examples of such intangible development costs came from the costs of drilling and preparing development wells: expenditures for labor, fuel, power, materials, supplies, tool rental, and repairs of drilling equipment. Intangible drilling and development costs, as Irving and Draper (1958, p. 14) and many other sources note, represent those expenditures that do not have salvage value incurred in the drilling and deepening of wells. One of the largest items included in intangible drilling and development costs represents payments to drilling contractors. Most oil companies capitalized intangible drilling and development costs of production wells, but expensed such cost for tax purposes. When oil operators chose to count intangible development costs as expenses, their allowable deductions under the percentage depletion option were not reduced unless the costs charged off to expenses came close to the 50 percent of net taxable income that limited the deduction for percentage depletion (McDonald 1963, p. 10). Unlike percentage depletion, which evolved through a legislative process, the option to expense intangible development costs developed through administrative regulations of the Treasury Department and the Bureau of Internal Revenue. In the Revenue Act of 1954, Congress gave its tacit approval to these provisions. During the 1945–1955 period, numerous legislative acts supported continued comprehensive coverage of the tax provisions. One effect of these provisions was their periodic inducement of overdrilling. Reduction of the effective cost of development wells encouraged the unnecessarily dense drilling of them (McDonald 1963, p. 83). This influence of charging intangibles to expenses was used by all firms in the oil industry but apparently was less well understood by the government.

Special exemptions under state prorationing tended to erode the economic effectiveness of prorationing policy. The special tax provisions tended to increase the excess capacity position of the nation and placed even greater pressure on state commissions to in-

---

of the exploratory well. All exploratory costs relating to dry holes are usually expensed for accounting purposes, while successful exploratory well costs are capitalized on corporate accounts. Development wells usually have 60 percent intangible costs, and by extending the expensing privilege for intangible development drilling costs, the financial risk of development outlays is relatively lessened.

crease shutdown days. Instead of attacking the basic causes of our national energy supply imbalance, both majors and independents sought to restrict the then lower-cost volumes of crude oil—foreign oil—in the name of national security. In addition, the rising importance of natural gas and gas liquids heavily influenced the concern for imports. The market for natural gas—once basically an intrastate commodity—expanded across state lines with the expansion of pipeline capacity. Because oil and gas are joint products in supply, rising imports could have undermined the joint profitability of both oil and gas.

Natural gas prices were rising in the early 1950's in response to increased demand. New natural gas pipelines extended to the east and west coasts, and competition among major and independent gas producers was fierce. However, market demand prorationing of gas was quite different from that of oil. The state function was mainly to prevent buyer discrimination within the same reservoir. Producers in a given reservoir were usually tied to one or a few buyers under long-term contracts. Potential buyer discrimination took the form of differential gas purchase agreements between large-volume and small-volume producers. Contract provisions were far more elaborate than mere direct price quotations. Fixed price escalation, tax sharing, inflation adjustment and spiral escalator clauses, and favored-nation and price redetermination stipulations were also characteristic features of these gas transactions. The effect of most of these provisions was to cause purchase contract prices to be adjusted upward. The objective of the favored-nation provision, as Neuner (1960) has noted, was much greater than that of securing an inflation adjustment. This clause assured the seller of some adjustment in contract prices if future market prices rose because of changing supply-and-demand relationships. This clause was one of the advantages accruing to the sellers. As a result of imperfect knowledge, prices acceptable to different sellers were really known only to the buyer. The buyer could discriminate by completing contracts in sequence, beginning with the seller offering the lowest-priced gas to whoever was the weakest, least knowing, or smallest in the field market (Neuner 1960, p. 93).

Periodic market demand estimates were made by state commissions and allocated among producers. Continuing litigation on control of the sales price of gas under the Natural Gas Act of 1938 was effectively settled in the famous Phillips Petroleum case of 1954, in which the Supreme Court reversed the Federal Power Commission and held that the act applied to sales of natural gas in interstate commerce.[9] Imposition of controls on gas prices was to set the stage for long and costly regulatory hearings before the FPC that engendered inappropriate arguments regarding the total cost of gas supply. "Directionality," a concept that emerged in those hearings, attempted to argue the mutual economic independence of oil and gas and thus the ability to earmark exploration and development funds specifically for gas. Although prices were not controlled for intrastate sales of gas, the impending ceiling price level on natural gas sealed the fate of imports of crude oil and products.[10] All these influences led to the next period of restrictionism.

The Return to Protectionism, 1954–1973

A program of voluntary restriction of imports, initiated by the Eisenhower administration, went through two phases. A special presidential cabinet committee concluded: ". . . if the imports of crude and residual fuel oils should exceed significantly the respective proportions that these imports of oil bore to the production of domestic crude oil in 1954, the domestic fuel situation could be so impaired as to endanger the orderly industrial growth which assures the military and civilian supplies and reserves that are necessary to the national defense" (Office of the President, Advisory Committee, 1957, p. 1). Voluntary restrictions to the 1954 import/production ratio on crude and residual fuel oil commenced in early 1955 and lasted to July, 1957. The second voluntary phase was marked by the establishment of quotas for individual importers; it was replaced by mandatory quotas in 1959.

National security, again, was the rallying theme for the need to restrict imports. For the first time, however, the focus of the threat

---

[9] The legal and economic history of controls on natural gas wellhead prices is contained in many excellent sources (Hawkins 1969; Brown 1972; Neuner 1960).

[10] The combined influence of seeking to increase production from "exempt" wells and reserves added through "extensions and revisions" worsened the surplus capacity conditions in 1950 (Lovejoy and Homan 1967).

to national security was placed solely on one major resource area, the Middle East. The Suez Canal crisis and the 1957 Arab-Israeli war featured a temporary boycott of oil supplies to the United States. Thus, the oil import policy of this period evolved largely into one of discrimination against the Middle East. Shortly after voluntary restrictions were announced, the Office of Defense Mobilization (ODM) exempted crude imports originating from Canada and Venezuela (ODM 1956). Later, the ODM exempted imports from all origins into the West Coast. These actions centered the full impact of controls on the East Coast and, given the exemptions, principally affected the Middle East. The early voluntary program had little effect until 1956 and 1957, when Venezuelan imports became dominant. Imports into PAD Districts I–IV from Venezuela nearly doubled from 1954 (351,000 barrels per day) to 1957 (531,000 barrels per day). Imports from sources other than Venezuela and Canada declined to 98,000 barrels per day in 1957.

Compliance with the voluntary program was largely based on the threat of compulsory regulation. An amendment to the Trade Agreements Extension Act of 1955 provided that if imports of any article were to threaten national security, the president "shall take any action he deems necessary to adjust the imports of such article" to eliminate that threat (Office of the President, Advisory Committee, 1957). This amendment became known as the National Defense Amendment. It was revised in 1958 to state that the president must take account of the effects of oil imports on the growth of domestic investment, exploration, and development in determining the requirements for national security. Regarding the pressure to do something about oil imports, W. L. Thorp (1960, p. 434) noted: "The Congressional debates suggest a very close relationship in the minds of some members of Congress particularly interested in oil and their attitude toward the extension of the trade agreement legislation. This then, was not a case which was considered in the light of some new national policy declarations, but one in which the policy declaration was written with a particular case in mind."

To initiate the second voluntary program, the ODM concluded in July, 1957, that crude oil imports threatened national security. The Special Committee to Investigate Crude Oil Imports confirmed the ODM finding (Office of the President, Advisory Committee,

1957) and at the same time considered three alternatives to quantitative restriction: (1) storage of imported oil within depleted fields or elsewhere; (2) government participation in exploring for oil reserves which, when discovered, would not be used until an emergency; and (3) encouragement of imports in order to conserve domestic oil resources. All three of these options were considered too costly. Storage was considered impractical due to the volumes involved. A government-run oil corporation was considered too politically offensive to be a workable option, as was the actual encouragement of imports. The voluntary system that was adopted brought Canada and Venezuela back in under restriction, while imports into the area east of the Rocky Mountains were set at a level equivalent to 12 percent of crude production in that area. The West Coast continued as a separate area, with imports allowed to make up the difference between local demand and domestic supply.

The second program attempted to implement voluntary quotas for each company. This program was an effort by the government to form an importers' cartel whose total output it could control. The government at first hoped that by persuasion it could get the companies to restrain their own imports. Between 1950 and 1954 the seven major companies engaged in importing on the East Coast, Standard Oil of New Jersey, Mobil, Gulf, Texaco, Standard of California, Atlantic, and Sinclair, accounted for almost three-fourths of total imports. These seven companies were asked to reduce their imports into PAD Districts I–IV to a level 10 percent below their average imports for 1954–1956. Smaller established importers were allowed to increase imports, while newcomers had to apply for quotas. East Coast refiners were asked to limit foreign oil imports to 35 percent of refinery input. Quotas were set *only* on crude oil, making attractive the importation of unfinished oils which required further processing at refineries. Unfinished oils were treated separately from finished products, and their tariff was lower. Further, no restrictions were imposed on finished products such as residual fuel oil.

The seven largest companies did make efforts to restrain imports. Indeed, their 1957–1958 import levels were comparable to their 1950 levels. However, largely because of loopholes, exemptions, and the apparent absence of penalties for noncompliance, the voluntary import cartel failed. Actual imports exceeded quotas throughout the period from 1957 to 1959. Newcomers in the importing market forced continued reduction of import levels by both large and small established importers. For example, at the beginning of the program there were thirty importers. By September, 1958, this number had grown to fifty-five, with over one hundred additional companies applying for quotas (Dam 1971; Shaffer 1968). This tremendous interest by new firms was significantly influenced by the growing discrepancy between foreign and domestic prices during the late 1950's. The right to import was valuable. With the failure to require any restriction on products and unfinished oils, the effective administration of the program was eroded, and by 1958 the voluntary cartel collapsed.

THE SHIFT TO MANDATORY QUOTAS

Mandatory quotas went into effect on March 10, 1959, after the Special Committee to Investigate Crude Oil Imports found that the scheduled level of imports under the voluntary program threatened national security as defined in the 1958 revision of the Trade Agreements Extension Act of 1955 (Office of the President 1959). Establishment of these quotas completed the return to a protectionist trade policy. The restrictionism of this program exceeded that of all previous governmental oil policies. Crude oil, unfinished oil, and finished products were included in the quota program. The amendments (1) authorized the president to take whatever action he deemed necessary, unless his own investigation showed that imports of a given article did not threaten national security; (2) authorized action at any time and for whatever period he felt was necessary; and (3) enumerated certain standards to measure the impact on national security of imports of any specific articles. These standards specifically included the economic welfare of the domestic industry involved, as it related to the general economic welfare and thus to the security of the nation. This authorization was included in the Trade Expansion Act of 1962 without substantive change and was the legal basis for the oil import control program.

No imports other than those of petroleum and its products have ever been restricted under this statute, in spite of the possibility of broad interpretations of the relationship between national security, the economic welfare of the nation, and the economic welfare of individual domestic industries. The inclusion of finished products, and specifically of residual fuel oil, added a new dimension to import controls. Residual fuel oil is used mainly for heating or as a boiler fuel, and it competed largely with coal in the 1950's. The coal industry, the coal-carrying railroads, and their respective unions, employing the usual "threat to national security" argument, combined to lobby for the restriction of fuel imports.

The mandatory program was characterized by two other major changes: the issuance of precise definitions to eligible importers and thereby the restriction of entry to specialized firms, and the explicit definition of a geographical element in the national security justification. The second change, a "continental oil policy," exempted overland imports into the United States (and shipments to Puerto Rico). This policy was designed largely to aid Canadian imports, since imports from Mexico had become insignificant. In addition, a "Western Hemispheric preference" principle was included in the program. Imported processed products had to be derived from Western Hemisphere crudes, thus mainly aiding Venezuelan production and Caribbean refiners and resulting in further discrimination against Middle Eastern crudes. However, the November, 1962, amendments to the mandatory program eliminated this exemption, thereby reducing imports from other countries which were subject to allocation.

Presidential Proclamation 3279, which established the Mandatory Oil Import Control Program, specified that the total quantity of permissible imports would vary directly with changes in total demand. In PAD Districts I–IV, imports of crude oil, unfinished oils, and finished products (except for residual fuel oil to be used as fuel) would approximate 9 percent of total domestic demand, based on Bureau of Mines estimates of demand for periods specified by the secretary of the interior, who was made responsible for the administration of the program. In PAD District V, total permissible imports would be that amount which, when added to domestic supply, would approximate total demand. In each area finished product imports were limited absolutely to 1957 levels. The balance of the total would be imports of crude and unfinished oils, with the latter category making up no more than 10 percent of the crude and unfinished oils allocated. In Districts I–IV, imports of residual fuel oil to be used as fuel were also restricted to 1957 levels; however, the secretary was empowered to make adjustments if permissible imports of residual fuel oil to be used as fuel were "consonant with the objectives" of the proclamation. Imports into Puerto Rico could approximate 1958 levels, with adjustments made to meet changes in local demand or demand for exports.

Two major problems were encountered in the use of the demand base to determine the overall level of imports. First, it was found that the projections of the Bureau of Mines consistently overstated actual demand for any given period and, therefore, that the ratio of imports to production rose each year (Manes 1961; Shaffer 1968). To alleviate this problem, Presidential Proclamation 3279 was amended in 1960 to allow for adjustment of the level of permissible imports in each allocation period by the amount of the estimation error in the previous period. Since estimates for period t were made in period $t-1$, the adjustment in period t corrected the error in period $t-2$. The imports-to-production ratio continued to increase, however, because of the second problem—the fact that the base used in determining the import level was the demand for products, some of which were derived from natural gas liquids (NGL). Production of NGL rose more rapidly during these years than production of crude, thus decreasing the percentage of total products derived from crude and increasing the imports-to-production ratio.

In November, 1962, the proclamation was again amended to change the base to "12.2 per cent of the quantity of crude oil and natural gas liquids produced" (Office of the President 1962). The problem of errors in estimation was eliminated by using actual production figures for the last six months. This practice, however, created a lag between changes in the production level of two allocation periods, since changes in production in period t were measurable only in period $t+1$ and incorporated into the import level in period $t+2$. In the period immediately following this amendment, imports would have fallen by 32,000 barrels per day as a result of decreasing production. Therefore, the base was once again changed to estimated current production.

The mandatory program granted the right to import petroleum

to all refiners in the United States. Import tickets were also granted under the mandatory program to terminal operators and petrochemical firms. Tickets, for example, were given for "petrochemical plant inputs," but considered only crude oil and unfinished oils.

METHODS OF ALLOCATION

The allocation section of Presidential Proclamation 3279 (Office of the President 1959, p. 4) states: "With respect to the allocations of imports of crude oil and unfinished oils into Districts I–IV, and into District V, such regulations shall provide, to the extent possible, for a fair and equitable distribution among persons having refinery capacity in these districts *in relation to refinery inputs* during an appropriate period or periods selected by the Secretary and may provide for distribution in such manner as to avoid drastic reductions below the last allocations under the Voluntary Oil Import Program" (italics mine). The class of importers was thus limited to persons having refinery capacity in the district for which they applied for an allocation. The quantity each refiner was to receive was more difficult to determine. However, the method of allocating quotas by the mandatory government cartel discriminated in favor of the smaller, independent refineries. The following program was worked out for the three classes of importers identified in the voluntary program (Dam 1971; Shaffer 1968):

(1) To retain the support of established (or historical) importers, it was necessary to grant them fairly large allocations. Thus, the mandatory program provided that no company would receive an allocation which was less than 80 percent of its last allocation under the voluntary program.

(2) To provide for the entry of newcomers into the import market and to maintain competition, the minimum percentage granted to established importers was to be reduced over time. However, it was not until January, 1971, that the last established (or historical) allocations were eliminated.

(3) The quantity allocated to each refiner (except for those whose allocation was protected by the historical minimum) was to be related to the size of that refiner's inputs. A graduated scale was created which granted a proportionately larger share of the total allocated to smaller refiners. The first scale that was used granted

allocations of 12 percent of inputs to refiners with inputs of 0–10,000 barrels per day, 10 percent for those with 10,000–20,000 barrels per day, and so on down to 4 percent for refiners with 300,000 barrels per day or more. For example, a refiner with an input of 100,000 barrels per day received 12 percent on the first 10,000 barrels per day, 11 percent on the second 10,000 barrels per day, and 8 percent on the last 40,000 barrels per day (for a total allocation of 9,200 barrels per day or 9.2 percent of total refinery runs). The specific percentage of refinery runs allocated in any given period varied with the total quantity available for allocation, and in 1962 the number of categories was reduced to four: (1) 0–10,000 barrels per day, (2) 10,000–30,000 barrels per day, (3) 30,000–100,000 barrels per day, and (4) 100,000 barrels per day and over. Table 13 compares several allocation years since 1962, a comparison which clearly demonstrates that the smaller *refiners* received favored treatment and that the percentages used also favored smaller *importers* at the expense of larger ones.

The graduated scale is a clear example of what Stigler (1971) has called "acquired regulation." Indeed, it was the political process through which the majors and the independents managed to extract limitations on the mandatory government cartel. In the formation of government policy on imports, major refining companies jockeyed to maintain the fewest possible restraints on their traditional import positions. The initial allocation mechanism *did* provide for a gradual

TABLE 13
Sliding Scale: Partial Comparison of Percentage Scale
in Various Periods

Average Input (bbl./day)	Allocation Percentage					
	July–Dec., 1962	Jan.–June, 1964	Jan.–June, 1965	Jan.–Dec., 1966	Jan.–Dec., 1967	Jan.–Dec., 1971
0–10,000	12.0	14.0	17.0	18.0	20.0	20.0
10,000–30,000	10.2	11.9	11.6	11.4	11.4	12.0
30,000–100,000	8.2	9.3	9.2	8.9	8.0	7.0
100,000+	5.2	5.45	5.53	5.26	4.28	3.5

SOURCE: *Oil Import Digest* A-51, cited in Dam 1971.

phasing out of quota allocation on a historical basis. Twenty-three firms, including both majors and independents, qualified under the historical category in March, 1959. These importers were granted a percentage of their 1957 quotas, and this percentage declined each year. As the historical percentages were reduced, many companies were automatically shifted to allocation on the basis of refinery runs, as it resulted in a higher quota. Nevertheless, their initial, historical division resulted in approximately 75 percent of the crude and unfinished oils being allocated to established importers.

By this policy, majors were in fact protecting their market shares by controlling the entry of potential rivals. The eventual rise of newcomers under the voluntary program undermined that program and acted as a destabilizing influence on oil prices that the majors desired to have more control over. Because the historical volumes were subtracted from the allowed quotas, the majors could at least anticipate a few years of internal control over the cartel. In turn, the policy of granting quotas only to refiners of crude oil, and not to the more numerous crude producers, also created an additional barrier to entry into refining. Newcomers had to invest sizable amounts of capital in refining facilities to become eligible for a quota. During the years of the import program in which historical quotas were most effective, 1960–1963, the smallest "new entry" capacity described in the previous chapter occurred. The phasing out of historical quotas appears to be related to the rise in the refining capacity of new entrants from 1964 to 1968. The period in which historical quotas were used also coincided with the rise in total operable capacity absorbed through mergers and acquisitions from 1960 to 1963, almost half of which was obtained by established importers. Thus, in planning for the restoration of their historical import levels that were being phased out, major companies acquired additional capacity that would bring them roughly equivalent import volume under the graduated scale.

The technique of enforcing quotas for the government cartel and special conditions for new entrants was a formidable barrier to entry, a situation that was quite satisfactory to the majors. However, subsequent employment of the sliding scale, new exemptions that began to depress entry barriers, and the mechanism of quota or import ticket exchange tended to eliminate the full entry-reducing and price-stabilizing purposes of the quota. All of these aspects of import controls tended to allow rivals to survive, to attract new rivals, and to further dissipate the advantages of the quota.

The Stigler theory of acquired regulation also explains the advantages granted to smaller, independent refiners under the quota program. Stigler postulates that the distribution of control of the industry tends to change under regulation because the political strength of each firm counts, and so "small firms have a larger influence than they would possess in an unregulated industry. . . . Thus when quotas are given to firms, the small firm will almost always receive larger quotas than cost minimizing practices would allow. . . . The pattern of regressive benefits is characteristic of public controls in industries with numerous firms" (Stigler 1971, p. 7). The sliding scale was different from traditional methods of cartel allocation in that import quotas tended to reduce the marginal cost of refining (Hay 1971). Each refiner's quota allocation was proportional to his expected output. Quota allocations were fixed interdependently with production. But for the smaller refiner, the favorable sliding scale provided relatively better access to the effective value of foreign oil. The mechanism by which this access was provided was the exchange of import licenses or tickets.

IMPORT TICKETS AND INLAND REFINERS

The sliding allocation formula introduced three new elements into the competitive structure of refining. The first was the granting of import tickets to inland refiners who had not previously imported foreign crude oil. Previously, because of their distance from shore facilities, inland refiners could not physically use their import rights. For example, of the eighty-four refining companies that had refining capacity of less than 30,000 barrels per day, only six (all majors) had refineries located near deep-water facilities.

The second element introduced into the industry's structure was the partiality of the sliding scale to smaller refiners. In particular, the percentage of allocation applicable to refiners with inputs up to 10,000 barrels per day for PAD Districts I–IV grew each year, while other steps in the scale remained relatively unchanged or declined. This special privilege granted to small refiners helps explain the size-class reversals in the minimum efficient size of refinery capacity discussed in chapter 1. The smaller size classes of refiners experienced a higher rate of growth during the years of import controls than they probably would have experienced under an unrestricted market. To this extent, the government achieved one of its goals in assuring the survival of the small, inefficient refiners at the expense of the growth of the larger, more efficient firms.

The third structural effect of controls and the sliding scale was the interregional shift in refinery runs. Most of the imported crude went to refineries on the East Coast. Import restrictions thereby increased demand for crude from the Gulf Coast and Southwest areas. This crude was shipped directly to the East Coast for processing or was refined on the Gulf Coast, with products moving to the East Coast by pipeline or tanker. Variations in delivered cost gave a slight advantage to Gulf Coast processing, and by early 1960 Gulf Coast refiners were accounting for over one-third of the annual increase in crude runs.

The competitive exchange market for import tickets was a great advantage to the small refiner. Several authors have argued that the quota program merely redistributed profits from larger companies to smaller ones (Manes 1963). Others have focused on what was popularly called "the cost of the oil import program" and have used the value of import tickets to measure the annual cost to consumers of controls (Office of the President, Cabinet Task Force, 1971).

Theoretically, the exchange of import tickets was not unlike the sale of taxicab medallions in New York City. Government regulates the supply of tickets, and only owners of tickets can engage in an exchange of tickets. According to governmental regulation, the tickets were not allowed to be sold for cash; thus, a roundabout exchange mechanism was developed so that inland refiners could reap some of the economic rent generated by the artificially large scarcity value of import tickets. The holder of the quota had either to run the imported crude in his own refinery or to exchange it for domestic crude, which also had to be processed in his own refinery. The exchange had to be on the basis of one barrel of imported crude for at least one barrel of domestic. In addition, quota rights were transferable. Thus, as a substitute for the purchase of quotas, refiners could purchase other refining companies.

The value of an import quota ticket was basically determined by comparing the delivery cost and the exchanged quantity of the foreign and domestic crudes. For example, as Boatwright (1971, p. 95) relates, an East Coast refiner had Venezuelan crude oil production and desired to import 32,292 barrels into the United States for use in its refinery. It contracted to supply an inland refiner with 33,145.64 barrels of domestic oil in exchange for the desired number of import quota tickets. The value of the ticket was calculated as follows:

Cost of Imported Venezuelan Oil	$1.92 per barrel
Transport from Venezuela to New York Harbor	.175 per barrel
U.S. duty	.0525 per barrel
Total c.i.f., New York	$2.1475 per barrel
Total aggregate cost	$69,347.07
Cost of Domestic Oil	
Grand Isle (La.)	$3.31 per barrel
Total aggregate cost	$109,712.07

The difference between the aggregate cost of the domestic and foreign crude oils is $40,365.00. This amount divided by the number of import tickets required (32,292) is $1.25 per barrel. The exchange ratio is 1.026435.

The relative distribution of the quota value to smaller refiners is shown in Table 14. As the table indicates, as refiners' inputs increase, the per-barrel cost decreases. Larger refiners received less than half the benefit in per-unit cost that was experienced by smaller refiners. Import tickets provided the refiners of less efficient size with an indirect subsidy, and for *some* smaller companies import quotas were the most valuable asset and were the difference between solvency and bankruptcy. The quota value remained at about $1.25 per barrel for crude on the average throughout the period of the control program. However, the value was greatly reduced by late 1970 and through 1971 as foreign crude prices and freight rates climbed upward. As ticket values narrowed, more firms began to exit the industry.

In 1966 import restrictions on residual fuel oil were removed, although ceilings on allowed amounts of other product imports continued. Throughout the mandatory program, the major leaks in import restrictions were the exceptions, special exemptions, and

TABLE 14
Effect of Sliding Scale Allocations
on Average Per-Unit Input Cost,
Districts I–IV, 1971

Refinery Inputs (bbl./day)	Ratio of Allowed Inputs (percent)	Allowed Imports (bbl./day)	Quota Benefit per Barrel of Input (cents/ bbl.)	Quota Benefit per Marginal Barrel of Input (cents/ bbl.)
0–10,000	20.0	2,000	25.0	10.0
10,000–30,000	12.0	3,600	15.0	6.25
30,000–100,000	7.0	7,000	8.75	4.38
100,000+	3.5	3,500	4.37	—

Source: Copp 1974b.

emergency grants made by the Oil Import Appeals Board (Dam 1971). Imports as a percentage of domestic production continuously exceeded the 12 percent limitation established in 1962. In addition, as Table 15 shows, by 1968 exempt imports accounted for one-third of *all* imports. These various exemptions (for "hardship" cases) included special quotas for terminal operators, petrochemical plants, and some Puerto Rican refiners. For example, in 1961 the regulations pertaining to imports of residual fuel oil were changed for PAD District I to provide allocations to all persons having operational control of terminals capable of receiving tankers. In addition, a new sliding scale for allocations was devised to help smaller terminal operators. Historical importers were to receive allocations equal to 85 percent of their total imports in 1957. This historical ratio declined three percentage points each year.

In 1965 the Johnson administration decided to allow allocations for petrochemical producers based on inputs to petrochemical plants. The entry of these newcomers to the mandatory cartel further reduced the import shares. Beginning in 1966 the definitions of petrochemicals, petrochemical plants, and refineries were expanded to allow even more participants in the program.

Also in 1966 a study by the Office of Emergency Preparedness

TABLE 15
Relationship between Exempt and Total Imports
of Crude and Unfinished Oils,
Districts I–IV,
1959–1971
(000 bbl./day)

Year	Total Imports*	Exempt Imports†	Ratio, Exempt Imports to Total Imports (percent)
1959‡	785	56	7.1
1960	769	64	8.3
1961	794	119	15.0
1962	839	141	16.8
1963	856	154	18.0
1964	872	171	19.6
1965	879	188	20.9
1966	931	221	23.7
1967	834	262	31.4
1968	1024	332	32.4
1969	1094	381	34.8
1970	1031	116	11.3
1971	1259	29	2.3

* Source: U.S. Bureau of Mines, *Crude Petroleum, Petroleum Products, and Natural Gas Liquids*, Mineral Industry Surveys, 1959–1971.
† Sources: 1959 calculated from U.S. Congress, Select Committee on Small Business, Subcommittee No. 4, *Hearings: Small Business Created by Petroleum Imports*, 87th Cong., 1st sess., 1961, p. 502; 1960–1967 calculated from U.S. Department of the Interior news releases; 1968–1971 calculated from U.S. Department of the Interior news releases, import totals.
‡ Figures given are for the entire year 1959, including the period before the imposition of mandatory controls. The program began March 11. Overland imports were exempted April 30.

(OEP) concluded that increased imports of residual fuel oil would not endanger national security, and controls on these imports were removed (Department of the Interior 1966). Because residual fuel accounted for over 48 percent of crude and product imports into PAD Districts I–IV (and 70 percent of total product imports into the United States), decontrol had a major dismantling effect on the mandatory quota program. In addition, the No. 4 fuel oil, which had formerly been categorized as a distillate, was reclassified as residual fuel oil. The decontrol of residual actually led to a major imbalance in the foreign price of naphtha, which in turn led to pressures to allow petrochemical plants to import naphtha. Decontrol induced construction of offshore refineries especially to provide domestic residual. In producing this residual, a surplus of naphtha was created, and this surplus led to a widening gap between its foreign and domestic prices. Tickets to import naphtha had a high value.

A further weakening of the control program was the special authorizations for Puerto Rico and the Virgin Islands granted to Phillips, Commonwealth, and Hess Oil companies. The allocations to Phillips and Commonwealth were subtracted from the overall allowable before the quantity of crude and unfinished oil available for mainland refiners was determined.

Toward the end of the 1960's, the imports-to-production ratio had become meaningless, and a somewhat different theme became popular for justifying import controls. This theme was the simple notion of the origin of certain presumably insecure oil as a percentage of total U.S. imports. Explicit consideration was given to national security arguments. Underlying this switch was the gradually developing fear of a new national oil shortage during the 1970's. Spare domestic production capacity had declined rapidly by the early seventies.[11] This capacity had been the reserve supply available for any emergency. During the 1967 Arab-Israeli conflict, increased output from this spare capacity was shipped to Europe, where large volumes of oil supplies had been curtailed. By 1972, all prorationing states reinstated the maximum allowable of 100 percent of the maximum efficient recovery for the first time since 1947. It has remained at that level to the present.

By 1972, the growing requirement for imports was worsened by the rising shortage of natural gas coupled with the environmental regulation of oil product sulfur emissions. The result was a large-scale substitution of low-sulfur residual and distillate fuel oils.[12] With the output of relatively low-sulfur U.S. crude oil experiencing an annual decline, and with the strong growth in oil demand, the

[11] The API statistics indicate that spare productive capacity was less than one million barrels per calendar day by 1973.

[12] An analysis of these substitutions is provided in chapter 3.

United States became more reliant on foreign oil supplies. Unlike the policy it had followed during the Free Trade phase, the announced reaction of the U.S. government was to encourage domestic development rather than to seek additional foreign oil. The fundamental reason was that OPEC began (1) demanding greater payments for its oil in 1971; (2) negotiating the eventual takeover of all foreign-based producing operations, especially in the Middle East; and (3) threatening to use oil as a political weapon against the United States because of its pro-Israeli policy.

Thus, the growing concern for the domestic energy crisis, the expected dominance of Middle East oil as a percentage of oil imports, the increasing oil balance-of-payments deficit, and the potential of an oil supply interruption forced the United States to consider policies designed to increase internal development. Dissatisfied with quotas, the Nixon administration seriously considered an auction program that would use the money from the sale of import tickets to foster research into new hydrocarbon resources or possibly finance an emergency storage program. However, energy policy was being formulated by the Treasury Department at that time, and Secretary George Shultz favored the abolition of quotas and the imposition of tariffs. As secretary of labor in 1970, Shultz had headed a special cabinet task force study of oil import controls, which concluded that a system of import tariffs would be less costly to consumers and to the national economy than would quotas (Office of the President, Cabinet Task Force, 1971).

In 1971 and 1972 extensive congressional hearings were conducted, especially by the Joint Economic Committee, on the cost of the oil import program. Opponents of the quota program (for example, New England consumer interest groups) maintained that quotas were weakening national security by reducing the real wealth of consumers. Other opponents, and several books that appeared during that period, argued that quotas vitiated national security by forcing greater consumption of domestic resources. The development of a national emergency storage program, of a "shut-in" capacity concept, combined with full abolition of import quotas, received widespread attention.[13]

---

[13] This attention resulted from the controversial Mead-Sorensen study (1971, pp. 211–224).

However, the abnormally cold winter of 1972/1973 caused spot shortages of fuel oil for home heating. Distillate fuels were rationed by oil companies, and by January, 1973, the oil industry was warning the Nixon administration of a possible gasoline shortage in the summer. Oil companies argued that the administration's price control program had caused a deterrent to the production of needed fuel oil in preference to gasoline, since the Cost of Living Council had frozen fuel prices at their seasonal low. Another factor that was becoming important in affecting the output of domestic refineries was the lack of a usable crude oil slate (that is, sweet crude) that met sulfur standards. Domestic crude oil wells had begun to decline in daily production despite the elimination of prorationing. President Nixon twice increased the amount of allowable imports of crude oil and, by December, 1972, lifted the preference for Western Hemisphere fuel oil imports.

Throughout this period Congress and the industry were calling for the development of a national energy policy. Energy became a major problem of the administration, and a special presidential council consisting of Henry Kissinger, Shultz, and John Erlichman was appointed to handle the energy problem. With the presentation of the president's energy message to Congress on April 13, 1973, the fourth era of national oil policy ended.

Deregulation, Boycott, and More Controls, 1973–1975

On April 18, 1973, the president terminated the Mandatory Oil Import Control Program (Office of the President 1973). A system of national security license fees replaced quotas for crude oil and product imports, thus ending the highly controversial quota allocation mechanism initiated under the Eisenhower administration. Moreover, this action brought the United States closer to a free-trade posture in international oil trade.

In addition to abolishing volumetric controls on oil imports, the new plan suspended existing tariffs on crude oil and refinery product imports. A separate tariff system was introduced which was applicable only to imports exceeding the quotas set for 1973. Thus, companies could import oil and products up to the amount of their original 1973 allocation duty-free, but beyond that level the special national security license fees had to be paid. Newcomers had to pay these license fees on all their imports.

In justifying the new program, William Simon, chairman of the Oil Policy Committee, found that "the Mandatory Oil Program no longer provided the proper climate to support a vigorous domestic petroleum industry, which is essential to the national security and the economic welfare of the nation" (Department of the Treasury 1973). Simon stated that oil policy was to be designed to get the federal government out of the business of regulating oil imports. Moreso, it appears the government did not want to be held responsible for any forthcoming shortage of crude oil products. This was a time of periodic shortages of low-sulfur crude oils and products; the supply-demand situation was tight, and the administration and Congress began to focus on the limited spare refining capacity and growing reliance on imports.

The initiation of this fifth era in U.S. oil policy grew out of a mixture of the Nixon administration's inflation control program and energy development proposals. However, the problem of the concentration of imports from the Middle East drew special attention in the administration's energy planning policies. The vast majority of world oil reserves are located in the Middle East; Saudi Arabia, Kuwait, and Iran account for most of them. Unlike some OPEC members, these nations had been somewhat moderate in their threats to use oil as a political weapon against the United States. Saudi Arabia had proposed in early 1973 that the United States grant it preferential status as an exporting nation, but this suggestion was declined. However, almost simultaneously with the president's energy message, the Saudi Arabian government formally threatened the United States with an oil boycott unless this nation's pro-Israeli policy changed. This threat, coupled with others from Libya, Kuwait, and Iraq, forced the administration to consider a national security storage program. By as late as September, 1973, the administration had not yet formulated a coordinated plan to alleviate crude oil and natural gas shortages—although at least *some* conciliatory negotiations had been initiated with the world's greatest oil reserve area, the Middle East.

In short, the initial U.S. policy in this latest phase was to deregulate imports of crude oil and products and to encourage development of domestic resources. Much of the initial impetus for this policy derived from the continuing debate on the costs of the mandatory quota program and its contribution to national security. As subsequent chapters will indicate, the Arab oil boycott of late 1973 restrained this initial deregulatory thrust and led directly to the imposition of a comprehensive range of controls on the petroleum companies.

Before 1973 the OEP had been charged with contingency planning for oil supply interruptions. The first official energy office within the Executive Office of the President, however, was the Energy Policy Office (EPO), which was organized in the summer of 1973. The EPO was replaced by the Federal Energy Office (FEO) in December, 1973. The FEO became the center for energy planning and coordinated compliance with an initial voluntary refined product allocation program that was initiated in May, 1973, to encourage major oil companies to share supplies with their competitors during the tight supply-demand period. This voluntary program later in 1973 became mandatory for propane and for middle distillate fuels, and then in January, 1974, it became required for all wholesale products. As the nation's policy makers, industry, and private consultants continued to study and to theorize about the causes of and solutions to what was popularized as the "energy crisis," the Middle East war erupted and supplies were curtailed.[14]

Several emergency measures which prepared the way for the formal evolution of the FEO to the Federal Energy Administration (FEA) were taken by the government. In November, 1973, Congress passed the Emergency Petroleum Allocation Act of 1973, which extended mandatory controls to crude oil and motor gasoline. The law provided for the mandatory allocation and pricing of crude oil, residual fuel oil, and each refined petroleum product. The program was designed to assure the suppliers and users of these fuels a pro rata share in proportion to their 1972 fuel demand and to guarantee supplies of these fuels to anyone whose use of alternate fuels was

---

[14] The period 1972–1974 was one in which an enormous allocation of resources was devoted to energy studies, most of which were obsolete by early 1975. Studies during this period included the FEA's Project Independence report (1974), the National Petroleum Council's *Energy Outlook* (1972), and the Ford Foundation's Energy Policy Project (1974).

curtailed because of government action. In addition, a state "set-aside" system was established for products that could be used by the states to resolve emergencies and hardships. With the passage of the Federal Energy Administration Act of 1974 in May of that year, authority under the Emergency Petroleum Allocation Act passed to the FEA. The FEA was charged with being the instrument of the domestic energy planning effort, and it supplanted many of the traditional roles of the Department of the Interior. The mood of Washington was that these established former agencies had failed in dealing with energy problems and that a new organizational structure for energy planning was required. With respect to international energy planning, the State Department generally commanded the effort to deal with OPEC and to coordinate energy planning among the major oil-consuming countries; one result was the formal organization of the International Energy Agency in late 1974.

The Crude and Product Allocation Programs

Under the allocation act, a total of eight specific allocation programs were established, including those for crude oil, residual fuel oil, aviation fuels, propane, middle distillates, gasoline, butane and natural gasoline, and naphthas and gas oils. A nonspecific program for "other products" was also developed. Not since World War II had there been such elaborate controls on the output of major and independent refiners. However, as in all the previous phases of U.S. policy, the magnitude of exemptions and special rulings for the independents and some majors tended to undermine the government's effort to redistribute by fiat the product shortages. The allocation program was only designed to equalize the economic burden of the product imbalance in supply and demand by essentially substituting regulatory decision for the market mechanism.

The allocation rules required that suppliers of crude oil and natural gas liquids and all refined products first determine their "allocation fraction" and then make allocations to wholesale purchasers and end users. The wholesalers and end users could not transfer their entitlement to an allocation. The FEA determined which industries were entitled to 100 percent of their requirements, and these requirements were multiplied by the allocation fraction to determine supplier allocation. The base period was 1972 for all products except naphthas, gas oils, and residual fuel oil, which were assigned 1973 base periods. The allocation fraction was to be equal to the allocable supply of each product divided by its supply obligation for all levels of distribution for that product. The total allocable supply—the numerator of the allocation fraction—was the sum of the suppliers' estimated production, imports, and oil and product purchases. It was adjusted for amounts designated as state set-aside, those amounts of allocation requirements not subject to an allocation fraction, and, finally, any amounts supplied to customers through exchange agreements. Amounts used to increase inventory were also excluded from the numerator. The supply obligation—the denominator of the allocation fraction—was the sum of its volumes in the base period, adjusted for unusual growth, plus volumes for new purchasers assigned to or accepted by the supplier. If allocation fractions were less than one, suppliers had to reduce, on a pro rata basis, the amounts supplied to end users and wholesale purchasers. If allocation fractions were greater than one—a condiiton of "surplus" product—the FEA could direct that the surplus be distributed among other suppliers, sold to other end users, or accumulated in inventory. Wholesalers were required to accept new customers if they would have been accepted under normal business practices in the base year. In controlling product supply, the FEA also had the authority to require refiners to adjust yield proportions at their plants whenever a particular product was in short supply. This particular refinery yield control program was tied to a special crude oil control program.

The effectiveness of the allocation program was questionable during its early operation, as long lines at retail gasoline pumps became a common scene during early 1974. Part of the problem emerged directly from the federal regulations, which tended to worsen the basic difficulties deriving from crude oil shortages. Each state had a "set-aside" program. On the first day of each month, each state received 3 percent of the total supply of motor gasoline and 4 percent of the middle distillates to be sold by prime suppliers. The states could dispose of this volume as they wished. However, several states experienced an additional growth in gasoline demand above that of the 1972 base period. According to the allocation law, only volume growth that was 10 percent more than 1972 levels could be added to the base-period volumes available for allocation. Allocation figures for monthly gasoline supply were set at fractions lower than 95 percent of 1972 levels after state set-aside. Thus, the queuing that inevitably resulted, particularly in major cities on the East Coast, occurred in part because FEA rules did not accommodate the first 10 percent of growth over 1972 base levels. Many retail outlets simply closed immediately following the sale of their allocated supply. Other retailers sold a maximum of three to five dollars' worth of gasoline to each customer as a means of stretching supply during a given week or sold gasoline only during specified hours of the day or days of the week. Some states were forced to adopt the practice in which cars with license plates ending in even numbers and those with odd numbers bought gas on alternate days.

This experience with motor gasoline was particularly damaging to the major refiners, who were viewed as somehow withholding supply while deliberately forcing prices upward. However, all increases in gasoline prices were controlled by FEO (later FEA) rules. The gasoline scarcity problem of 1974 was seen by various congressional committees as further evidence of the threat to the small, independent retailers and wholesalers who relied upon the majors for supply. Indeed, independent marketers consistently protested that they were being squeezed out of the market by the majors. The long lines at service stations from December, 1973, through May, 1974, however, reflected a demand for gasoline of some 500,000 to 600,000 barrels daily in excess of available supply. Federal allocations allowed basic industries to receive 95 percent to over 100 percent of their 1972 consumption, which limited supplies at service stations to below the 1972 level. Statistical evidence nevertheless suggests that during the embargo winter of 1973/1974, the early switch in yields away from distillates to motor gasoline by all refiners prevented what could have been an even more serious decline in available gasoline. High distillate stocks built up to avoid cold weather crises in some states, the mildness of the winter, and apparently some public conservation contributed to the feasibility of the early switching.

The allocation program later provided greater flexibility in allowing suppliers to allocate crude products themselves. However, this flexibility was overshadowed by the FEA rules controlling product price increases and by the imposition of crude oil price controls and the oil cost equalization program.

REFINER MARGINS, PRICE CONTROLS, AND CRUDE OIL ENTITLEMENTS

Among the most controversial aspects of the government's intervention into petroleum refining were its price controls on domestic crude oil and on the ability of refiners to recoup the increased cost of crude oil and other inputs to refineries through increased product prices. Initially, the Cost of Living Council (CLC) and the FEO held the allowable refiner and marketer margin increases to the equivalent of the wholesaler's base margin on May 15, 1973. Increases in product and nonproduct costs were allowed to be passed along on a dollar-for-dollar basis with the limitation that only 10 percent of costs could be passed along in a given month. Remaining increased costs were then "banked" to be passed along in the future. The FEA extended control over some product cost increases by its controls over crude oil.

The FEA distinguished between "old" or nonexempt crude oil and "new," exempt crude oil. Old crude petroleum was defined as the total number of barrels produced and sold from a given property using the base level of 1972. This volume of crude oil represented about 60 percent of total domestic production and about 40 percent of aggregate supplies of oil to the United States. A ceiling price on all old oil was eventually set at $5.25 per barrel.[15] New crude oil was exempt from price controls. Thus, the total available oil supply for the United States in the fifth phase of the nation's oil policy history consisted of three bureaucratically established but disconnected

---

[15] In March, 1973, U.S. crude oils of about 34° API were priced about $3.65 per barrel. By early fall, 1973, the U.S. price had increased to $4.25 per barrel. The Cost of Living Council (CLC) in August, 1973, established the maximum price at which "old" crude oil could be sold as the May 15, 1973, posted price in the applicable field plus $0.35 per barrel. On December 19, 1973, the CLC increased that price by $1.00 per barrel, resulting in the $5.25 per barrel price. This price varied from field to field depending on the May 13, 1973, posted price of that field for the grade and quality of crude, and it was as low as $3.50 per barrel and as high as $7.00 per barrel.

segments: (1) a perfectly elastic segment defined as old oil receipts ($5.25 × 5.5 million barrels daily in mid-1974); (2) a new crude segment whose exempt price ranged from $9.95 per barrel in mid-1974 (approximately 3.8 million barrels daily) to over $12.00 per barrel by mid-1975; and (3) imported crude oil (2.8 million barrels daily in 1974), the average price of which, when landed at U.S. ports, moved from about $12.75 per barrel in mid-1974 to over $13.50 per barrel by mid-1975. Imports of crude oil increased up to 4 million barrels daily by 1975.

The FEA later found that their own price control system imposed inequities on refiners who relied substantially on open-market purchases of crude oil. Refiners with large amounts of old oil had a competitive edge over those whose cost of inputs from new domestic and foreign oil was relatively greater. Therefore, the FEA designed the Old Crude Oil Entitlements Program to allocate low-priced old oil proportionately among all refiners. In addition, the FEA decided to extend its cost equalization scheme to cover imported distillate oil and residual fuel oil. Each month, the FEA established a national average ratio of old crude supplies as a percentage of the total of crude runs to refinery stills and imported products. All refiners were issued entitlements equal to the national average ratio, with additional entitlements being issuable to small refiners. Refiners with less than the national average ratio would then sell entitlements to old crude, and refiners with more old crude than the national average would have to buy entitlements in order to process the old crude they had. For example, if 80 percent of a major refiner's runs for a month were old crude, and if the national old oil supply ratio was 40 percent, the refiner would have to buy old oil entitlements equivalent to 40 percent of its total refinery runs for the month from refiners who had less than 40 percent old oil and therefore excess entitlements. Importers of distillate and residual fuel oil were also issued entitlements to old crude which they could sell. Again, the small refiner was treated preferentially in the interest of assuring his survival. Small refiners with less than 175,000 barrels per day in capacity received a proportionately greater number of entitlements to compensate them for their "high operating costs and proportionately greater capacity expenditure requirements." Later, a temporary special rule was established that exempted small refiners through their first 30,000 barrels per day from having to purchase all of their mandatory amount of entitlements. Thirty-eight refiners were eligible under this special rule. In another example of "acquired regulation" the smaller refiners were granted a special sliding scale of entitlements in addition to their base entitlements level, as shown in Table 16.

It is apparent that there was an economic incentive to maintain a small-refiner status and to reopen small, shutdown refineries that could become eligible for entitlements. The relatively greater benefit accrued to refiners in the range of 30,000 to 100,000 barrels per day. The FEA would set an entitlement level (1,258), adjust this amount for the difference between the crude runs of a refiner (175,000 barrels per day) and a set volume (100,000 barrels per day), and multiply the difference by a set fraction. This number was subtracted if the base entitlement value was above 30,000 barrels daily and added if it was below 30,000 barrels daily.

Unlike the market for import tickets under the mandatory oil import quota program, the value of an entitlement was determined monthly by the FEA. This value was set with reference to the difference between the price ceiling for old oil and free market prices for new and imported oil. The FEA also set separate entitlement values for qualified importers of residual fuel oil and home heating fuel oil. These entitlements were arbitrarily assigned to be worth 30 percent of the per-barrel value of entitlements for crude runs to

TABLE 16
Additional Allocations by the FEA of Old Oil Entitlements
to Small Refiners (less than 175,000 bbl./day)

Crude Runs to Stills (bbl./day)	Entitlement	Entitlement Adjustment	Actual Number of Additional Entitlements
100,000–175,000	1,258	$-(175-100)(16.7733)$	$+1$
30,000–100,000	1,690	$-(100-30)(6.1714)$	$+1,258$
10,000–30,000	1,238	$+(30-10)(22.6)$	$+1,690$
0–10,000	123.8 per 1,000 bbl.	—	$+1,238$

SOURCE: *Federal Energy Guidelines* (New York: Commerce Clearing House, 1975).

stills. In January, 1975, the first buy/sell entitlements list and values were defined at $5.00 per barrel for crude oil and $0.615 per barrel for qualified importer entitlements. The national old oil ratio was set at 41 percent, and refiners whose crude oil runs were greater than that had to buy entitlements. The importers' value was developed by multiplying $5.00 by 41 percent and then multiplying again by 30 percent.

It was apparent that the FEA had extended its controls to virtually every phase of the petroleum refiners' business. Rules were later set defining the value of intracorporate transfer prices between foreign affiliates of major refiners. Within this atmosphere of regulation, the administration attempted a campaign to begin to phase out price and output controls on the industry, and through August, 1975, a virtual stalemate with Congress prevailed over which direction—continuation, gradual phaseout, or total decontrol—the nation would take toward its petroleum refiners.

For the new Ford administration's part, an effort to force reduction in oil and product imports via the price mechanism was imposed in early January. The United States by that time was importing 40 percent of its total petroleum consumption. Through Proclamation No. 4341 under authority of Section 232 of the Trade Expansion Act of 1962, as amended by the Trade Reform Act of 1974, a license fee on imported oil of $1.00 per barrel was imposed and later increased to $2.00 per barrel in June; fees on petroleum products were increased up to $1.20 per barrel. The Ford administration also favored decontrol of crude oil prices along with decontrol of interstate natural gas prices. However, by late 1975 policy makers still failed to agree on the role of government in oil pricing and hence whether the fifth phase of our nation's oil policy would give way to another period of reduced controls and consequently introduce a new phase. The earliest indications were that a gradual phaseout of price controls would be adopted, which would extend the fifth era to the end of the 1970's.

On December 22, 1975, President Ford signed the Energy Policy and Conservation Act, which effectively extended price controls on all U.S. crude oil but introduced a forty-month phaseout period on these price controls. This act assured continued governmental pricing intervention in the oil industry to 1980 and probably well beyond that year. Because of the significance of this piece of legislation, it is discussed in greater detail in the following chapter. The fifth era of interventionist oil policy was being extended; by design, price controls would ostensibly phase out to a free-market level by 1980. On paper, the fifth era was to evolve toward a return to uncontrolled markets and prices—a Phase Six. However, this new omnibus energy legislation signed by Ford will allow prices to eventually rise to ten or eleven dollars per barrel by 1980. It seems apparent that foreign oil prices could rise well above this level from 1975 to 1980. Consequently, a large domestic/foreign price differential would remain in 1980, with the likely consequence that controls on crude pricing in the oil industry will be continued beyond that year.

False Assumptions in Energy Policy, 1948–1975

In retrospect, the nation's energy policies since 1948 have often been inconsistent and even conflicting with their stated ends and have been almost totally uncoordinated. Government import policy was clearly contradictory with respect to the treatment of crude oil, unfinished oil, and products. As Table 15 showed, the percentage of exempt imports to total imports of crude and unfinished oils into PAD Districts I–IV had reached nearly 35 percent by 1969. Although the reimposition of restrictions on overland imports tended to amend this weakness, the government released control of residual fuel oil in 1966, and in 1970 it released control of distillate fuel oil within the Western Hemisphere.

Confusion over the mandatory control program resulted in a search for other forms of control. The 1971 cabinet task force report suggested tariffs; others argued for the auctioning of import tickets; still others argued for replacing the sliding scale with an exponential scale. The task force's argument for a tariff was based on its finding that "reasons support the conclusion that the landed price of foreign crude by 1980 may well decline and will in any event not experience a substantial increase" (Office of the President, Cabinet Task Force, 1971, p. 124). In fact, one year after the report was issued, foreign prices began to exceed domestic prices.

Earlier state control policies had been ineffective in increasing crude oil price because the various exemptions tended to offset the true price effect of prorationing. Federal tax policy tended to stimulate unnecessarily the addition to surplus productive capacity; later, at a time when spare productive capacity was declining (after 1967), these tax provisions were reduced by Congress. Natural gas prices were controlled at the wellhead, and such artificially low prices created an excess demand for natural gas. Because one of the main purposes of energy policy was to create a positive economic environment for the discovery and development of proved reserves of oil, gas, and natural gas liquids, and since additions to proved reserves were always less than production during this period, energy policy can only be considered a failure. The government attempted to regulate imports through its own cartel of importers, yet in its response to political pressures the government undermined its own cartel with its numerous exemptions and gradual decontrol of products. By reducing controls on products, it created the incentive to *export* refining capacity. Foreign location of refineries showed greater profitability at the expense of refinery expansion in the United States. Thus, the government was creating a deterrent to the expansion of new refinery capaciy while it was supporting the survival of smaller, less efficient refiners.

How could such an uncoordinated and conflicting set of policies develop? Because oil and politics are inseparable, the individual segments of the oil industry operating in pursuit of their own self-interest often created a political tug-of-war among policy makers and among themselves. In effect, both industry and government attempted to equate the public interest of the country with the private interest of a particular segment of the oil industry. Whatever real merit there was in the equation of national security with preferential privilege for the industry was obscured in the pre-1970 era; when security considerations became more apparent and the requirement for effective policy action increased after 1970, policy makers and legislators seemed more hesitant to adopt the advice or counsel of the industry. Cumbersome regulations were to follow, and only through the mid-1970's was there evidence of a growing need for the mutual cooperation of industry and government to develop the energy resource potential of the United States. There seems little doubt that both majors and independents, in their pursuit of reasonable or equitable acquired regulation, created much to confuse the policy makers. But the government, in addition to submitting to the pressure for acquired regulation, added to the inconsistencies of oil policy with government-initiated support for natural gas regulation and for special exemptions for special-interest groups under the import program. Finally, the unexpectedly rapid increase in demand for energy since 1966, and specifically for gasoline and distillate fuels, tended to exacerbate the negative effects of government policy.

In general, this policy was based upon a set of five assumptions that either were basically false or became false during the period 1948–1975. These assumptions were the following: (1) the United States had a cushion of spare refining capacity and spare productive capacity, and supply would always exceed demand; (2) the long-term supply curve of foreign oil was perfectly elastic, and restrictions on foreign oil would increase national energy security; (3) energy policies could be developed for specific petroleum raw materials and refined products, and consideration of the costs of crude oil and natural gas as joint products could be ignored; (4) national security is enhanced by a healthy oil industry, with "healthy" defined as the ensured survival of small, independent firms; and (5) regulation and planning could supplant the market system.

As Figure 4 showed, the United States had a cushion of excess refinery capacity between 1948 and 1975 for all but three periods: the early 1950's, the mid-1960's, and the early 1970's. The refinery undercapacity of 1971 to early 1973 soon gave way to temporary excess capacity as the economy of the United States and other oil-consuming nations suffered the most serious economic recession since the 1930's. Spare refining capacity was the exception rather than the rule. Spare crude oil productive capacity was a different case: the nation had spare capacity up to the late 1960's, when shutdown days in oil prorationing states began gradually to decline. Even by the early 1970's there was still substantial optimism regarding surplus capacity in the United States (Van Meurs 1971). However, by 1972 all states were producing at full productive capacity, that is, at 100 percent MER. From 1948 the ratio of foreign crude oil to domestic crude oil used as an input to U.S. refineries gradually increased, and of course some East Coast refineries were built to handle foreign crude exclusively. But by the mid-1970's foreign oil accounted for some 35 percent of all inputs to U.S. refineries. The assumption of the supply elasticity of foreign oil was soon violated by the actions of OPEC and other foreign oil-producing countries. The analysis and economic history of these events are discussed in subsequent chapters because of their importance to the development of United States oil policy.

Of the five major assumptions listed above, the third deserves special notice. A major policy flaw has been the failure to view energy supply and demand as being highly interdependent on each other. Particularly, the failure to recognize that crude oil, natural gas, and natural gas liquids are really joint products in supply and limited substitutes in consumption for various end users directly explains the current crisis in declining proved reserves in oil and gas. In the finding, developing, and producing process, firms are concerned with the commercial discovery of hydrocarbons. Both crude oil and natural gas are now produced on 95 percent of all leases in the United States. Firms, in their resource allocation decisions, are consequently interested in the total profitability of the joint production of oil, gas, and gas liquids. Thus, factors that influence crude oil supply and prices will also have an impact on gas output and prices. In other words, the cross-elasticity of supply is positive.

Because existing national petroleum policy did not coordinate both natural gas and oil policy, the end effect has been an apparent conflict in policy. Crude oil import controls were designed to stimulate or stabilize crude prices only while gas prices were being controlled. Moreover, in the regulatory proceedings for natural gas, firms inadvertently contributed to the situation of oil and gas policy independence by concocting the spurious "directionality" argument, which tended to indicate that oil policy had no effect on gas supply and price.[16] By arbitrarily allocating jointly incurred costs of finding, developing, and producing natural gas in an effort to support arguments for greater ceiling price levels before the

[16] "Directionality" meant that oil companies earmarked funds for the specific production of crude oil. Thus, an average cost per barrel of crude or per thousand cubic feet of gas could be calculated. Because of the Federal

Federal Power Commission, the independence argument gained credibility. The petroleum industry's position was an expected reaction to the influences of FPC gas price controls.

More than ever before, the challenge of new government policy today stems in part from the need to generate new policies that are productive for one of the joint products but not counterproductive for the other. The inability to do so clearly worsens national energy security. In the government's efforts to placate both major and independent factions, the government has undermined its own efforts at achieving energy security. Indeed, the numerous exemptions granted under the mandatory oil import program directly induced the overseas location of refinery capacity and contributed to the absense of spare refining capacity that characterized the early energy crises from 1970 to 1973. Moreover, less efficient plants were maintained longer, and to this extent the import program after 1959 reduced the incentive for the rapid adoption of process innovations. Majors and the larger independents maintained their permanent shares of the market by mergers and acquisitions and by expansion to units of more efficient size that were more competitive with the subsidized smaller refiners.

One implication of the joint-supply policy failure was the ancillary treatment of the United States as a homogeneous geologic area. The United States, from the geologic viewpoint, is a series of geologic provinces, each of which has a unique potential for yielding hydrocarbons. In economic terminology, the theoretical production function or schedule for oil and gas is somewhat unique for each province, since petroleum exploration and development within each often requires its own specialized technologies. Discovery potential varies by geologic province; for example, policies affecting price will have a different impact on discoveries of oil and gas on the Gulf Coast compared to more inland areas. There are high-cost and lower-cost provinces, which is simply indicative of the increasing-cost characteristic of the industry. Several statistical studies of the interrelationships between long-run and short-run supply and de-

---

Power Commission pricing regulations, firms had to concoct complicated cost allocation schemes to justify higher prices. Directionality assumes away the problem of joint cost (see the discussion of the third period of oil policy).

mand for oil and gas have been made by Fisher (1964), Khazzoom
(1971), Bradley (1967), Erickson (1968), Erickson and Spann
(1971, 1973), and Adelman (1962). Only recently, in work by
Erickson and Spann (1973) and by MacAvoy and Pindyck (1973),
are estimates based on joint-product hypotheses attempted. However, all these studies have treated the United States as a homogeneous geologic unit; data unfortunately are more frequently
collected according to political units (that is, states) than by geologic areas.[17]

The argument that oil and gas are jointly produced and that
the functions of joint production are unique for each geologic
province in the United States implies that the impact of government
policy will vary significantly from region to region. Because U.S.
policy makers are concerned with meeting enormous future energy
requirements, they will need to understand how to stimulate the
maximum development of areas of potentially high resource yields.
The United States will require massive additions to proved reserves
of oil and gas over the next decade to meet its expected energy requirements. Policy focus therefore should be placed on the specific
geologic provinces where the payoff is expected to be the greatest.

To this end, it is obvious that the estimates of resource potential at present and future prices should be the guiding focus of a
national petroleum policy. Studies of petroleum resources by geologic province have been conducted by the American Association
of Petroleum Geologists (Cram, 1971), the National Petroleum
Council (1970, 1973b), the U.S. Geological Survey (1975), the
Potential Gas Committee (1973), and the National Academy of
Sciences (1975). Estimates of current proved reserves of oil and
gas have been published by the American Petroleum Institute and
the American Gas Association, and by special studies by oil consultants and oil companies. The great weakness of most of these
studies is that the role of economics and particularly price is not
explicitly defined in these estimates.[18] At a minimum, a concerted

---

[17] In a previous study I have used an Erickson-Spann model based on
the Gulf Coast province as a test area relative to the rest of the United States
to support the argument for a regional energy policy (Copp 1974b). See also
the recent study by MacAvoy and Pindyck (1973).

[18] See the discussion of the role of price in estimating proved oil and gas

effort to define the general long- or short-run elasticity of resource price should be undertaken. This range of responses of resources to price should include the joint price effect of crude oil, natural gas, and gas liquids along with the impact of prices of competing substitutes such as coal.

The fifth false assumption that became prevalent in the 1960's was the assumption that regulation and planning could supplant the market system—that the price mechanism could not be relied upon to solve the energy problem. Much of the belief in this assumption was based upon one of two general philosophies: either resource potential was limited, and hence higher prices would only add wealth to petroleum companies, or petroleum companies were deliberately withholding resource development. However, the misallocative effects of FEA regulation on the industry were quite evident in their essential thrust at redistributing scarcities as opposed to stimulating productive supply. The price mechanism was clearly evident in 1975 with the decline in the demand for petroleum products, and, indeed, significant domestic and worldwide excess refining capacity was apparent through most of the year. The demand for petroleum seemed surprisingly responsive to price change. Moreover, it was eminently apparent that the assumption of a perfectly elastic supply of foreign oil was false. Since 1970 the price of foreign oil has risen fivefold and exceeds the price of domestic oil. Because of the apparent weaknesses of the import program, state control programs, and natural gas ceiling price control programs, the additions through discoveries induced by the price system have been less than the production. This "decline rate" now affecting the United States indicates that the original purpose of governmental energy policy to assure national energy security has failed to be met or maintained since 1948.

---

reserves—"the price elasticity of proved reserves"—in Copp and Garrett (1975).

3

Government Policy and Product Supply and Demand

FROM 1948 through the mid-1970's, small and large refiners continued to maximize yields of higher-profit gasoline. To do so they adopted technical processes designed to minimize yields of residual fuel oil. However, various federal energy policies over the period 1948–1975 greatly altered the technological thrust of refiners and, consequently, the level of regional capacity. Therefore, government policy not only influenced both the supply and the price of jointly produced crude oil and natural gas, but also directly influenced both the yields and the prices of major refined products. In addition, by the mid-1970's there was growing evidence of a recession-induced excess in worldwide refining capacity. This excess capacity also affected the operational strategy of refiners.

Product Demand and Joint Cost in Refining

The desire to increase the yield of light refined products (that is, the desire to maximize profits) was the primary influence on the evolving process technology (NPC 1967). While the market for gasoline and distillates grew continuously from 1940 to the mid-1960's, the percentage of demand for residual fuels declined. Before the mid-1960's the major contributing factors to the decline of residual fuel oil were the price of crude oil and the import policy of the United States. In the mid-1960's residual's share of the market increased. The major contributing factor to this increase was the growing imbalance of natural gas relative to demand reinforced by the environmental movement toward clean-burning fuels. Use of high-sulfur coal by industry and utilities was beginning to be constrained.

Concurrent with changing trends in demand for refined products was the gradual effort to develop refining processes that allowed not only greater flexibility in shifting the output yield between gasoline and other products but also greater ability to improve the yield and quality of gasoline. As noted in the previous chapters, since 1948 technical growth of refining was characterized by modernization toward catalytic processes and the gradual increase in the minimum efficient size of plant. Ideally, refiners would have preferred to produce multiple, non-joint products in response to these changing demand patterns, but of course the joint-supply and joint-cost nature of refining, as discussed in the previous chapters, made that type of production impossible. From standard joint-cost theory we know that a firm cannot apportion all costs among its various products so that it can draw up a unique marginal cost curve for each product independent of the others (Carlson 1965; Henderson and Quandt 1958). The refiner's problem is not that of choosing a single optimal output of one product, but rather an optimal product mix (Griffin 1971). Moreso, the cross-elasticity of refinery supply—the response of the supply of one product, such as No. 2 fuel oil, to a rise in the price of another product, such as gasoline—for some major refined products is positive. An increase in the price of gasoline, *ceteris paribus*, will increase the supply of gasoline.[1]

Federal Policy and Residual Fuel Oil

Since refined outputs are inseparably produced, more gasoline also means more residual fuel and middle distillate. It is true that some refinery yields can be shifted to produce more gasoline, but only within certain technical limits. As chapter 1 indicated, the major technical advances during the earlier part of the study period involved minimizing yields of residuals to accommodate a rising de-

[1] In the real world, of course, not all things are equal. A rise in the price of gasoline, if the rise is significant, may cause a reduction in the quantity demanded. The short-run effect is relatively insignificant.

mand for motor gasoline and middle distillates. Even so, increasing the output of higher-valued gasoline still resulted in an increased output of residual fuel oil at a selling price even lower than the cost of crude oil—both domestic crude and that imported from the Caribbean. Thus, since there was no control on imports of residuals before 1959, it became less costly to import residuals than to import crude, which furnished an additional incentive for domestic refiners to rapidly adopt technology that would minimize residual yields. This technological trend continued even after the 1959 imposition of controls on the import of residuals. As increasing amounts of higher-boiling-point materials were charged to catalytic cracking, the remaining oil, which was sold as residual fuel, became progressively heavier. It became common industry practice to blend these heavy stocks with a distillate to lower their viscosity for a salable fuel. This practice led to the development of visbreaking, a process which allowed a smaller mixture of distillate with the residual (NPC 1973*a*).

Federal import policy on residual fuel oil (or resid) before 1966 clearly made it more attractive to reduce domestic yields and to import the majority of total requirements. Understandably, independent crude oil producers as well as coal mining interests strongly supported restrictions on foreign resid, while major petroleum companies resisted these controls. The final residual fuel oil quota program was, again, ineffective, and again the ineffectiveness was due to the loopholes allowed importers. Although imports were restricted to their 1957 levels, the secretary of the interior was empowered to make monthly revisions, if necessary, on an ad hoc basis to take care of emergencies such as unseasonably cold winters. In 1961 the 1957 ceiling was revised to apply only to PAD Districts II–IV. PAD District I, where the largest demand for resid was concentrated, was allowed to import an amount equal to the difference between expected demand and expected supply (NPC 1973*a*), with the Bureau of Mines responsible for forecasting both. In 1961 the government concluded that a relaxation of controls was consistent with the national security. After 1961 the secretary of the interior raised the allowable amount forecast by the Bureau of Mines by 10 percent each year. Finally, in 1966 the secretary granted importers permission to bring in as much residual as they needed to meet contractual obligations or to make spot sales (Department of the Interior 1966).

This decontrol was critically influential on refinery residual yields. With import controls, many refiners could not reduce residual yields to the level allowed by "best-practice" technology. Most of the residual fuel oil sold was on a long-term contract basis, and because of these long-term contracts import restrictions prevented some refiners from taking complete advantages of technology that would reduce residual. Controls forced these refiners to produce more resid from domestic capacity. Had import restrictions *not* been lifted, it is likely that the decline in domestic production of resid would have been more pronounced than that which actually occurred. In particular, much of the residual fuel oil consumed on the East Coast before 1950 was provided by refiners in PAD District III. The shipments of residual to District I declined rapidly from the early 1950's to 1959. When controls were imposed in 1959, these shipments increased in 1960 and then returned to their decline pattern. Table 17 shows this long-term pattern for District I under the voluntary and mandatory control programs. By 1972 imports of resid provided 90.3 percent of total resid demand in PAD District I, and in 1975 over 85 percent.

For PAD Districts I–IV only, Table 18 shows the importance of resid imports to total imports and to total crude oil production. Residual fuel imports accounted for 35 percent of total imports under the voluntary program in 1954 and over 50 percent of total imports by 1971. After 1971 the percentage of resid to total imports declined as crude import volumes grew. Thus, accompanying the decline in total residual demand through 1965 was the continued substitution of imported for domestic resid and the technical substitution of resid-reducing processes for resid-producing processes.

The resid control program worked mainly to the advantages of major refiners. The majors owned and operated most of the East Coast refining capacity, most of the distillation capacity on the Gulf Coast, and processing capacity in Venezuela, Netherlands Antilles, and Trinidad. In turn, they held the primary concessions in Venezuela, where most of the heavy crude oil attractive for processing into resid was located. Thus, these refiners had an incentive to locate new refining capacity in places easily accessible to Vene-

TABLE 17

Relationship of Residual Fuel Oil Imports to Total Product Demand
and Domestic Residual Production, District I, 1951–1975

Year	Domestic Production (000 bbl./day)	Shipments from District III (000 bbl./day)	Imports (000 bbl./day)	Total Demand* (000 bbl./day)	Ratio, Residual Imports to Total Demand (percent)
Imports prior to Mandatory Controls					
1951	242	164	326	732	44.5
1952	247	166	350	763	45.9
1953	246	179	361	786	45.9
1954	220	159	354	733	48.3
1955	216	152	417	785	53.1
1956	214	159	442	815	54.2
1957	217	138	471	826	57.0
1958	191	131	489	814	60.4
Imports during Mandatory Controls					
1959	178	121	608	907	67.0
1960	163	139	579	881	65.7
1961	158	129	588	875	67.2
1962	157	108	651	916	71.1
1963	121	87	693	900	77.0
1964	109	89	749	947	79.1
1965	98	89	873	1,060	82.3
1966	108	85	981	1,174	83.6
Imports following Decontrol					
1967	112	83	1,050	1,254	84.3
1968	112	96	1,078	1,286	83.8
1969	116	75	1,208	1,399	86.3
1970	96	78	1,471	1,638	89.8
1971	102	89	1,531	1,715	89.3
1972	102	83	1,686	1,867	90.3
Imports during OPEC Boycott and Domestic Controls					
1973	143	46	1,752	1,940	90.3
1974	154	99	1,459	1,706	85.5
1975†	168	143	1,469	1,903	85.0

SOURCE: U.S. Bureau of Mines, *Crude Petroleum, Petroleum Products, and Natural Gas Liquids*, Mineral Industry Surveys, 1951–1975.
* Total demand excludes some small shipments from PAD Districts II, IV, and V.
† Preliminary.

TABLE 18
Relationship of Residual Fuel Oil Imports to Total Oil Imports and
to Domestic Crude Production, Districts I–IV, 1954–1975

Year	Residual Imports* (000 bbl./day)	Total Imports* (000 bbl./day)	Ratio, Residual Imports to Total Imports (percent)	Domestic Crude Oil Production (000 bbl./day)	Ratio, Residual Imports to Crude Production (percent)
Imports prior to Mandatory Controls					
1954	354	997	35.5	5,367	6.6
1955	417	1,149	36.3	5,835	7.1
1956	442	1,245	35.5	6,193	7.1
1957	471	1,301	36.2	6,239	7.5
1958	489	1,464	33.4	5,851	8.4
Imports during Mandatory Controls					
1959	610	1,523	40.0	6,207	9.8
1960	620	1,501	41.3	6,199	10.0
1961	622	1,542	40.3	6,345	9.8
1962	685	1,652	41.5	6,491	10.6
1963	729	1,724	42.3	6,687	10.9
1964	782	1,798	43.5	6,763	11.6
1965	916	1,979	46.3	6,906	13.3
1966	1,015	2,116	48.0	7,309	13.9
Imports following Decontrol					
1967	1,072	2,072	51.7	7,738	13.9
1968	1,105	2,415	45.8	7,878	14.0
1969	1,243	2,657	46.8	8,000	15.5
1970	1,513	2,935	51.6	8,383	18.0
1971	1,560	3,268	47.7	8,259	18.9
1972	1,718	3,921	44.0	8,291	20.7
Imports during OPEC Boycott and Domestic Controls					
1973	1,798	5,252	34.0	8,086	22.2
1974	1,513	5,046	30.0	7,685	20.0
1975†	1,509	6,431	23.0	7,186	20.9

SOURCE: U.S. Bureau of Mines, Crude Petroleum, Petroleum Products, and Natural Gas Liquids, Mineral Industry Surveys, 1954–1975.
* Bonded and military imports destined for re-export are included in figures. Total imports consist of crude and products.
† Preliminary.

zuelan crude and close to East Coast markets. Because import rights were only provided to historic importers—all of which were majors —the full value of the import ticket for residual was captured by the majors.

Table 19 shows that the average wholesale price of residual fuels in the United States, excluding PAD District V, was generally stable during the early 1960's. As the table demonstrates, the long-term residual price trend was relatively stable after the 1959 imposition of controls until 1966, when controls were lifted. From 1966 to 1969 fuel oil prices tended to decline. With the decontrol of residual imports, European refiners (mostly Italian) started to compete with those in the Caribbean in supplying the massive U.S. East Coast market. Table 17 showed that the total requirements of the East Coast had risen from a volume of over 600,000 barrels daily in 1959 to some 1 million barrels per day by 1966 and to 1.3 million barrels per day by 1969. This was an annual average growth of 7.4 percent for the ten-year period.

Residual fuel oil has historically been the lowest priced of all major oil products, and it is the *only* major refined product whose price was generally below that of crude oil (Department of the Interior 1966). During the 1960's residual prices were 50 percent or more below the wellhead price of domestic crude oil. The reason for the low price of this product relative to crude cost is that in the United States residual fuel oil in several of its key markets must compete with coal and interruptible natural gas (Adelman 1972). This factor has determined both the domestic price of residual fuel oil as well as the worldwide export price of the Caribbean product, for which the U.S. East Coast is the principal outlet.

Before 1969 the highest resid prices had occurred during the 1947/1948 winter fuel shortage and following the closing of the Suez Canal in 1957. But in 1970 residual prices rose sharply to their "Suez" levels on both spot purchases and new contracts. The factors influencing this dramatic rise in the price of resid can be summarized as follows: (1) shortage of refining capacity with a high yield of resid; (2) the reversal of an expected decline in the demand for resid, (3) an unexpected coal shortage, (4) increased European demand for resid, (5) a world tanker shortage, and (6) rising short-

TABLE 19
U.S. Average Wholesale Prices for Heavy Fuel Oil, 1948–1975
Excluding California*

Year	Price (cents/gal.)	Year	Price (cents/gal.)
Prior to Mandatory Controls			
1948	5.90	1954	3.92
1949	3.10	1955	4.66
1950	4.10	1956	5.34
1951	4.47	1957	6.03
1952	3.76	1958	4.56
1953	3.59		
During Mandatory Controls			
1959	4.70	1963	4.57
1960	4.86	1964	4.56
1961	4.82	1965	4.82
1962	4.67	1966	4.72
Following Decontrol			
1967	4.55	1970	6.35
1968	4.33	1971	7.55
1969	4.34	1972	7.36
During Arab Boycott and Domestic Controls			
1973	8.48	1975	23.57
1974	21.62		

SOURCE: *Platt's Oil Price Handbook and Oilmanac*, 52d ed. (New York: Mc-Graw-Hill, 1975); Independent Petroleum Association of America, statistical releases, 1948–1975.
* U.S. including California—Individual product prices are weighted as follows: Oklahoma 16.8%; Midwestern group 3, 20.8%; New York Harbor, 11.2%; Philadelphia 4.0%; Jacksonville, 2.4%; Gulf Coast, 22.4%; and Los Angeles, 20%. Four products' average is weighted as follows: gasoline, 50%; kerosine, 5%; distillate, 15%; and residual fuel, 30%.

age of natural gas. The total demand for residual fuel oil increased while the short-run ability to supply more resid at the current schedule of prices became more limited (a leftward shift in the short-run supply curve of residual).

Shortly before 1970, and because of the stable low price of residual fuel, only slight expansion of heavy refinery capacity was completed in either the Caribbean or the United States. Therefore, resid production capacity was not expanded at a rate sufficient to meet requirements. Another deterrent to expanded heavy refinery capacity was that excess gasoline and middle distillates would have been produced along with additional resid, and these products—at least those from the Caribbean—would have been difficult to dispose of in light of U.S. import controls on lighter products.

There had been few expectations of improvement in the long-term price of residual. It had been assumed that after 1969 atomic energy would make substantial and rapidly growing inroads into residual's largest and most dynamic market—electric power generation. In 1967 half of all new power plants ordered in the United States were designed for nuclear power. Simultaneously, the first restrictions were placed on residual fuel oil with a high sulfur content. It was stated in congressional testimony that these restrictions would greatly curtail residual fuel oil consumption. The Clean Air Act Amendments of 1966 and the Air Quality Act of 1967 set the pattern for both federal and state implementation and enforcement of air pollution control. Sulfur content restrictions varied widely by states, with the lowest content limit of 0.5 percent or less in effect in the New York–New Jersey area and in Boston (Adelman 1972, pp. 176–177). By 1969 it was recognized that nuclear power was costlier than had been expected—and took longer to construct. By that time the United States had a nuclear power capacity of only 2,840 megawatts, compared to the 4,200 megawatts which had been forecast by the Federal Power Commission (NPC 1973a, app. 3). Also, as evidence of the pollution and public health hazards of nuclear power plants became known, public resistance to such stations developed.

In 1969 it also became evident that sulfur restrictions would actually increase instead of curtail the demand for low-sulfur residual fuel oil. The reason was simply that the supply of substitutes was extremely limited. Low-sulfur resid was much more readily available and more economical than low-sulfur coal at the U.S. East Coast (FPC 1971). Thus, East Coast utilities affected by the restrictions increased their share of liquid fuel at the expense of coal. Most of the low-sulfur coal was used further inland from the East Coast. Besides this scarcity of low-sulfur coal there was an overall decline of 1.3 percent in the consumption of all varieties of coal by East

Coast electric utilities in 1969, even though fuel requirements increased 10 percent. Coal, largely of metallurgical quality but also including steam-grade coal, was being exported to more profitable European and Canadian markets (Comanor 1966, pp. 212–225; Larson 1967, pp. 173–183; Council on Environmental Quality 1973). Coal exports rose 16.9 percent in 1969 and 38 percent in 1970. The shortage in domestic coal supplies therefore forced a return to resid.

A situation of short supply was also developing in another substitute utility fuel, natural gas. Natural gas prices had been regulated at the wellhead by the Federal Power Commission (FPC) since 1960. These less than market-clearing ceiling prices created an excess demand for this clean-burning fuel, and very little interruptible gas was available to electric utility users (Adelman 1966, pp. 199–211). Thus, only residual fuel was available to meet the demands of the East Coast utilities, and the demand for electricity on these utilities from 1967 forward grew at an average annual rate of almost 9 percent (MacAvoy 1971). Finally, extremely high tanker freight rates and growing European demand also influenced the increase in prices of resid (FPC 1972).[2] It is quite interesting to note that this fuel, the only one to be totally decontrolled under U.S. import policy, was in persistently scarce supply shortly after the controls were lifted. A similar result was to occur with middle distillates after 1970, when controls on their imports were lifted. This early 1970's period was punctuated by a series of hearings on the impact of the fuel crises on small business. Hearings on shortages of fuel oil and coal to electric utilities tended to focus on the market power of the major oil and coal companies and, in particular, on the entry of oil companies into the coal business (Congress, House, Select Committee on Small Business, 1970, 1971).

The historic price parity of resid with crude oil was reversed after 1969. In 1970 the Caribbean f.o.b. market price of resid was significantly above that of Venezuelan crude oil. The premium on resid is directly traceable to the low-sulfur standards enacted in 1966 and the increased demand for electricity. Figures for 1970 to 1972 East Coast residual fuel consumption by sulfur levels are provided in Table 20. Low-sulfur supplies are those with sulfur levels

[2] In 1970, for example, high tanker rates on the Worldscale index made import tickets worthless.

of less than 1.0 percent. The changes in consumption have occurred in the lowest and highest sulfur ranges, with the middle range remaining basically unaffected. Resid under 0.5 percent sulfur increased from 7.8 percent to 34.6 percent of East Coast consumption, suggesting that users of residual fuel switched from the consumption of natural gas, a product with virtually no sulfur limitation, to the product with the most severe limitation and the highest price.

In spite of the fact that residual fuel oil reached its highest price in history (before the Arab boycott of 1973) consumption of it increased rather than diminished. The influence of the Clean Air Act and its amendments imposed standards that made clean-burning fuels mandatory. With the regulation-induced shortage of natural gas and limited supplies of low-sulfur coal, resid was the logical alternate. Increased desulfurization capacity in the Caribbean and in the United States was needed. Problems with the technology of desulfurization units, however, contributed to a continued deterioration of the supply-demand ratio of resid, and its prices increased through 1971, 1972, and 1973. As early as 1970 this predictable trend led to a dramatic turnabout in the demand from electric utilities. Consumption of resid by utilities grew from some 250 million barrels in 1969 to over 500 million barrels in 1973.

The role of residual fuel oils following the Arab boycott con-

TABLE 20

East Coast Residual Fuel Oil Consumption by Sulfur Levels,
1970–1972
(000 bbl./day)

Sulfur Level	1970		1971		1972	
	Volume	Share (per-cent)	Volume	Share (per-cent)	Volume	Share (per-cent)
0.5 and under	110	7.8	300	20.6	555	34.6
0.51–1.00	390	27.8	448	30.8	440	27.4
1.10–2.00	227	16.2	210	14.4	212	13.2
2.1 and up	675	48.2	497	34.2	396	24.7
Total	1402	100.0	1455	100.0	1603	100.0

SOURCE: U.S. Bureau of Mines, *Availability of Heavy Fuel Oils by Sulfur Levels,* Mineral Industry Surveys, 1970–1972.

tinued its pre-boycott pattern through mid-1975 in spite of the administration's announced goal of reducing oil imports by one million barrels daily at the end of that year. The growing pressure of natural gas curtailments and declines in domestic low-sulfur crude oil supply, plus the impetus of environmental regulations, added to increased imports of resid. There was evidence that coal would take up some of the short-term excess demand for resid, as coal increased its share of U.S. energy production to about 24 percent, and aside from the negative impact of the 1974 strikes, coal production volumes and prices rose appreciably in 1974. Indeed, this demand for low-sulfur coal initiated an industrywide push to develop greater productive potential by 1980 at newer midwestern locations.

Nonetheless, the huge East Coast demand for residual fuel oil tempered substantially through 1974 and 1975 as the nationwide recession worsened. Heavy fuel oil inventories along the East Coast, and indeed around the world, increased by over 20 percent. Many of the key East Coast importers—Exxon, Asiatic, and Amerada Hess among them—were forced to roll back prices of imported resid. This rollback, however, was market-induced. In late 1975 and early 1976 resid prices improved, largely because of colder East Coast weather. However, following the imposition of the Energy Policy and Conservation Act and the resulting rollback of "new" crude oil prices, the prices of resid were again lowered.

Federal Policy and Middle Distillates

In contrast to residual fuel oil, nearly all middle distillates and motor gasoline consumed in the United States have been produced by domestic refineries. The bulk of these products consumed on the East Coast are shipped by pipeline or tanker from PAD District III refineries. The growth in consumption of upgraded gasolines, No. 2 heating oil, diesel fuel, and jet fuel has characterized most of the postwar growth in product demand.

The demand for No. 2 heating oil is concentrated in the Northeast section of the United States (Gonzalez 1968, pp. 177–181). Sales of this fuel are highly seasonal, with consumption of No. 2 greatest during winter months and lowest during summer months. Inventories of distillate are important in meeting winter demand, one-third of which is generally met by a reduction of inventories. In contrast, gasoline consumption is greatest in the spring and summer months and lowest during winter. Thus, inventory accumulation of motor gasoline, normally occurring during late winter, provides about one-third of total summer gasoline demand. Figure 8 shows the cyclical nature of gasoline and distillate production, inventory, and demand.

Before the imposition of sulfur requirements, the federal government limited the importation of No. 2 fuel oil to the historic levels of 1957, or some 76,000 barrels daily. This mandatory program excluded newcomers from gaining a quota (Office of the President 1959). There were few changes in the quotas to all eligible companies from 1959 to 1966. However, in 1960 Texaco acquired one of the larger independent importers, Paragon, Inc., and obtained a historic quota.

The first major reduction in quota allocations came when the government decontrolled residual fuel oil and arbitrarily defined No. 4 fuel oil as residual (Department of the Interior 1968). Before 1966 a large portion of the finished light imports had been No. 4 oil. When residuals were decontrolled, the quota to all companies was reduced appreciably. But in 1968 the government granted licenses to twelve additional companies to import about seven thousand barrels daily of No. 2 (Office of the President 1967b). One of the more controversial aspects of this quota was the special allocation to Hess Oil Company of fifteen thousand barrels daily (Department of the Interior 1968). This allocation was granted by the government to help promote employment in the Virgin Islands. A similar concern by the government for the development of Puerto Rico resulted in the exception of that island from quotas for PAD Districts I–IV. Therefore, official quotas set for PAD Districts I–IV were supplemented by a highly flexible import allowable from Puerto Rico.

This supplement benefited major refiners like Gulf, Phillips, Sun, and Texaco that managed to gain entry into Puerto Rican refining and ship products to the continental United States. Distillate fuel oil and gasoline were the primary imports from Puerto Rico, but shipments from the Hess Oil complex in the Virgin Islands consisted mainly of distillate, residual, and unfinished oils. By 1965 light product imports totaled 35,000 barrels per day or almost 50 percent of

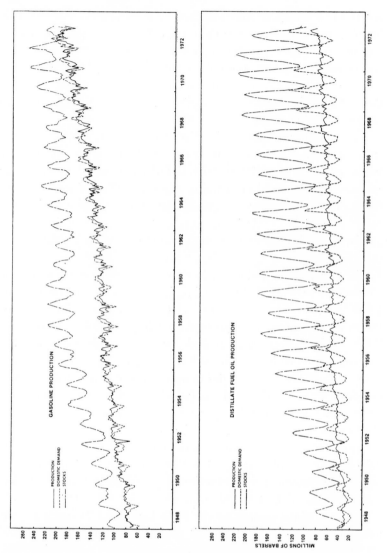

FIGURE 8. Gasoline and Distillate Fuel Oil Production, Domestic Demand, and Stocks in the United States by Months and by Years, 1948–1973

total imports allowed under historic quotas to PAD Districts I–IV. In short, government import policy for distillate and gasoline was essentially flexible and basically under the operative aegis of the major refiners. In 1970 the government effectively decontrolled imports of No. 2 fuel from all Western Hemisphere sources (Office of the President 1967c).

By 1968 and 1969 the air quality laws passed by the federal and various state governments began to exert pressure on the price and the supply of low-sulfur residual fuel oil. To help fill the rising demand, No. 2 and gas oil from which No. 2 is made, both of which have low sulfur content, were blended in the Caribbean with high-sulfur residual fuels. This additional use for No. 2 contributed to the scarcity of that product in the early 1970's. And the blending with high-sulfur residual fuels to meet the requirements of the air quality laws eventually linked the price of No. 2 to the price of domestic low-sulfur resid. Previously, Caribbean No. 2 prices were influenced by world market trends.

Under normal conditions, the real price of heavy or residual fuel oils was lower than the real price of the crude from which they were made. The real price of lighter products was generally above the real price of crude. This price structure existed for reasons basic to the joint cost of refining products. For example, if gasoline and fuel oil are the products jointly produced at a refinery, then an increase in the output of gasoline unavoidably entails an increase in the output of fuel oil. The cross-elasticity of supply is positive. However, the elasticity of demand for gasoline (or distillates) is less than the elasticity of demand for heavy fuel oil. Therefore, for a given supply, an increase in demand for gasoline will increase gasoline prices more than a similar increase in demand for fuel oil will increase fuel oil prices. Conversely, for any given demand, an increase in output will lower fuel oil prices relatively more than an increase in gasoline or distillate output will lower their prices. These relationships of supply hold for a stable yield pattern. They are short-run relationships; in the long run, yield patterns are more flexible and can more easily respond to demand increases. If the rise in demand for one product is expected to be consistently high, refiners can and will develop technical processes to provide for a unique increase in the output of that product while leaving the output of the other product relatively unchanged. The advent of hydrocracking was a prime example of this kind of development. A stronger link between the price of gasoline and heating oil, a link that made them competitive with natural gas and electricity, was created with the introduction of hydrocracking units capable of converting a given quality of crude oil entirely into gasoline (Office of the President, Cabinet Task Force, 1971). This innovation reduced the number of "crude runs" necessary to achieve a certain yield or output of gasoline. An increase in crude oil costs, in the long run, would result in greater substitution of hydrocracking facilities for cat cracking facilities in order to economize on crude costs and simultaneously increase yields of higher-value products.

As earlier chapters have shown, hydrocracking experienced a rapid growth among both majors and independents—a growth that tapered off after 1970. The economics of hydrocracking depend largely upon access to low-cost supplies of hydrogen. As the effects of the natural gas shortage began to be felt, the increase in hydrogen costs forced the shelving of new hydrocracking expansions and simultaneously led to more intensive development of other cracking processes, including the use of zeolite catalysts and riser cracking.

On the demand side, the shortage of natural gas plus low-sulfur requirements led directly to increased demands for low-sulfur residual fuel and No. 2 fuel. In fact, as the scarcity of low-sulfur resid, low-sulfur coal, and natural gas became apparent, the demand for low-sulfur No. 2 increased dramatically more than had been forecast by either industry or government sources.

The price of No. 2 and sales of oil boilers were quite stable before 1969. Average prices were about 8.9 cents per gallon in 1960 compared to 9.89 cents per gallon in 1969. However, with the impending shortage of natural gas and the rising price of low-sulfur residual, oil furnace and boiler sales experienced their highest growth rate in history. A major component of this increase in demand again was from the electric generating sector on the U.S. East Coast. Failing to obtain increased supplies of low-sulfur coal and residual, utilities began to use No. 2 as fuel for their gas turbines. From 1963 to 1973 demand for No. 2 from electric generating plants had increased by more than 300 percent. No. 2 prices jumped from 9.89 cents per gallon in 1969 to over 22 cents per gallon in 1975.

Thus, the domestic shortage of No. 2 and other distillates that was experienced by late 1973 was the culmination of the influence of seemingly unrelated government policies that changed the traditional price structure relationships of refined products. The sulfur requirements, natural gas policy, coal scarcity, and changing import policy on distillate all contributed to generating the energy crisis that became more apparent by 1973. Both major and independent companies gained by the increased prices on distillate and residual that resulted, but because of the more advantageous position of the majors with respect to their import program and access to foreign distillate supply, their dominance in maintaining market shares for these products went relatively unchallenged. The total competitive impact of these policies among refined products inadvertently reinforced the permanent component of market power of the majors, and the price of fuel oils, in the absence of corrective forces, seemed to be irreversibly rising.

From 1973 to mid-1975, distillate fuel oil demand continued strong, but its use for heating declined for the first time below 50 percent of total annual distillate sales over one billion barrels. Government allocation and price control programs described in the previous chapter tended to distort the conventional economics of the distillate supply-price pattern. As it did for other products, the recession of 1974–1975 caused a temporary slowdown in distillate demand, but the growing problem of natural gas shortages made it clear that growth would be renewed.

Federal Policy and Gasoline Supply and Demand

From 1948 to 1975 imports were never a significant source of gasoline supply for the domestic market. A complex of factors, however, has changed this situation—in particular, the proportion of domestic gasoline derived from foreign crude oil. Historically, all domestic refiners have maximized yields of gasoline for a given level of rated capacity. Most of the gasoline produced in PAD Districts I–IV originates in the Gulf Coast refinery complex and is transported by pipeline, tanker, and barge to other districts. For example, in 1974 refineries in PAD District III supplied 65 percent of the East Coast's gasoline. However, about 10 percent of PAD District II's supply came from District III. Table 21 shows that in 1974 about one-third of total motor gasoline demand derived from interdistrict shipments, mainly from PAD District III to District I. Other districts are essentially self-sufficient in providing for gasoline demand,

TABLE 21

U.S. Motor Gasoline Interdistrict Shipment, Imports, and Domestic Demand, 1974

(000 bbl./calendar day)

From PAD District	(1) To PAD District					(2) Total Inter-district Shipments	(3) Total Imports by District	(4) Total Domestic Demand by District	(5) Total Percentage of District Demand from (2)	(6) Total Percentage of District Demand from (3)
	I	II	III	IV	V					
I	—	126	—	—	—	126	176	2,150	.65	.08
II	34	—	54	7	—	95	1	2,238	.18	—
III	1,364	254	—	14	37	1,669	19	992	.05	.02
IV	—	14	—	—	36	50	1	209	.16	—
V	—	—	—	12	—	12	7	948	.08	.01
Total	1,398	394	54	33	73	1,952	204	6,537	.30	.02

Source: Data compiled from U.S. Bureau of Mines, *Crude Petroleum, Petroleum Products, and Natural Gas Liquids*, Mineral Industry Surveys, 1974.

and imported gasoline was only about 2 percent of total U.S. demand but about 8 percent of East Coast demand. Over 85 percent of all gasoline imports went to the East Coast.

The establishment of import controls on gasoline and the relatively higher tariff of 1.25 cents per gallon (or almost 10 percent of the wholesale gasoline price) tended to effectively insulate the domestic market from foreign price influence. Furthermore, 100 percent of the imports going mainly to the U.S. East Coast came from U.S. possessions: 94 percent from Puerto Rico, and the rest from the Virgin Islands. Two major refining companies, Phillips and Commonwealth Oil Refining, accounted for most of this supply through the use of their special import quotas of 58,000 barrels per day of finished products from Puerto Rico (Gonzalez 1968, pp. 177–181). Amerada Hess, another major, accounted for all shipments from the Virgin Islands. Before 1973 gasoline shipments from Puerto Rico and the Virgin Islands were duty-free except for a small portion of Hess's special quota.

One impact of controlling foreign imports of motor gasoline was to create the incentive to import crude oil of relatively higher gravity. Statistics collected by the Department of Commerce indicate that from 1959 to the present, a relatively greater proportion of crude over a gravity of API 25° has been imported. This higher-gravity crude has yielded greater volumes of gasoline, which is more salable in the insulated market. More important, higher-gravity crudes commanded a greater import ticket value.

Domestic gasoline supply and demand have become controversial subjects in the United States, with controversy centered mainly on the question of whether or not major companies are using unfair, monopolistic practices to weaken competition from independent marketers. In the 1950's independents were credited with 10 percent of the total domestic gasoline market (Department of the Interior 1968). By 1973 this figure had risen to 25 percent. But before the year was out, this latter percentage was declining because of the difficulty of independents to obtain product.

The relationship of supply and price is more difficult to define here due to changing gasoline marketing practices by both majors and independents. For example, during periods of excess crude supply and falling real crude prices—and also low growth of demand for gasoline—refiners continued to emphasize production of gasoline. It was the continued availability of surplus gasoline that led to the development of independent marketing, in which both spot and contract market purchases were made from the majors. Indeed, some major refiners, such as Ashland and Marathon, sell more gasoline and fuel oil to independent private branders than they sell through their own company outlets.

Government import controls resulted in an insulated domestic market. The influences these controls exercised on pricing must therefore be examined on a regional basis. Regional price variations were stimulated by the value of import tickets for more inland refiners and hence by their capacity to provide lower-priced products to wholesale purchasers.

Although the majors control the bulk of the nation's gasoline supply, they have limited control over their retail outlets—the service stations from which the consumer must purchase major-brand products. A very small percentage of all service stations in the United States are owned and operated by major producers. Most are operated by a lessee/dealer. Some majors do not market gasoline directly to consumers; much of their gasoline is supplied through jobbers and commissioned agents. In 1974 major-brand gasolines produced by the top twenty firms accounted for 76.3 percent of actual retail sales on the national market, a slight decline from the previous year. The share of the top ten firms from 1969 to 1974 is shown in Table 22. The top ten firms have gradually experienced a decline in market shares, although their market shares exceed their shares of distillation capacity.

From 1959 to 1968 the annual average growth rate in demand for motor gasoline had been about 3.5 percent per year. The demand for gasoline is derived from the demand for transportation services. It was to be expected that with rising real incomes the stock of gasoline-consuming vehicles would also rise, thereby increasing the demand for gasoline. In addition, the consumption efficiency of automobiles in terms of miles per gallon also affects gasoline demand.

From 1948 through the sixties, refiners were preoccupied with meeting requirements for higher octane numbers for new automobiles and with the effort of differentiating their primary product— gasoline—with "no-knock" performance standards applicable to all

TABLE 22

Shares of U.S. Gasoline Sales for the Top Ten Oil Companies, 1969–1974

Company	1969	1970	Percentage of Share 1971	1972	1973	1974
Texaco	8.33	8.13	8.35	8.13	8.09	8.07
Shell	8.19	7.87	7.36	7.14	7.54	7.39
Exxon	7.55	7.42	7.05	6.85	7.62	7.38
Std. of Ind.	7.48	7.30	7.07	6.93	6.99	6.99
Gulf	7.60	7.12	6.68	6.53	6.53	6.55
Mobil	6.70	6.60	6.40	6.36	6.73	6.54
Atlantic Richfield	5.66	5.55	5.48	4.94	4.41	3.98
Std. of Calif.	5.21	5.02	4.70	4.70	4.97	4.90
Sun	4.33	4.15	4.08	3.85	3.72	3.72
Phillips	3.95	3.97	3.94	4.11	4.05	3.81
Top ten total	65.00	63.13	61.11	59.54	60.65	59.40
Residual total	35.00	36.87	38.89	40.46	39.35	40.60
Total volume of motor gasoline sold (million gal.)*	85,756	89,748	94,163	100,616	105,759	101,856

SOURCE: Lundberg Survey, Inc., 1975; *Federal Highway Administration News*, August, 1974.
* Excludes Puerto Rico.

makes of cars (Allvine and Patterson 1972; Lundberg Survey, Inc., 1975). With full-scale development of automatic transmissions and air conditioning on new cars, gasoline consumption per mile began to rise. A second factor in the rise in gasoline demand was the emission control devices later imposed by states and the federal government on new cars.

An even more controversial policy problem concerned the quality of future gasoline supplies. The debate focused on the trade-offs between fuel economy and emission control. The government desired a phaseout of leaded gasoline, and the Environmental Protection Agency required that refiners provide a lead-free gasoline by July 1, 1974, for the 1975 model cars. The problem was that the 1975 models, equipped with catalytic converters, did not perform well with lead-free gasoline. Automobile manufacturers had apparently designed their models for research octane number (RON) 95, while oil company officials claimed that the automakers had prescribed RON 91 gasoline. With this octane gap, the possibility of a government-induced octane race was growing.

By 1974 there were over 107 million passenger cars registered in the United States, an increase of about 5.5 percent over the previous year. Total production in 1974 was slightly over 7.3 million passenger cars, almost 25 percent fewer than in the previous year. New imported car registrations totaled 1.4 million units in 1974, also a decrease of some 20 percent from the previous year. Virtually all of the new domestic automobiles featured automatic transmissions, large engines, power brakes and steering, and air conditioning —items that limited gasoline mileage efficiency.

In 1968 motor gasoline consumption rose 6.1 percent, and in the following year 5.0 percent. A decline in 1971 was followed by another increase of 6.0 percent in demand for 1972. Simultaneously, the growth of refinery crude runs was only 3.0 percent per year. Between 1972 and 1974 the rate of increase in gasoline demand was slightly lower, although rates of total crude runs continued to grow. To meet this divergent demand pattern, refiners steadily increased the yield of gasoline per barrel of crude oil from 43.8 percent in 1968 to 45.7 percent in 1974. However, because in the short run a shift in yields can only come at the expense of other products (due to the effects of joint supply), the emphasis on gasoline tended to reduce the normal quantities of distillates and residual fuels produced. Only by increasing crude runs and using up all spare refining capacity could normal jointly produced supplies be provided.

With refiners increasing their requirements for crude oil, the state prorationing agencies, for the first time since 1948, allowed all regulated wells to produce at 100 percent of the MER. In spite of the anticipated increase in crude oil supply, the spare productive capacity of all wells had become insignificant, and the annual output level of crude oil and natural gas liquids was static at about nine million barrels daily. In the short run, the only recourse for refiners was to import more crude oil, distillates, and motor gasoline. However, because of the sulfur requirements imposed by the Clean Air Act, refiners could import only sweet crude, for which most U.S. refineries had been designed. The federal government was pressured into abandoning the oil import quota program because of the expanding requirement for crude. The greatest sources of new "growth" supply of crude were North Africa and the Middle East. Domestic output was inadequate to provide for total U.S. energy needs. In April, 1973, the Nixon administration announced the national security license fee system for petroleum and product imports to replace the old import quota program, and later the Ford administration attempted to limit import growth by supplemental fees on crude and products. These supplemental fees were later removed, and with the imposition of the Energy Policy and Conservation Act of 1975, gasoline prices were temporarily reduced between two cents and four cents per gallon. Thus, a period of relatively lower and stable gasoline prices was evident for the early part of 1976, but it was evident that higher price levels would be restored over the longer term.

In summary, the cause of the shortages of motor gasoline, distillates, and residual fuel oil in the early 1970's was the untimely culmination of government policies which had conflicting impacts on refined products. Demand was stimulated, supply was contracted, and the incentive for increasing refining capacity diminished. To help reduce the demand for refined products, the government considered the imposition of additional taxes on gasoline and, alternatively, a gasoline rationing program. As a short-run policy expedient, increased focus was placed on estimating the price elasticity of demand for motor gasoline.

Gasoline Demand Elasticity and the Debate on Gasoline Rationing

In the spring of 1973 shortages of gasoline and fears of a continuing energy crisis led to consideration by the U.S. Treasury Department of an increased excise tax on gasoline. According to the theory of demand, all other things being equal, an increase in the price of a commodity will result in a reduction in the quantity demanded. However, policy makers were unsure of the elasticity of response to any price increase. For normal goods, price elasticity is expected to be smaller in the short run and larger in the long run. However, there was growing congressional sentiment to avoid imposing any increase in the price of gasoline. Instead, many congressmen desired a gasoline rationing program. Indeed, through the early months of 1974 the block-long queues at retail outlets resulted in the government setting lower national speed limits and urging voluntary measures to attempt to alleviate the level of gasoline demand.

In 1973 gasoline prices rose slowly from an average of 36.98 cents per gallon for regular grade in January to 39.16 cents per gallon in September on the eve of the Middle East hostilities.[3] Following the Arab posted price increases and embargo, prices jumped to a peak of 55.50 cents per gallon in July, 1974. Thereafter, retail prices eased off to 52.25 cents per gallon by December, 1974. With subsequent increases in posted prices, however, the retail price inched upward in 1975 to about 53 cents per gallon. By mid-1975 retail prices for majors, as estimated by the *Lundberg Letter*, were over 58 cents per gallon, and for independents, over 55 cents per gallon (Figure 9). As indicated earlier, gasoline marketers lost some 13.2 billion gallons of sales in 1974 which might have been expected if the conditions of the period before 1973 had continued. Sales in

---

[3] *Lundberg Letter* 2, no. 28 (May 16, 1975): 3. The volumes of foreign crude used to produce domestic gasoline were also increasing to 30 percent of total output.

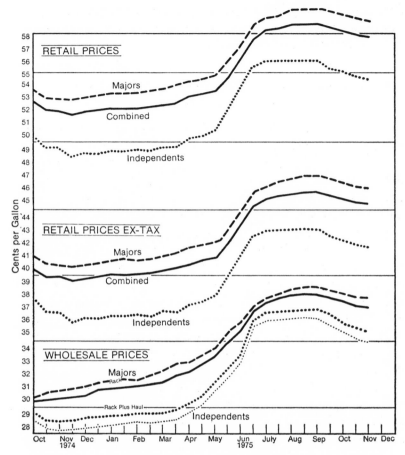

FIGURE 9. Prices of Regular-Grade Gasoline of Majors and Independents (Reprinted, with permission, from *Lundberg Letter*, December 5, 1975).

1974, however, were 101.8 billion gallons, 11.0 percent below the demand of normal growth.[4] The deviations among majors and independents with respect to price tended to narrow in 1975, partially as a result of the refiner cost equalization program. However, the distortions imposed by the price controls on old crude and the prod-

---

[4] See *Lundberg Letter* 2, no. 17 (February 28, 1975). Note that there are only fifteen "majors" in the Lundberg study. Data on sales agree with those compiled by the Federal Highway Administration, Department of Transportation.

uct price and allocation control program also tended to distort the pricing patterns within the major categories. Some companies were as much as two cents per gallon over or under the average. Price realignments continued through 1975, although the recessionary market conditions tended to limit the ability to recover all costs through higher gasoline prices.

Government oil policy for the short run was designed to force greater reductions in the demand for imported crude oil through various consumption-constraining programs specifically for gasoline. As Figure 10 shows, the gasoline derived from foreign crude oil accounted for over one-third of total gasoline production. The national policy objective was to reduce reliance on crude imports and thus lower the gasoline volumes produced from foreign crude. A reduction of one million barrels per day in imports of crude oil would involve a gasoline cutback of about half that size, as Figure 10 illustrates. The focus on gasoline was so prevalent that the outlook for refining capacity in the United States—designed to maximize yields of gasoline—was for a persistent level of spare refining capacity throughout the 1970's. However, in spite of efforts to curb imports, the apparent level of gasoline supply derived from foreign crude oil increased from about 22 percent in 1973 to over 33 percent in 1975. This anomaly can be attributed in part to the two-tier price system on domestic crude oil and in part to declining domestic production. Oil field producers had an incentive to limit production from wells declared by the FEA to be old oil at fixed prices of $5.25 per barrel. There was a definite incentive to prematurely abandon old wells or even cut back production on some wells to achieve an exempt status from price controls. Stripper wells were exempt from price controls. With the Arab price increases and the development of adequate gasoline supplies, the pressure to impose the policy option of new gasoline taxes or government rationing abated through 1975.

Nonetheless, a number of previous attempts have been made to estimate the percentage change in the quantity demanded of gasoline from a percentage change in price—the price elasticity of demand for gasoline—and the majority of these attempts have been made with complex macroeconometric models of the U.S. economy such as the Wharton model and the model developed at Data Resources Institute (Preston 1973; Verleger 1973). Other macroesti-

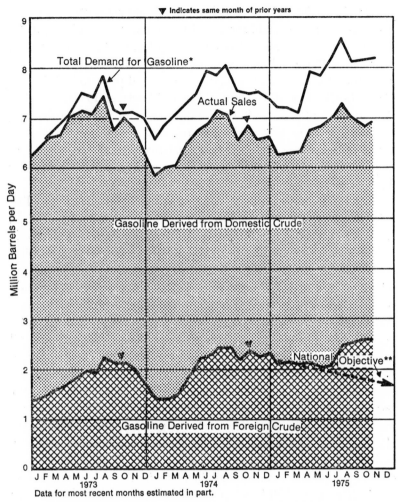

▼ Indicates same month of prior years

Total Demand for Gasoline*

Actual Sales

Gasoline Derived from Domestic Crude

National Objective**

Gasoline Derived from Foreign Crude

Million Barrels per Day

J F M A M J J A S O N D J F M A M J J A S O N D J F M A M J J A S O N D
1973   1974   1975
Data for most recent months estimated in part.

* Projected demand if prices and trends before 1973 had continued unabated.

** A million barrel per day reduction in imports of crude oil would involve a gasoline
cutback of half that dimension, as illustrated.

FIGURE 10. The Gasoline Market's Reliance on Foreign Oil Supply
(Reprinted, with permission, from *Lundberg Letter*, November 14, 1975)

mates have been attempted by Phlips (1972, pp. 450–488), Adams
and Griffin (1968), and the report on the National Petroleum Council energy study (Avramides and Cross 1973, pp. 304–315).

In the Griffin-Adams model, no significant short-run price relationships could be established, and the authors concluded that demand for gasoline was independent of price. Of the other studies, only in the Phlips estimate was price significant. Verleger, in a recent study for the Ford Foundation, has found price to be fairly inelastic in the short run (Houthakker and Verleger 1973). His elasticity coefficient was -0.43 for the short run and -0.75 for the long run. Shortly after this study was released, several analyses published in the press concluded that a relatively small tax increase of 10 percent would reduce short-run aggregate consumption by over 4 percent.

Such conclusions about the short-run magnitude of gasoline price elasticity were strongly challenged by oil industry officials, who argued that it would take a larger tax increase to effectively reduce domestic consumption. The industry viewpoint was that imposing excise taxes would only add new tax collection burdens on oil companies while failing to provide economic incentives for companies to invest in petroleum exploration. Later, a study by Ramsey and others (1974) analyzed the price elasticities by end use category and by income group. This study confirmed the essential oil industry position that small price increases had little effect on quantity demanded while large increases did. For every 1 percent increase in price, quantity demanded by private users fell about 0.7 percent and that by commercial users about 0.4 percent. Ramsey concluded that a price of sixty cents per gallon would be the market clearing level and would alleviate shortages, allocation schemes, and long lines. Ramsey contested a popular political view in concluding that even a substantial increase in the price of gasoline would have a negligible effect on the lowest third of the nation's income groups, even after consumers have had time to adjust. He concluded, however, that the burden on higher-income groups was much greater. In an earlier study I found that the long-run price elasticity was -0.54, while the short-run elasticity was much smaller, at about -0.20 (Copp 1974b). In most of these later price elasticity studies it became apparent that gasoline consumption was not independent of price changes and that federal policy could work through the price mechanism to achieve significant results in holding down long-term increases in rates of consumption of gasoline. More questionable was the ability of federal policy to affect consumption with small increases in tax on gasoline prices.

One option that was kept alive throughout this period was that of gasoline rationing through the issuance of coupons.[5] The FEO designed a rationing system as a contingency plan for future emergencies; its essential factors were price controls below the market level, exchangeable coupons, and ration banking. Assume, for example, that the U.S. market is in equilibrium at its 1974 sales volume of 101.8 billion gallons at the average national price of $0.5225 per gallon. Assume also that OPEC countries reimpose an oil embargo that results in a sudden 30 percent shortage of gasoline to the U.S. market (approximately the level of motor gasoline derived from foreign crude). Under free market conditions this shortage would result in upward pressure on domestic gasoline prices. If a short-run price elasticity of demand of −0.20 is assumed, the 71.3 billion gallons of gasoline (70 percent of the sales volume) available from domestic crude would generally clear the market at about $1.36 per gallon. The contingency government rationing scheme would freeze domestic gasoline prices at $0.5225 per gallon and distribute exchangeable coupons for 71.3 billion gallons to private and commercial users. These coupons could then be used by the coupon holder or traded in a coupon market. Post offices were to be used to allocate the coupons to licensed drivers. Service station retailers would require coupons in exchange for gasoline and would bank the coupons to obtain gas from wholesalers. Thus, gasoline would go where the coupons indicated demand. The competitive market for coupons would establish a market coupon value equal to the difference between the controlled price of $0.5225 per gallon and the free-market clearing price of $1.36 per gallon, or about $0.84 per coupon. The coupon exchange market would bid the values of coupons above the frozen price and would allocate gasoline among users so that the value of gasoline at the margin to the user would be equal to the opportunity cost (that is, the cost of the next best alternative) of the pump price plus the coupon price.

With coupons valued at $0.84, the rationing of 71.3 billion gal-

[5] See Edwards (1974) and the studies on the economics of rationing by Neisser (1943) and Tobin (1952).

lons of gasoline would generate a coupon market of about $60 billion. The unique aspect of rationing is the income redistribution effects to gasoline consumers from the oil industry. With a free-market price of $1.36 per gallon, the gross revenue to the oil industry would be about $97 billion. However, with prices frozen at $0.5225 and with coupons worth $0.84, gasoline consumers theoretically would receive $60 billion and the oil industry $37 billion. If the government would allow the pump price to rise—for example, in response to the desire for acquired regulation or exemption by independent refiners, marketers, and majors—the value of the coupons would fall. The rationing program would allocate scarce supplies of gasoline, but the opportunity for inefficiencies in such a program are manifest. Black markets could easily develop, and a new, massive bureaucracy would be required to enforce and administer the program. Program costs would be substantial, and it is likely that rationing would distort the normal product distribution system. It would be a form of welfare program—possibly not quite as efficient as outright welfare grants.

All of the above studies suggest certain avenues for government policy toward gasoline. It is apparent that as long as gasoline is perceived by consumers to be a normal, nonluxury commodity, habit will strongly influence short-term auto use, and thus past consumption patterns will be important determinants for current consumption patterns. The view that some quantum jump in price is necessary to affect demand implies a relatively constant level of real disposable income. There is a threshold level at which consumers will alter their habits, possibly first by switching away from the major-brand gasolines to the presumably lower-priced unbranded ones and then by eliminating all unnecessary driving. Finally, a point would result at which drivers would decide to substitute cars with better mileage for less efficient ones—the classic example of economizing on gasoline use. Of course, if real incomes are falling, these final economizing decisions may be put off for the future while interim substitute transportation methods such as car pools, buses, subways, and the like are used. Moreover, consumers may extend the economic lives of their current motor vehicles; such conservation would be reflected by a tremendous increase in demand for maintenance and replacement parts services. As real incomes increase, however, the ability to accommodate high-priced gasoline will increase so that relatively the consumer's price expectations will not be violated. Thus, driving habits could still continue relatively unchanged, and the government's policy may more appropriately be geared to affecting the annual rate of increase in gasoline price as opposed to attempting absolute reductions in annual consumption.

4

Government Policy and the National
Security Rationale

THE legal basis for oil import controls, proposed and supported by the petroleum industry, was national security. As previously noted, oil is the only commodity to which the national security amendment of the Trade Expansion Act of 1962 has been applied. The quota scheme appears to have helped the majors maintain their permanent component of market power, while independent firms were assured survival as long as the quota rights had a positive value. Thus, the policy was tailored to attempt to ameliorate both classes of refiners. The national security justification for quotas was designed to assure proper structuring of "acquired" import regulation. In 1959 no shortage of domestic crude oil existed, and substantial spare refining capacity was available. Therefore, to protect domestic crude oil and crude oil product suppliers from the competitive influence of foreign crude prices, quotas were imposed. It was assumed at the time that the foreign supply of crude oil was highly, if not perfectly, elastic and that the domestic price protection provided by quotas would tend to stimulate the discovery of additional domestic proved reserves of oil. Indirectly, the continuation of a "cushion" of excess refining capacity was also hoped for. Quotas were selectively distributed to refiners, establishing in effect a government-controlled cartel of importers. However, political pressures for favoritism, applied by both majors and independents, weakened the cartel, and for all practical purposes the cartel was ineffective after 1970.

Chapter 2 argued that import controls on crude oil were a great weakness of federal policy in that the nature of oil and gas as joint products was ignored, as was the geologic heterogeneity of the United States. A price ceiling on natural gas, combined with ineffectively stabilized domestic crude oil prices, reduced the economic incentive to explore and develop new oil and gas resources. The imposition of import quotas and the almost simultaneous imposition of controls on the wellhead price of natural gas about 1960 coincided with a decline in the number of exploratory and development wells drilled, which is shown in Table 23. Total drilling declined by more than 40 percent from 1959 to 1972, and the decline persisted until late 1973. Assuredly, some of this decline can be attributed to the increased efficiency of each well drilled (Copp 1974*a*, 1976), but only until real prices increased did a significant increase in drilling result in 1974 and 1975. As Tables 24, 25, and 26 indicate, the total annual crude oil, natural gas, and natural gas liquids reserve additions were consistently lower than annual production levels from about 1967 to 1975. In terms of providing a continued "cushion" of proved reserves and productive capacity, federal petroleum policy was self-defeating. The most revealing data in Table 25 show that the annual marketed production of natural gas far exceeded reserve additions. The momentum of energy demand stimulated by low ceiling prices had exceeded available supply.

It is pertinent to consider what alternative policies on crude oil and natural gas should have properly been considered. For example, would an increased tariff on crude oil and products have been more effective than a quota? Would the auctioning of import tickets, as opposed to granting them freely, been a more effective tool? Would a national program of "storage" have been a less costly national energy security alternative than a quota program? Would free trade have been a superior policy from a resource allocation viewpoint? What are the implications for market structure in refining for these alternative policies? The following sections address some of these major policy questions.

Shifts in World Oil Supply and Demand

As a trade flow control technique, the voluntary and mandatory oil import programs of the United States were not unique. Import

TABLE 23

Drilling Activity and Producing and Abandoned Oil Wells in the United States, 1951–1975

Year	Total New Wells Drilled*	New Oil Wells Completed	Service Wells Drilled	Exploratory Wells Drilled	Number of Producing Oil Wells at Year End	Oil Wells Abandoned†
1951	44,516	23,473	1,380	11,256	474,990	10,574
1953	49,279	25,762	1,262	13,313	498,940	13,278
1955	56,682	31,567	760	14,937	524,010	9,968
1957	55,024	28,012	1,409	14,707	569,273	8,651
1959	51,764	25,800	1,670	13,191	583,141	11,451
1960	46,751	21,186	2,733	11,704	591,158	15,434
1961	46,962	21,101	3,091	10,992	594,917	16,977
1962	46,179	21,249	2,400	10,785	596,385	16,224
1963	43,653	20,288	2,267	10,664	588,657	14,363
1964	45,236	20,620	2,273	10,747	588,225	14,476
1965	41,423	18,761	1,922	9,466	589,203	15,456
1966	37,881	16,447	1,497	10,313	583,302	16,207

TABLE 23 (continued)

Year	Total New Wells Drilled*	New Oil Wells Completed	Service Wells Drilled	Exploratory Wells Drilled	Number of Producing Oil Wells at Year End	Oil Wells Abandoned†
1967	33,630	15,329	1,396	9,059	573,159	14,986
1968	32,038	14,331	1,439	8,879	553,920	20,496
1969	33,667	14,368	1,490	9,701	542,227	15,618
1970	29,341	13,020	1,221	7,693	530,990	15,631
1971	27,250	11,858	1,399	6,922	517,318	18,483
1972	28,725	11,306	1,434	7,539	508,443	13,483
1973	27,551	9,902	959	7,466	497,378	13,756
1974	32,756	12,784	1,058	8,619	497,631	13,779
1975	37,092	16,336	1,454	9,242	—	—

SOURCE: American Petroleum Institute, *Quarterly Review of Drilling Statistics for the United States, 1951–1975.*
* Excludes stratigraphic and core tests.
† Abandonments are the number of producing oil wells that have been abandoned during the year. The bulk of these are stripper wells abandoned as of January 1 of a given year.

TABLE 24

Changes in U.S. Crude Oil Proved Reserves, 1959–1974

(000 bbl.)

Year	Revisions	Extensions	Discoveries	Total Additions to Proved Reserves	Annual Production	Proved Reserves* (end of year)	Net Change from Previous Year
1959	1,518,678	1,778,705	369,362	3,666,745	2,483,315	31,719,347	1,183,430
1960	787,934	1,323,538	253,856	2,365,328	2,471,464	31,613,211	−106,136
1961	1,087,092	1,209,101	361,374	2,657,567	2,512,273	31,758,505	145,294
1962	759,053	1,041,257	380,586	2,180,896	2,550,178	31,389,223	−369,282
1963	966,051	858,168	349,891	2,174,110	2,593,343	30,969,990	−419,233
1964	899,292	1,419,182	346,293	2,664,767	2,644,247	30,990,510	20,520
1965	1,783,231	792,901	471,947	3,048,079	2,686,198	31,352,391	361,881
1966	1,839,307	814,249	310,422	2,963,978	2,864,242	31,452,127	99,736
1967	1,900,969	716,467	344,686	2,962,122	3,037,579	31,376,670	−75,457
1968	1,320,109	776,780	357,746	2,454,635	3,124,188	30,707,117	−669,553
1969	1,258,142	614,710	247,184	2,120,036	3,195,291	29,631,862	−1,075,255
1970	2,088,927	631,354	368,637	3,088,918	3,319,445	29,401,335	−230,527
1971	1,600,426	560,596	156,710	2,317,732	3,256,110	28,462,957	−938,378
1972	820,107	459,311	278,430	1,557,848	3,281,397	26,739,408	−1,723,549
1973	1,551,777	390,141	202,913	2,145,831	3,185,400	25,699,839	−1,039,569
1974	1,300,929	368,918	313,726	1,993,573	3,043,456	24,649,956	−1,049,883

SOURCE: American Petroleum Institute annual, 1959–1975.

* Does not include the 9.6 million barrels of crude oil discovered on the Alaska North Slope in 1969. Alaskan crude was expected to be in production by early 1978.

TABLE 25

Changes in U.S. Natural Gas Proved Reserves, 1959–1974

(millions of cu. ft.)

Year	Revisions	Extensions	Discoveries	Total Additions to Proved Reserves	Annual Production	Proved Reserves* (end of year)	Net Change from Previous Year
1959	14,852,004		5,769,245	20,621,249	12,373,063	261,170,431	8,408,639
1960	7,293,015		6,600,963	13,893,978	13,019,356	262,326,326	1,155,895
1961	10,258,692		6,907,729	17,166,421	13,378,649	266,273,642	3,947,316
1962	13,184,794		6,299,164	19,483,958	13,637,973	272,278,858	6,005,216
1963	12,586,733		5,577,934	18,164,667	14,546,025	276,151,233	3,872,375
1964	13,342,838		6,909,301	20,252,139	15,347,028	281,251,454	5,100,221
1965	14,775,570		6,543,709	21,319,279	16,252,293	286,468,923	5,217,469
1966	4,937,962	9,224,745	6,057,725	20,220,432	17,491,073	289,332,805	2,863,882
1967	6,570,578	9,538,584	5,695,171	21,804,333	18,380,838	292,907,703	3,574,898
1968	3,016,146	7,758,821	2,922,041	13,697,008	19,373,428	287,349,852	−5,557,851
1969	(1,238,261)	5,800,489	3,812,776	8,375,004	20,723,190	275,108,835	−12,241,017
1970	(99,721)	6,158,168	5,137,912	11,196,359	21,960,804	264,746,408	−10,362,427
1971	(1,227,400)	6,374,706	4,678,115	9,825,421	22,076,512	252,805,618	−11,940,790
1972	(1,077,791)	6,153,683	4,558,671	9,634,563	22,511,898	240,084,846	−12,720,772
1973	(3,474,756)	6,177,286	4,122,519	6,825,049	22,605,406	223,950,207	−16,134,639
1974	(1,333,285)	5,847,251	4,165,218	8,679,184	21,318,470	211,132,497	−12,817,710

SOURCE: American Petroleum Institute annual, 1959–1975.

* Does not include the 26 trillion cubic feet of gas discovered on the Alaska North Slope in 1969. Gas production in Alaska was not expected to be available before 1980.

TABLE 26
Changes in U.S. Natural Gas Liquids Proved Reserves, 1959–1974
(000 bbl.)

Year	Revisions	Extensions	Discoveries	Total Additions to Proved Reserves	Annual Production	Proved Reserves (end of year)	Net Change from Previous Year
1959	593,905		109,539	703,444	385,154	6,522,308	318,290
1960	603,621		121,509	725,130	431,379	6,816,059	293,751
1961	590,537		104,149	694,686	461,649	7,049,096	233,037
1962	580,570		151,979	732,549	470,128	7,311,517	262,421
1963	700,183		177,937	878,120	515,659	7,673,978	362,461
1964	457,702		151,042	608,744	536,090	7,746,632	72,654
1965	721,605		110,707	832,312	555,410	8,023,534	276,902
1966	634,233	131,583	128,300	894,116	588,684	8,328,966	305,432
1967	671,112	159,725	98,921	929,758	644,493	8,614,231	285,265
1968	469,689	155,940	60,030	685,659	701,782	8,598,108	−16,123
1969	106,192	106,815	68,021	281,028	735,962	8,143,174	−454,934
1970	35,446	103,740	168,393	307,579	747,812	7,702,941	−440,233
1971	135,144	93,909	118,667	347,720	746,434	7,304,227	−398,714
1972	38,796	112,537	86,940	238,273	755,941	6,786,559	−517,668
1973	231,460	121,835	55,684	408,979	740,831	6,454,707	−331,852
1974	393,484	149,996	76,361	619,841	724,099	6,350,449	−104,258

SOURCE: American Petroleum Institute annual, 1959–1975.

quotas on petroleum and petroleum products have been imposed in international energy trade since the late 1920's. Trade restrictionism, however, contradicted the spirit of the General Agreement on Tariffs and Trade (GATT) (Baldwin 1970). A fundamental principle of GATT was that quantitative restrictions should not be used to regulate international trade. The articles of agreement specified that, except on most agricultural products or for national security reasons, new quantitative restrictions could be introduced only temporarily for balance of payments or development purposes. This exception was the fundamental rationale for oil import quotas.

International barriers to trade in energy seem to have been a universal exception. For example, the "trade loss" from the multinational system of quotas and subsidies on coal falls almost entirely on the United States. It has been estimated that quotas and subsidies on coal in the European Common Market amount to a 50 percent duty on coal imports and account for an annual export trade loss to the United States of more than two billion dollars (Baldwin 1970, p. 35). The United States partially (and indirectly) compensates the domestic coal industry by imposing high excise taxes on oil products. By raising oil prices, the tax tends to inhibit the substitution of oil for coal and to maintain the demand for coal.

Other major energy-consuming nations also have supporting energy policies (usually subsidies) which reinforce the protective effect of quotas. The French government, for example, has protected domestic producers by means of import controls for oil and oil products since 1928 (OECD 1966). The French government directs its companies to seek sources of supply in which French interests are paramount. For example, French import controls were tightened against Middle East oil when Algerian oil was found in 1955. In addition, the French government provides subsidies and development grants to its industry. An oil depletion allowance is also provided for in France. Although Germany has formal quotas on products from East European sources, licenses and a system of voluntary quantitative controls are applied to the international oil companies. In Germany loans are provided for prospecting outside the European Economic Community and are repayable *only* if oil is found (Hartshorn 1967). In Belgium and Great Britain, tax concessions are made for all firms discovering indigenous oil, and in Great

Britain, taxes paid abroad can be deducted (Gordon 1970). In Italy and the Benelux countries there is free entry for imports from all countries except for imports of crude oil and products from Eastern Bloc countries (Gordon 1970, chap. 2). It is also true that except for coal these nations had no major indigenous energy resources until the discovery of North Sea oil and gas. The United States, in contrast, has a huge potential in energy resources. Estimates of 1975 proved oil and gas reserves in the North Sea were 23 billion barrels and 75 trillion cubic feet, respectively. Significant North Sea oil production only commenced in 1974, although the Ekofisk Field off Norway was producing some oil by mid-1971.

The United States has been the traditional "energy rich" nation, and indeed, before 1950 the world oil price structure was founded on a "Gulf Coast Plus" basis. The discovery and development of 70 percent of the known world crude oil reserves in the Middle East shifted the world price structure from the "Gulf Coast Plus" basis to a "Persian Gulf Plus" basis (Frank 1966). The potential impact of Middle East production is one factor that led the United States to abide by the regulatory preferences of the majors and independents to erect import barriers.

However, it was not U.S. import barriers that led to the formation of the cartel known as OPEC. OPEC developed from the need for budget stability of Middle East governments and because the primary source of development funds for these countries was taxes collected from multinational oil companies. The growing supply of extremely low-cost Middle East crude oil contributed to substantial downward pressure on world crude prices. In August, 1960, oil companies initiated major posted price reductions (Rouhani 1971). By late 1960 OPEC was formed by the major oil-producing countries expressly to put pressure on the oil companies to restore the prices in effect before the reductions made in August and to maintain stable prices in the future. From 1960 to 1971 the new OPEC posted prices remained virtually unchanged (Lubell 1963; Schurr 1971; Tanzer 1964; Stocking 1970; Longrigg 1968). In fact, actual market prices for oil were lower throughout this period. Major oil company refiners who owned concessions in the Middle East were behaving in a manner predictable from economic theory. The availability of low-cost crude in quantities that would outlast the life of producing concessions was the compelling motive for extending the marketing range of Middle East oil. The attempted reduction in posted prices was followed by the use of widespread discounting of these prices for market sales of Middle East crude. Quotas provided a "kink" to the sales radius of Middle East crude.

Since 1971 the producing nations of OPEC have made aggressive demands for increased tax payments and participation in concessions and company profits.[1] Underlying their success in securing these demands was the apparent inelastic demand for crude oil.[2] The forcefulness of OPEC demands coincided with a rapid increase in world demand for crude oil from 1967 to 1973. The worldwide recession from 1974 through early 1976, however, reduced world petroleum demand and may have contributed to the delay in full takeover of oil operations in some OPEC countries.

To place in perspective the market position of the OPEC nations, Tables 27, 28, and 29 provide the historical overview, from 1960 to 1974, of world petroleum demand (or consumption), production, and spare productive capacity. In 1960 Western Hemisphere demand for petroleum was almost twice that of the Eastern Hemisphere, as shown in Table 27. From 1960 to 1964 petroleum demand in the West was relatively static, while Eastern Hemisphere demand (including Western Europe) almost doubled.[3] United States demand from 1960 to 1964 grew barely over one million barrels daily. Beyond 1965, however, both Western and Eastern Hemisphere demands grew rapidly. Consumption in the United States from 1965 to 1969 increased by over 2.5 million barrels daily, and from 1969 to 1974 U.S. consumption increased an additional 3.3 million barrels daily. Western Europe's consumption increase

[1] By 1973, Middle Eastern members were demanding an accelerated takeover of oil-producing properties. Libya simply nationalized the properties (Rouhani 1971, chap. 1).

[2] There were few major substitute sources of energy for Japan and Western Europe (Adelman 1972).

[3] *Demand* here is used in the businessman's sense, which, in economics terminology, would be "consumption" or "total quantity demanded and supplied." In the oil trade, *demand* most often means "disappearance" from refineries, terminals, and the like.

TABLE 27

Trends in World Petroleum Demand, 1960–1974

(millions of bbl./day)

	1960	1962	1964	1966	1968	1970	1972	1974
Western Hemisphere	12.3	13.1	13.9	15.2	16.9	18.8	20.8	21.8
Canada	0.9	0.9	1.1	1.2	1.4	1.5	1.6	1.8
Latin America	1.7	2.0	2.0	2.1	2.4	2.8	3.2	3.4
United States	9.7	10.2	10.8	11.9	13.1	14.4	15.9	16.4
Miscellaneous	—	—	—	—	—	0.1	0.1	0.1
Eastern Hemisphere	6.7	8.8	11.3	14.3	17.6	22.3	24.7	26.8
Western Europe	4.1	5.3	6.9	8.6	10.3	12.8	14.4	14.4
Africa	0.4	0.4	0.6	0.6	0.7	0.9	1.0	1.0
Middle East	0.5	0.6	0.7	0.7	0.8	1.0	1.2	1.4
Far East and Oceania	1.4	1.9	2.8	3.6	4.8	6.4	7.4	8.2
Miscellaneous	0.3	0.6	0.3	0.8	1.0	1.2	0.7	1.8
Noncommunist World (excluding United States)	9.3	11.7	14.4	17.6	21.4	26.7	29.6	32.1
Noncommunist World (including United States)	19.0	21.9	25.2	29.5	34.5	41.1	45.5	48.5
Sino-Soviet Bloc	3.0	3.6	4.3	4.9	5.7	6.9	8.0	9.6
World Total	22.0	25.5	29.5	34.4	40.2	48.0	53.5	58.1
Net Soviet Bloc Exports to the Western World	0.4	0.6	0.7	1.0	1.2	1.2	1.0	0.9

SOURCE: Gulf Oil Corporation, *World Petroleum Productive Capacity*, 1973, 1974.

was even greater, rising from 7.8 million barrels daily in 1965 to 11.6 million barrels daily in 1969 and to 14.4 million barrels daily in 1974. Thus, the 1962 U.S. import quotas were imposed during a period in which domestic demand was relatively static and foreign demand was rising. With a static consumption level, it would seem that quotas were designed to "reserve" the U.S. market for owners of domestic production and refining. However, a review of world productive capacity suggests an alternative explanation. By 1972 the total non-Communist world was consuming 45.5 million barrels of petroleum daily, and by 1974 it was using 48.5 million barrels daily.

The productive capacity to provide for these rising demands is shown in Table 28. Spare productive capacity is shown in Table 29. Productive capacity is the maximum volume of petroleum that can be produced at any given time without jeopardizing remaining recoverable reserves. It is the significant factor for short-term petroleum supply, not proved reserves. Only in the long run, with the impact of production decline relative to net reserve additions, are proved reserves relevant to supply. There are actually several categories of capacity. Wellhead or field capacity is the sum of producing rates of all wells within a given area. Connected capacity is the volume which existing gathering and transmission facilities are equipped to handle. Terminal capacity is the tanker loading capacity. In addition, the API defines productive capacity as "the capacity that existing wells and facilities can be brought to within a specified time period, usually 90 days." Spare or surplus productive capacity is the difference between actual production and total productive capacity developed for a given area. In 1960 Western Hemisphere spare productive capacity was over 3.9 million barrels daily, while Eastern Hemisphere spare productive capacity, including that of the Middle East, was only slightly over 1.9 million barrels daily.

The dominance of Western Hemisphere production capacity reinforced the belief that the "national security" argument for quotas was adopted by majors and independents to support the desired form of acquired regulation. Before the imposition of quotas, new majors and a substantial number of smaller newcomers had entered

TABLE 28

World Productive Capacity of Oil, Natural Gas Liquids, and Synthetic Liquids,
1960–1974

(000 bbl./day)

	1960	1962	1964	1966	1968	1970	1972	1974
Western Hemisphere	16,212	17,224	17,909	19,261	20,087	20,091	19,328	18,100
Canada	1,050	1,264	1,501	2,000	2,125	2,200	2,200	2,100
Latin America	4,762	5,110	5,243	5,521	5,732	5,691	5,543	5,200
United States	10,400	10,850	11,165	11,740	12,230	12,200	11,585	10,800
Eastern Hemisphere	8,383	11,025	12,813	15,812	20,164	25,110	29,672	36,900
Western Europe*	402	439	489	486	509	502	513	300
Africa	594	1,876	2,524	3,577	5,228	6,788	6,079	7,300
Middle East	6,580	7,880	9,010	10,855	13,347	16,300	21,035	26,700
Far East and Oceania	807	830	790	894	1,080	1,520	2,045	2,600
Noncommunist World (excluding United States)	14,195	17,399	19,557	23,333	28,021	33,001	37,415	44,200
Noncommunist World (including United States)	24,595	28,249	30,722	35,073	40,251	45,201	49,000	55,000
Sino-Soviet Bloc	3,360	4,153	4,973	5,841	6,749	7,842	8,928	11,900
World Total	27,955	32,402	35,695	40,914	47,000	53,043	57,928	66,900

SOURCE: Gulf Oil Corporation, *World Petroleum Productive Capacity*, 1973, 1974.
* Excludes all North Sea potential, since production there was only established in 1975. North Sea productive capacity was expected to grow to 800,000 bbl./day by 1977 and substantially more thereafter.

TABLE 29

World Spare Productive Capacity of Oil, Natural Gas Liquids, and Synthetic Liquids,
1960–1974

(000 bbl./day)

	1960	1962	1964	1966	1968	1970	1972	1974
Western Hemisphere	3,941	3,857	3,753	4,051	3,194	2,068	1,375	600
Canada	506	530	649	987	928	723	378	100
Latin America	1,000	830	708	903	665	438	640	300
United States	2,435	2,497	2,396	2,161	1,601	907	357	200
Eastern Hemisphere	1,972	3,073	2,450	2,527	3,543	3,300	3,705	6,800
Western Europe	80	66	55	35	53	51	63	—
Africa	305	1,068	815	478	1,224	699	437	1,700
Middle East	1,332	1,706	1,415	1,553	2,110	2,408	2,990	5,000
Far East and Oceania	255	233	165	191	156	142	215	100
Noncommunist World (excluding United States)	3,478	4,433	3,807	4,417	5,136	4,461	4,723	7,200
Noncommunist World (including United States)	5,913	6,930	6,203	6,578	6,737	5,368	5,080	7,400
Sino-Soviet Bloc	—	—	—	—	—	—	—	—
World Total	5,913	6,930	6,203	6,578	6,737	5,368	5,080	7,400

SOURCE: Gulf Oil Corporation, *World Petroleum Productive Capacity*, 1973, 1974.

the worldwide search for oil and had made a great many discoveries in Canada and Latin America. Quotas were desirable for those seeking preference for Western Hemisphere imports of crude products and unfinished oils and protection from the competition of Middle Eastern oil. The quota program eventually evolved toward a program favorably discriminating toward Western Hemisphere crudes. Besides the surplus capacity of the Western Hemisphere, another factor discriminating against the Eastern Hemisphere was the sulfur content of their crudes. Most Middle East crudes were of the "sour," high-sulfur type. By contrast, most U.S. crudes are of the "sweet," low-sulfur variety, and most U.S. refineries were engineered to handle this type of crude. Several East Coast refineries were nevertheless engineered for and capable of processing Middle East crudes in 1960. As new refining techniques evolved in the 1960's, one net effect was to increase the ability to substitute sour for sweet crudes. This capability, of course, had an effect on the value of import tickets, as more Middle East crudes were imported in the late 1960's.

As Table 28 shows, productive capacity of the Western Hemisphere has been relatively stable since 1966 and reached a maximum in the 1969–1970 period. Thereafter, productive capacity declined. Spare productive capacity (Table 29) in the United States by 1970 fell below 1 million barrels daily for the first time in the nation's history. Spare productive capacity for the entire Western Hemisphere, which had peaked in 1966, was only slightly over 1 million barrels daily by 1972 and only 600,000 barrels daily by 1974. On the other hand, Middle East spare productive capacity rose continuously to nearly 3 million barrels per day in 1972, with Saudi Arabia alone accounting for some 2 million barrels per day. In 1974 Middle East capacity rose to 5 million barrels daily. Total Eastern Hemisphere spare productive capacity was 3.7 million barrels per day in 1972 and 6.8 million barrels per day in 1974. In 1972 the United States had less than 400,000 barrels per day of spare productive capacity, and in 1974 only 200,000 barrels daily.

Thus, by 1972 the United States could not count on its domestic resources to provide additional supplies of crude oil for major increases in quantity demanded. Canada's spare productive capacity also had declined to a level almost identical with ours. And even Venezuela had less than 600,000 barrels daily of surplus capacity. The only remaining surplus existed in the Middle East. World demand for crude oil was assumed to be highly inelastic, and development of oil substitutes such as synthetic crude from oil shale and tar sands was not considered to represent any real threat to OPEC's dominance before 1985. Recognizing that the existence of its own surplus capacity could cause a decline in world oil prices, OPEC pressed its position as a strong cartel in 1970 and 1971. OPEC would finally control its own output and unilaterally fix world oil prices. The Middle East price was no longer controlled by supply and demand, but by the power of the OPEC monopoly. The question of whether there was, at that time, an energy crisis or an oil shortage could only be answered in relative terms. From the viewpoint of domestic productive capacity, by 1972 there was clearly an oil shortage. In terms of world productive capacity, there was (and is) no shortage of crude oil in a physical sense. The economic shortage, however, is real. OPEC used its monopolistic control to set worldwide prices at a level more than triple the level of domestic crude prices. The physical overabundance, however, made it possible for "buyers'" markets to exist over short periods of time because of demand considerations. Such a condition existed in 1975 and 1976.

The goal of national energy security, in terms of adequate domestic spare capacity of both crude oil and natural gas, had clearly failed by 1972. In late 1972 refineries on the Gulf Coast and in the Midwest began using foreign crude oil for the first time in history. Major refiners began to clamor for a new energy policy, and independents found that, for the first time, import tickets would have no real value. By 1972 the Nixon administration had imposed price controls on crude oil and all refined products. It is no surprise that in terms of well drilling effort, 1972 was one of the worst years ever recorded.

If the argument for national energy security was contrived to support the quota program in 1959, the argument had a more substantive basis in 1973. As Adelman (1973) has argued, security of supply becomes the dominant concern when there are no substitute possibilities. In the present case, the power of OPEC constituted the real threat to energy security in the United States. A concerted oil boycott appeared to be able to force the elimination of many independent refiners (and marketers) in the absence of a direct rationing of domestic crude oil supplies by the federal government. By September, 1973, crude oil rationing appeared to be the intent of the government. With the Arab embargo, as discussed in previous chapters, the response by the government was total regulation. Even after the normalization of supplies, the government continued to allocate product output and to monitor domestic prices. Moreover, it appeared to see a clearer national security threat in OPEC's future policies, but tended to relate OPEC's ability to carry out such future oil embargo threats to the international role of the major oil companies. It was in this light that, recognizing the resource role of Middle East crude, the government attempted to focus on curtailing imports and, hence, on monitoring effectively all major and independent importers.

Resource Allocation: Quotas, Tariffs, or Storage?

In all the testimony regarding energy policy, few of the participants ever engaged in a formal consideration of the implications to resource allocation of a quota policy or of possible alternatives such as a tariff or a stockpile policy. Recent analyses, such as those by Burrows and Domencich (1970), President Nixon's Cabinet Task Force on Oil Import Control (1971), Areskoug (1971), and Hay (1971), analyze only crude oil. The implicit assumption of U.S. petroleum policy (and most analyses) had been that oil and gas were independent, with no cross-supply elasticity, and that the foreign supply elasticity of crude oil was virtually infinite. Earlier chapters have shown the fallacious nature of the assumption of product independence, and the previous section described how the assumption of infinite supply elasticity was not realistic in the long run.

The 1970 Burrows and Domencich study indicates the type of policy analysis conducted to analyze the U.S. oil import program of the late 1960's. Its analytical approach apparently influenced the fundamental conclusions of the Cabinet Task Force on Oil Import

Policy in 1970. Possibly the most startling conclusions of the Burrows-Domencich report were that:

> . . . it appears extremely unlikely that OPEC members could co-operate effectively to achieve a price increase. The member nations have little in common and competition from the other oil-producing nations is increasing.

> . . . the extreme importance of oil in the economies of the Arab nations makes it highly unlikely that these nations would intentionally cut off supplies of oil to the West for a protracted period of time.

> . . . OPEC appears to be a loose cartel that will gradually disintegrate in the future. As a result the world market price for crude oil will gradually decline from its present level. [Pp. 94, 96]

Within one year all these conclusions were known to be false. Figure 11 provides the competitive analysis of the Burrows-Domencich study. *S* is the long-run supply from domestic sources, and *D* is the long-run aggregate demand for oil in the United States. The vertical axis measures price in dollars per barrel, and the horizontal axis, quantity in billions of barrels per year. The curve *F* represents the foreign crude oil supply curve.

Hence, those authors assume that foreign supplies are available at constant marginal cost—in spite of the fact that import supply, including the traditional Venezuelan and Canadian crudes, is clearly characterized by increasing costs similar to those of the United States. *S'* is the total supply of crude oil, and equilibrium is at *J*, under quota policy. Under free trade, *OM* of domestic production and *BH* of imports would result. Because of the assumed shapes of these curves, Burrows and Domencich concluded that the world price of crude would drop to the foreign price level. Had they predicted foreign crude supply more realistically, they would have reached decidedly different conclusions. For example, if the foreign supply curve reflected the more realistic increasing cost characteristic, and given a quota program, decontrol of quotas would not necessarily lead to lower prices but to *higher* prices. This is in fact what has occurred since 1971.

A more realistic illustrative analysis of the U.S. energy problem would provide for the joint supply of both oil and gas. Furthermore,

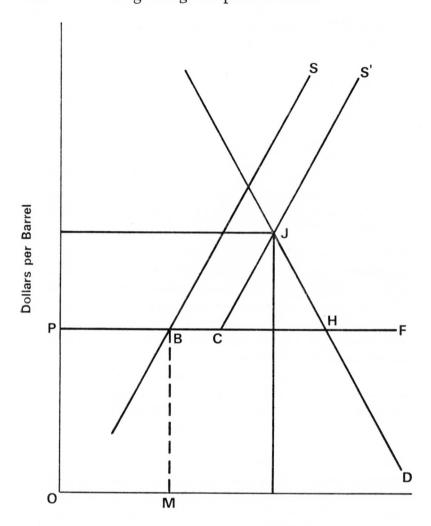

Quantity (Billions of Barrels per Year)

FIGURE 11. Long-run Supply and Demand Equilibrium for the U.S. Crude Oil Industry's Foreign Supply Based on Infinite Elasticity

this study has provided evidence of the importance of permanent components of market power among major refiners and of their price leadership structure. I characterize this market as a competitive oligopoly and assume that the federal government has decided to create a cartel through the imposition of quotas on foreign crude oil imports.[4] This characterization is realistic because almost 80 percent of the quotas granted by the government went to established firms—the "historical" importers. As domestic suppliers of crude oil and products, these companies were also suppliers of natural gas and gas liquids.

The joint-cost industry analysis depicted in the following graphs shows profit maximizing behavior simultaneously for both oil and gas markets in the absence of regulation and then under real-world conditions of regulation. The point of the illustration is to show how policy makers could have evaluated the behavior of the petroleum industry under various regulatory constraints. The realistic conditions of both intra- and interstate markets for natural gas are shown along with the imposition of quotas and/or tariffs on oil. Assumptions of foreign supply elasticities are also considered. Even under the simplistic conditions based on the assumption of profit maximization portrayed in these graphs, the direction of behavior is clear for various policy alternatives.

Figures 12 and 13 illustrate conditions in a joint-product industry which enjoys price leadership power with respect to domestic output but has to take into consideration imports at the world price. In Figure 12 crude oil supply and demand curves are provided. The vertical axis shows the average price per barrel of crude, while the horizontal axis shows the quantities of crude oil measured in billions of barrels per year. The curve DD' is the domestic demand curve for crude oil; the domestic industry's marginal cost curve is MC. If production were on a competitive basis, OQ_1 would be produced at price OP_1. However, since production is dominated by the price leaders, only OQ_2 is produced. This quantity corresponds to the point at which marginal revenue equals marginal cost. If the monopolistic power of the refiners was complete—that is, if there was no threat of entry by potential competitors and if the com-

---

[4] A competitive oligopoly, particularly when spatial location of firms is considered, refers to the case of price leadership or retaliatory pricing and inherently provides for business security for smaller firms already in the industry. It does not, however, imply direct collusive behavior (see Greenhut 1970). More importantly, a structured oligopoly with majors and independents provides for competitive behavior among firms. Indeed, the existence of workable competition is a characteristic of the petroleum refining industry.

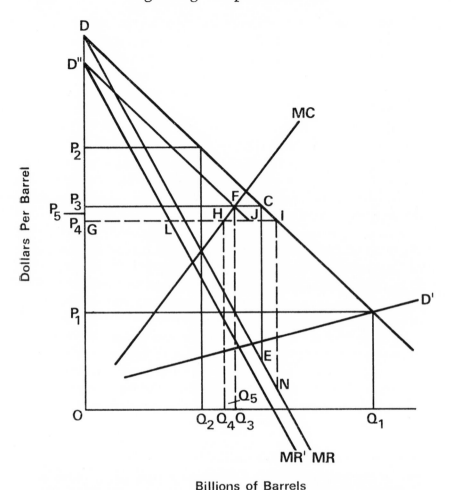

FIGURE 12. Crude Oil Supply-and-Demand Equilibrium under Conditions of Quotas, Tariffs, and Free Trade

modity was not produced abroad (or, conversely, if the elasticity of import supply is zero)—then the unit price OP_2 would be charged for OQ_2 output. However, we now allow for the existence of foreign supply which becomes available to the United States at price OP_3. This supply of foreign crude changes the domestic demand curve to P_3CD'. The marginal revenue changes to P_3CEMR. Domestic refiners extend their output to OQ_3, where the new marginal revenue

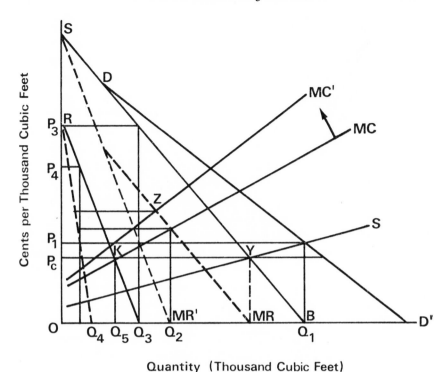

Quantity (Thousand Cubic Feet)

Figure 13. Natural Gas Supply-and-Demand Equilibrium under Gas
Price Regulation

curve cuts the marginal cost curve. At price OP_3, FC is imported
and OQ_3 is produced by the domestic industry.

Before introducing the implications of a quota or tariff on crude
oil, observe Figure 13 for natural gas.[5] In this figure, natural gas
demand consists of two submarkets: sales to interstate and intrastate purchasers. Intrastate purchasers are represented by the demand curve RA, and the interstate market is indicated by SB; the
horizontal summation for total demand, including both markets, is
SDD'. Under competitive conditions, OQ_1 would be produced and
OP_1 would be the price per unit or per thousand cubic feet of
natural gas. However, under price leadership, the intersection of

[5] Under a specific set of conditions a tariff can be set that achieves the
same level of imports as a quota. This is the famous equivalence theorem
(Bhagwati 1969; Ophir 1969, pp. 1002–1005).

marginal cost with the aggregated marginal revenue will determine the respective outputs and prices in each submarket. The results are analogous to a price discriminating monopolist. The intrastate price and output are OP_4 and OQ_4, and the interstate price and output are OP_3 and OQ_3. What happens if the government imposes a price ceiling on interstate sales of natural gas? Assume that the ceiling price of P_c is imposed. In this case, under competition, total quantity produced would decline by the total amount YQ_1. However, under the price leadership case, the imposition of ceiling prices reduces output to the interstate market at K, equal to OQ_5, which is less than the price leadership output for interstate sales, OQ_3. The effect of a price ceiling is to reduce natural gas output while creating an artificial attraction for intrastate sales of gas at relatively higher prices. Indeed, this has been the experience in the United States. In 1975 interstate gas prices were regulated at $0.52 per thousand cubic feet while unregulated intrastate prices were recorded at up to $2.00 per thousand cubic feet.

Now we can introduce a quota and/or tariff on foreign crude oil supplies and trace the effects in both markets.[6] We assume that the cross-elasticity of supply of oil for gas is positive. Assume that a dramatic increase in world supply reduced world price and that imports to the domestic economy are expected to rise. To protect the domestic market, the government imposes import quotas.[7] Before the fall in world price, OQ_3 was domestic production and FC was imports. The fall in world price from OP_3 to OP_4 reduced domestic production to GH, while imports rose to HI. To stabilize domestic production and domestic prices, the government introduced a quota equal to the former base-period imports. Here, $FC = JI$. Hence, while the demand curve confronting price leaders had become infinitely elastic at world oil prices OP_3 and OP_4, the demand curve facing the domestic monopolist with quotas is only infinitely elastic by the amount of the quota. For additional quantities in excess of quota volumes, price leaders face their original

---

[6] A huge literature has developed over the question of the "effective tariff" and "effective protection." The most comprehensive source on this question is Corden (1971).

[7] The standard sources on the various effects of imposing quotas and tariffs are Kindleberger (1969), Corden (1971), and Heuser (1938).

demand curve. However, the demand curve relevant to the government cartel has been shifted to the left by the amount of the quota. The new demand curve is $D''JID'$, and the marginal revenue curve for the domestic market is $D''LJINMR_1$. This latter marginal revenue curve cuts the marginal cost curve at about H, and industry crude oil output declines from OQ_3 to OQ_4. Total quantity supplied is OQ_4 plus JI. Therefore, in this case domestic output actually falls while the price to the producers increases.

The quota has two general effects. By restricting imports it increases demand for output of the domestic industry, which *should* induce the industry to raise output and replace imports, the normal effect when industry is competitive. However, quotas also reduce elasticity of the demand facing producers. Because elasticity of import supply becomes zero beyond a given point, the elasticity of domestic demand is reduced. This lower elasticity of demand reinforces the price leadership power of the domestic industry, which is given the incentive to limit output and raise prices. The smaller the quota, however, the more likely that output would increase. The lower the elasticity of total demand, the more likely that output would fall. By restricting imports to their previous level, there is no incentive for import substitution, and domestic output will fall as shown in Figure 12. By expanding the size of the quota, the elasticity of domestic demand would increase and the incentive to limit output and raise prices would lessen.

However, there are feedback effects on the natural gas market. By the very nature of joint production, a change in the volume of production of crude oil changes the marginal costs of producing natural gas. In this case, an increase in output of crude oil in response to an increase in price of that product shifts the marginal cost of natural gas and leads to a change in the volume of production of natural gas. Therefore, the volume of production of natural gas is a determinant of the marginal cost of crude oil. Based on our earlier assumption, an increase in the output of either product reduces the marginal cost of the other product.

The initial impact of quotas is to support the price of limited domestic output. The reduction in domestic output of crude oil causes a leftward shift in the marginal cost of natural gas. This shift is indicated by MC' in Figure 13. The shift in turn causes a wider disparity between unregulated intrastate and regulated interstate prices of natural gas while increasing excess demand from interstate consumers.

Note that if a tariff had been imposed instead of a quota, it would have caused an upward shift of OP_4 to OP_5, which would have the effect of increasing domestic production from OQ_4 to OQ_5. Thus, domestic output of the industry would actually rise with a tariff. An increase in crude oil output would cause a rightward shift in the marginal costs of natural gas, thereby eliciting greater supply at all prices. This would have worked to alleviate somewhat the excess demand for interstate natural gas. Therefore, on theoretical grounds a tariff would seem to be preferable to a quota. Such a technique instead of the quota program would have contributed to expanding the level of domestic output of both oil and gas and probably would have reduced the "permanent component" of the market power of major refiners. According to the theory of acquired regulation, it would be consistent for major refiners to oppose a tariff as an unacceptable form of regulation.

For refiners who are not self-sufficient in crude inputs, a tariff tends to increase the refiner's foreign unit or per-barrel costs, and this increase in turn tends to create the import substitution effect— that is, substitution from foreign oil—toward domestic production. In addition, a tariff does not erect the entry barriers that a quota provides. Hence, use of a tariff, as one of the parameters of this import demand elasticity, would have increased the demand elasticity, since the elasticity of import supply would have increased from zero.

The auctioning of import licenses was never seriously considered as a policy alternative because the system would have broken down with the existence of a monopoly buyer or a buyers' cartel. The majors, in this case, could have outbid other companies for the limited supply of import licenses and left nothing for the independents. An auctioning system would have taken away the advantages of a quota subsidy to independents and probably would have caused their exit from the industry. Therefore, all things being equal, the shares of output among the majors would have increased at the expense of the independents. If all petroleum firms in the world could have participated in the auction, OPEC would have been provided a grand opportunity to become a crystallized cartel long before 1970. OPEC could have outbid the majors for most of the quota rights. In such a case the value of import rights would have accrued to the United States Treasury, but domestic companies would then have faced monopoly prices for foreign oil. In addition, if foreign crude oil has a positive elasticity, the results of Figure 12 will be somewhat altered. A foreign supply curve that intersects at point H and is below MC thereafter would clearly have increased prices beyond the competitive level, and in the absence of quotas. The incentive for domestic output to increase is present.

The quota program was often considered to be a kind of national insurance scheme designed to protect the American economy against excessive oil shortages whenever the supply of oil is interrupted. As shown above, the program failed to provide adequate insurance in terms of additions to proved reserves or productive capacity.

With the existence of minimal surplus capacity within the Western Hemisphere by late 1973, and with the growing power of OPEC, the policy alternative of oil stockpiling or storage, although quite costly, was widely debated. The opportunity for stockpiling low-cost foreign oil was lost after the 1970's; it was apparent that any program of storage that involved foreign oil would increase upward pressure on world oil prices and particularly lead to the special premium prices for oil earmarked for strategic storage. What would have been the expected consequences of imposing a stockpile insurance scheme on the domestic industry? If the program were designed to "shut in" domestic production for future emergencies, the MC of both oil and gas would have shifted to the right.[8] This shift would have caused greater excess demand for natural gas while increasing the imports of foreign oil. A "shut-in" program would have increased the natural gas shortage and weakened national energy security by increasing reliance on imports. Thus, a shut-in storage policy was not an effective insurance solution.[9] On the

[8] The proposal to "shut in" domestic capacity was made by Mead and Sorensen (1971, pp. 211–224).

[9] In conjunction with McRae I have demonstrated the high cost of constructing and maintaining an emergency storage program (Copp and McRae 1974).

other hand, the United States could have introduced a program designed to use foreign crude as storage material. By stockpiling foreign crude during the early 1960's, the United States could have provided for future supply interruptions. Increasing the demand for foreign crude would have led to higher foreign crude prices and would have reduced the difference in foreign and domestic prices. This price reduction, in turn, would have increased the incentive to develop domestic resources.

The United States instead decided to heed the pressures of the major companies. Neither quotas, price ceilings, nor state prorationing had achieved the goals of replenishing the oil and natural gas reserves of the nation, nor had they stimulated refinery expansion. By 1973 the Nixon administration decided to introduce new energy policies designed to take away the advantage of foreign crude supply and foreign locations for refinery capacity. Since it was clear by 1973 that OPEC intended to use oil as a political weapon, the United States was faced with the task of seeking all available alternatives to minimize the expected effect on the U.S. economy of an oil boycott. When the boycott was imposed, the limitations of any meaningful short-term responses by the United States were apparent. Besides punitive controls on the U.S. oil industry, additional import fees were proposed, and a formal move to establish an oil storage system was being developed. The U.S. returned to a policy of attempting to curb imports. Meanwhile, during the period of the Arab embargo the severity of the growing natural gas problem was somewhat ignored. The shortage of crude oil and petroleum products was much more acute than the gas shortage, and interstate gas customers were in a more favorable position from the standpoint of supply and price than were users of petroleum products. However, in 1974 and 1975 this illusory well-being was shattered by the FPC's announcement of gas curtailments.

Conclusions on the National Security Rationale

National security has been an ill-defined and much abused rationale for the interests of both majors and independents and government. From the economic viewpoint, nevertheless, a national security rationale has legitimacy. A national security argument is effectively an effort to impose external criteria on the efficient allocation of petroleum industry resources. The relevant questions of how much national security, for whom, and at what cost are questions that have received little or no attention.

In essence, a national security rationale is an effort to justify the increased costs of resource misallocation on the basis of the cost necessary to insure petroleum resource supplies for the United States. For most oil policies, the insurance costs were presumably those of overcapacity of oil and gas production plus a cushion of refining overcapacity. In time of emergency or for national defense requirements the costs of overcapacity presumably would be outweighed by the benefits of assured supplies of crude oil and oil products. Government intervention in the petroleum industry, whether the regulation was acquired or not, constitutes the formation of a national energy insurance policy whereby consumers supposedly pay the premiums while being the main benefactors. Political pressures, however, have subverted this sequence. The acquired regulation by both majors and independents has tended to increase the cost of insurance over and above what it might be in the absence of such pressure. What might have been a reasonable cost for that national security oil policy was worsened by the political tactics of small and large refiners. However, even in the absence of this acquired regulation, the insurance cost of oil import policy became unreasonable with the additional influence of national monopoly policy. The government not only desired to stimulate a reasonable level of overcapacity but also attempted to enforce a preferred industry structure in refining.

The achievement of national defense does not imply any particular industry structure. Although 60 percent of the crude oil and natural gas production is controlled by the major integrated firms, a substantial amount of the exploratory drilling effort is conducted by smaller independent firms. More than five thousand firms engage in exploration for oil and gas. More than one hundred firms engage in petroleum refining. There is no real evidence to conclude that the top ten or twenty firms in refining have acted in concert to raise prices or restrict output at monopoly levels. As earlier chapters have shown, the limit price–price leadership theory of oligopoly provides a more accurate description of the industry. The industry is best described as a competitive oligopoly. Normal technological and economic factors have tended to encourage investment in larger-scale operations in refining. Because many firms in refining have been smaller ones, these factors inevitably forced smaller firms to expand, merge, or leave the industry. This process of survival is patently not a signal of monopolistic behavior but of the actual workings of competition. As defined, the government attempted to subvert this firm growth process.

To restore legitimacy to the national security rationale, government policy should abandon its effort to infuse monopoly policy with national energy security policy. Rather, it should limit its efforts to increase productive raw and synthetic energy supplies, it should provide for a reasonable level of emergency capacity in secure supplies of crude oil, and it should consider a special program of limited excess refining capacity. The cost of this excess refining capacity, which could be less than 10 percent of operating refining capacity distributed regionally and possibly among conversion processes, could be carried by the government with special tax credits to refiners similar to the accelerated amortization benefits of early 1951. In periods of excess refining capacity these credits could be extended, while refiners with uneconomic plant capacity would not be eligible for them.

Crude oil and natural gas joint supply is the central issue of the current energy crisis. Virtually no spare productive capacity exists. Imports of foreign crude and products are rising, and the vulnerability of the United States to boycotts of crude supplies increases with rising imports. A national security rationale should provide some protection or insurance against a cutoff of foreign supply. Such a rationale should evaluate the alternate costs of various policy options. The relevant concern is how much foreign oil needs insurance and for how long a period. The most apparent options include (1) an emergency oil storage program, (2) an aggressive government program to develop new surplus capacity from known domestic fields where higher-cost secondary and tertiary projects are feasible and foreign areas, including OPEC countries that have not participated in boycotts against the United States, (3) a subsidy program to develop high-cost substitutes such as shale oil, (4) a national emergency conservation program that would implement arbitrary programs to allocate supplies, and (5) some combination of these. These options should essentially be designed to encourage capital formation in the energy industry and to facilitate the financing of energy projects by both majors and independents.

In the past, the United States implemented a quota program that theoretically should have stimulated the continued development of oil and gas proved reserves and productive capacity. The weaknesses of that program have been demonstrated. To achieve a given level of national energy security, foreign imports, presumably all from Arab countries, would require insurance. A minimum period of ninety days' supply should be considered, although this minimum could be lowered in combination with a conservation program. Imports from Arab countries accounted for 20 percent of total oil imports to the United States in 1972. This figure increased to 40 percent by early 1974. As a percentage of total U.S. oil demand, Arab oil accounted for some 17 percent in 1974. If we allow that 10 percent of U.S. demand to be reduced through conservation efforts, then it appears reasonable that 10 percent of total oil demand is a level that should be ensured against possible interruption. Defining the appropriate strategy will depend on the insurance costs of the various policy alternatives. These considerations for the national security rationale should have been apparent. But, as the next chapter will show, the policy initiatives of 1973 through 1975 appeared to worsen the supply position of the United States. However, through the Energy Policy and Conservation Act of 1975 an oil storage program was initiated. It was a beginning for energy security, but it also created a permanent governmental presence in the oil business.

5

Recent Federal Response: Continued Regulation of Competition

AS petroleum supply and demand imbalances worsened in the early 1970's, the piecemeal, uncoordinated response of the government became more apparent: there simply was no effective national policy. During the winter 1972/1973, certain regions of the United States experienced scarcities of heating oil, diesel fuel, and propane similar to shortages that occurred during the winter of 1948/1949. The likelihood of these seasonal shortages had been predicted by petroleum industry spokesmen as early as 1971. Heating oil supplies, particularly in New England and Midwest regions, were persistently tight. Apparently, increases in domestic yields of distillates, imports of additional quantities of distillates, and the short duration of severe winter weather temporarily alleviated the supply imbalance. Because refineries had to sacrifice gasoline output to increase yields of distillates, the deliverable seasonal supply of gasoline was relatively lower by early April, 1973. Refiners began to initiate their own allocation of gasoline to major-brand and "unbranded" outlets. This practice forced arbitrary reductions in normal stock for many of the independent marketers, and some of them had to leave the market.

The government pressured refiners to maximize the output of middle distillates at the expense of gasoline. Refiners complained that the domestic supply of sweet crude oil was insufficient. The government responded by allowing refiners to receive advances on their 1973 import quota allocations. By late 1972 oil companies had an incentive to pay the rising foreign crude and product prices, expecting that historical import volumes would be an important factor in a new energy policy. In particular, the "oil psychology" of the period was that following the presidential elections price controls would be lifted. A survey of all refiners conducted by the API in October, 1972, indicated that the main reason for low levels of operating capacity was "lack of sweet crude oil at a *reasonable price*" (italics mine). Other reasons given included unscheduled maintenance and turnaround and environmental regulation of emissions. At controlled product prices, only integrated refiners with over 70 percent self-sufficiency in crude oil could still profit by higher crude prices. All other refiners, even though partially self-sufficient, could not profit by a crude price increase under conditions of controlled product prices.

Natural gas firm curtailments, in addition to massive interruptible curtailments, occurred for the first time in 1972.[1] Industries that had assumed that long-term supplies of gas were available were suddenly faced with the prospect of shutting down a substantial amount of industrial capacity for lack of fuel. The industrial demand for propane as a substitute for natural gas tripled by the end of 1973.[2] By bidding up the price of propane, the industries obtained supplies that otherwise could have been consumed by agriculture for its seasonal requirements.

Although most refineries by early 1973 were producing at maxi-

[1] Increased requirements for natural gas during the first half of 1972 led to firm volume curtailments by interstate natural gas pipeline companies. During the summer of 1972, eleven major pipeline companies reported firm volume curtailments totaling nearly 555.4 billion cubic feet, followed by volume curtailments by fourteen companies of an additional 565.6 billion cubic feet for the 1972/1973 winter. This curtailment constituted over 5 percent of the total annual marketed production of natural gas in 1972. The volume curtailments for the summer of 1973 were estimated to be 910.8 billion cubic feet, and for the winter months of 1973/1974 the estimate was 670.2 billion cubic feet (FPC 1973).

[2] Most of the firm curtailments affected users of interruptible in the Gulf Coast, Midcontinent, and Midwest areas. As natural gas curtailments increased, users of interruptible increased their demand for substitutes such as propane, low-sulfur residual fuel oil, and distillate fuel oil. As weather in the Midwest deteriorated, propane demand doubled, and spot propane prices were at 6.25 cents per gallon and probably would have been higher except for Phase II controls. Propane prices increased 8 percent during this period with no appreciable effect on demand.

mum rated capacity, the total demand for refined products had increased far beyond the nation's existing capacity. Refinery capacity was inadequate. The foreign supply of refined products was almost completely price inelastic. By December, 1972, the Western Hemisphere preference on products was lifted to allow refiners and other license holders to import from any source. However, foreign product prices were 50 to 60 percent greater than comparable domestic product prices. With domestic price controls on products, and limited, high-cost foreign supply, it was economically unfeasible to rely on imported products.[3] For reasons pointed out in earlier chapters, spare productive capacity of both oil and gas and spare refinery capacity were virtually nonexistent by early 1973.[4] However, these conditions soon changed.

Liberalized Natural Gas Pricing

Federal reaction to the "energy crunch" began to synthesize in early 1972 with the provision of optional pricing for new supplies of natural gas. Old ceiling gas prices would remain for all supplies committed before April, 1972, but new gas supplies were allowed to be priced for long-term contracts at higher levels subject to FPC approval. The immediate benefactors of this policy were firms already engaged in the search and development process whose payout was based on the joint profitability of pre-April gas and crude

[3] Environmental regulations had reduced high-sulfur coal as an economically feasible input for East Coast users. Also, during 1972 new state and federal laws regarding particulates and emissions at industrial plants became effective. These plants were faced with a decision to either install costly emission control equipment or switch from residual fuel oil to low-sulfur distillate. The 1971–1972 period was also characterized by substantial investments by electric utilities for gas turbine generating facilities, which were induced by delays in construction and permits for nuclear generating facilities. Gas turbines have a low investment cost but high operating cost and use No. 2 low-sulfur distillate.

[4] As noted earlier, most U.S. refineries are designed to process either sweet crude or sour crude. A National Petroleum Refiners Association report (1973) stated that "if U.S. refiners had to substitute sour crude (1 to 2 per cent sulfur content) runs, the reported runs of 12.5 million barrels per day would be reduced to 11.3 million barrels per day. This decrease would be due to limitations imposed by environmental regulations, metallurgy of crude units, and lack of sulfur recovery units and other downstream processing units. Some 700,000 barrels per day of refining capacity would be left unuseable."

oil prices. Firms with marginal productive potential in developed gas fields also benefited by committing these marginal proved reserves to production at higher prices. Because of their dominance in natural gas production, majors and a few large independents were primary beneficiaries of this new pricing policy, but because FPC approval was required, the potential delay of litigation was still present. By releasing prices for new interstate gas sales, the incentive was provided to commit increased volumes of new gas to interstate markets.

At the same time, intrastate markets, particularly in Texas and Louisiana, had expanded, and competition for new gas led to higher intrastate prices with no regulatory lag (Hawkins 1969). The net result was that by late 1973 relatively more new gas sales were contracted for intrastate markets. With this competing market for gas, greater interest was created for importing natural gas. Liquefied natural gas (LNG) supplies from Algeria were contracted at prices almost triple the highest known interstate price. Other supplies from Libya, the Middle East, and the USSR were also being considered. However, the federal government was faced with the contradictory policy of refusing to increase domestic old and new gas price ceilings while allowing the importation of higher-priced natural gas. The reaction of the FPC and Congress was that such LNG importation ventures were unreasonable. While the administration argued for domestic decontrol of natural gas prices, sentiment in Congress and the FPC was for a total policing of U.S. natural gas reserves by field and company. The sentiment was that the cure for the nation's energy imbalance was to impose the right kind of regulation to replace previous regulation. Congress and the FPC were considering what can be called balanced regulation in which prices were flexibly controlled and output was flexibly allocated by the FPC. At issue was the elimination of barriers to interstate markets. Thus, the attempt to allow the price mechanism to perform its function was considered a temporary measure to allow the development of a new structure of regulation.

The liberal FPC pricing policy, however, still remained ineffective in attracting adequate new volumes of gas to interstate markets. Indeed, a continuing debate between U.S. producers and interstate pipeline companies with the FPC over the appropriate price level led to the development of Commission Opinion 699-H, wherein the FPC adjusted its basis for determining the cost of finding and producing new supplies of natural gas. In this opinion a discounted cash flow basis with a 15 percent return generally replaced total reliance on historic cost experience in setting prices. Under this basis, prices for new gas contracts were set at $0.5298 per thousand cubic feet. Although this opinion was something of a breakthrough in FPC policy, it was soon obvious that selectivity in the cost data used by the FPC tended to result in gas prices still substantially lower than intrastate prices. By 1975 intrastate prices, depending on location, ranged from $0.56 per thousand cubic feet to a high of $2.43 per thousand cubic feet—almost five times the "liberalized" rate. Indeed, the unregulated Texas intrastate market entered a period of temporary surplus supply by mid-1975, in striking contrast to the interstate market—particularly pipelines transmitting gas to the U.S. East Coast. By 1974 and 1975, gas curtailments—reductions in the contracted volumes of available supply—were up to 15 percent of annual requirements.

In this atmosphere of energy crisis, the Ford administration pushed harder for the decontrol of natural gas prices. Nevertheless, given the political vagaries of gas legislative issues, it was apparent that more liberal pricing policy by the Federal Power Commission provided the best possibility for gas producers. Indeed, on December 31, 1975, the Federal Power Commission issued Opinion No. 749 (FPC 1975b) authorizing a rate increase for producers of "old" gas, that is, gas that began flowing in interstate commerce before January 1, 1973. For the first time, a uniform national-area base rate for "old" gas, supplanting the multiple-area rates for this gas established in prior rate cases, provided for an immediate increase to 23.5 cents per thousand cubic feet. By mid-1976, sellers would be permitted to file for increased rates up to a base rate of 29.5 cents per thousand cubic feet. The added amount of 6 cents was to account for the income tax liability that would be incurred by virtue of the elimination of the percentage depletion allowance. In 1975 depletion had been eliminated for most gas producers. The FPC estimated that under the new national-area rate ceiling, the average price of old gas after July 1, 1976, would rise from 22.90 cents per thousand cubic feet to 27.68 cents per thousand cubic feet. This increase would add new revenue to producers of about $503 million per year.

At the same time, the FPC ended the advance payments program to natural gas producers. This program, initiated in 1970, allowed pipeline companies to lend money, at no interest cost, to producers for exploration and development and to collect the interest costs of the loan from customer utilities. Pipelines would have a call on the gas. Also, under FPC regulations, advances were allowed as rate base items. Under the program, over $2 billion had been committed, with the largest amounts going to exploratory programs in South Louisiana and offshore areas. Total proved natural gas reserves related to advance payments amounted to over 12.5 trillion cubic feet by mid-1975, and the pipelines obtaining the greatest productivity per dollar advanced included Natural Gas Pipeline of America, Tennessee Gas Pipeline, Trunkline Gas Co., Texas Eastern Transmission, Northern Natural Gas, and Michigan Wisconsin Pipeline. These companies tended to support continuation of the program, while those with lesser success tended to oppose continuation. The prime argument against continuation was that financially stronger producers looked to pipelines for loans without having to carry the loans as outstanding debt. Nevertheless, another example of conflicting acquired regulation characterized this gas issue.

The FPC next turned its attention to "new" natural gas prices; that is, those jurisdictional sales of natural gas dedicated to interstate commerce on or after January 1, 1973. The FPC's Bureau of Natural Gas (BNG) and Office of Economics differed in their studies on the cost of finding and producing new natural gas. The allowable interstate rate by early 1976 was 52 cents per thousand cubic feet, but the BNG estimated that new gas costs ranged from 85.32 cents per thousand cubic feet to $1.69 per thousand cubic feet (FPC 1975a). The Office of Economics recommended a continuation of the base rate of 52 cents per thousand cubic feet established in Opinion 699-H. While the FPC mulled its decision in early 1976, a key piece of legislation for gas price decontrol failed to pass in the House of Representatives. Barring a reversal of administration and industry position, it appeared unlikely that the 1976 Congress could be looked to for total price decontrol legislation acceptable to both government and the petroleum industry. Therefore, there was growing expectation that the FPC would act to adopt higher national area rates.

Nixon Administration Policies

Another major switch in government policy concerned federal regulation of oil imports and domestic oil and product prices. Government policy was designed to phase out its quota-imposed cartel while increasing the cost of using foreign crude oil in domestic refineries as well as the cost of foreign refined products to domestic consumers.

On April 18, 1973, the Nixon administration announced a complete overhaul of the Mandatory Oil Import Control Program to become effective May 1, 1973 (Department of the Treasury 1973). The presidential proclamation modifying Proclamation 3279 stated that William E. Simon, chairman of the Oil Policy Committee of the Department of the Treasury, had recommended in the interest of national security,

> after consultation with the Oil Policy Committee, that the method of adjusting imports of petroleum and petroleum products be modified by immediately suspending tariffs on imports of petroleum and petroleum products and *by shifting to a system whereby fees for licenses covering such imports shall be charged and whereby such fees may be adjusted from time to time, as required in order to discourage the importation into the United States of petroleum and petroleum products in such quantities or under such circumstances as to threaten to impair the national security;* to create conditions favorable, in the long range, to domestic production needed for projected national security requirements; to increase the capacity of domestic refineries and petrochemical plants to meet such requirements; and to encourage investment, exploration, and development necessary to assure such growth. [Italics mine.]

Thus, the new program terminated volumetric quotas on oil imports and substituted a system of license fees on imports of petroleum and petroleum products. Furthermore, all existing duties on crude oil and refinery product imports were suspended. The president noted that the mandatory oil import program was not to be abandoned but only modified. In justifying the new program, the administration stated that the mandatory quota program "was not so much a failure as it was obsolete." An objective of the new program was "the need to get the federal government out of the business of regulating oil imports" (Department of the Treasury 1973). However, the modified program could hardly be described as a scrapping of the government-imposed importers' cartel. The program was, in effect, a joint tariff-quota program designed to phase in a complete tariff program.

OUTPUT-RELATED CONTROLS UNDER THE NATIONAL SECURITY
FEE SYSTEM

Under the new program, the participants were to be granted yearly allocations, exempt from license fees, equal to import levels in effect as of April 1, 1973, for residual fuel oil and quota levels in effect as of January 1, 1973, for crude oil and petroleum products other than residual fuel oil. The exempt allocations were to be granted through April 30, 1974, after which the level upon which allocations were based was to be reduced by a fraction of the original level each year for the next seven years. No allocations were to be exempt from fees beyond April 30, 1980. Table 30 shows the percentage of initial allocations exempt from license fees.

Each of the refiners, petrochemical plant operators, deep-water terminal operators in PAD District I, and asphalt marketers in PAD Districts I–IV retained their import allowables, fee-exempt, with

TABLE 30
Initial Import Allocations Exempt from License Fees

Year (after April 30)	Percent Exempted
1973	100
1974	90
1975	80
1976	65
1977	50
1978	35
1979	20
1980	0

SOURCE: Department of the Treasury 1973.

nonexempt allowables increasing each year from the 1973 base volume. Increases in import volumes from each importer above 1973 allocations were subject to fees. For PAD Districts I–IV the maximum level of imports of crude oil, unfinished oils, and finished products (other than residuals to be used as fuel oil) from sources other than Canada and Mexico totaled 1,992,000 barrels per day (Department of the Treasury 1973). In addition, 50,000 barrels per day of fee-exempt No. 2 fuel oil manufactured in the Western Hemisphere from crude oil produced in the Western Hemisphere was to be allowed for District I only. Holders of No. 2 import licenses could also import an equal volume of crude oil if so desired. Thus, licenses were interchangeable.

For PAD District I only, a fee-exempt ceiling was established of 2,900,000 barrels per day of residuals to be used as fuel oil (Department of the Treasury 1973). Added to this amount was a ceiling of 42,000 barrels per day of residual fuel oil for PAD Districts II–IV. Thus, for the first time since 1966, residual fuel oil was again under the control of government allocation. Special limitations, as under the quota program, were set for imports from Canada and Mexico. For Districts I–IV, fee-exempt Canadian imports of crude and unfinished oils were set at 960,000 barrels daily. Total fee-exempt imports of crude and products from Mexico were 32,500 barrels daily. In PAD District V, fee-exempt imports from origins other than Canada and Mexico totaled 670,000 barrels per day of crude and unfinished oils and finished products except for residual fuel oil. For resid, District V fee-exempt volumes from other sources totaled 75,600 barrels daily. Fee-exempt imports of crude oil and products into District V from Canada totaled 280,000 barrels daily. Fee-exempt imports into Puerto Rico were to average 227,221 barrels daily. Imports of asphalt, ethane, propane, and butanes were allowed to be imported without a license requirement. Furthermore, crude oil imported into District I that was "topped" for use as a burner fuel was decontrolled but was not fee-exempt. However, these decontrolled volumes were not to be subtracted from the total fee-exempt volumes. The Puerto Rican program was novel in that it integrated its imports into the United States system. Imports to Puerto Rico were subject to license fees, while finished products shipped to the United States mainland from Puerto Rico were fee-exempt. Conversely, for the Virgin Islands imports of crude oil and products were fee-exempt while exports of products to the United States mainland were subject to fees.

NATIONAL SECURITY LICENSE FEES AND CRUDE OIL PRICE

The system of national security license fees was designed to reach a level of 0.5 cent per gallon on crude oil and 1.5 cents per gallon on petroleum products by November 1, 1975. The fee was designed to achieve this level gradually. Table 31 provides that national security license fee schedule. It is apparent that the initial import fees on motor gasoline were almost 3.5 times the fees on other products and about 5 times the fees on crude oil. The government's objective in setting discriminatory fees on products relative to crude oil was to eliminate the attractiveness of foreign locations for refineries. The new regulations also required that import fees be paid at the time of application for import licenses. This additional regulation tended to increase the effective tariff on imports. Two additional aspects of the program evolved after April, 1973. The government considered using license fee program revenues to initiate the Energy Research Trust Fund, which was to be used to subsidize research in new production technology for crude oil and natural gas and which committed resources to study a program for strategic crude oil storage.

Although the government appeared to let the price system become the regulator of imports and domestic production, a more fundamental price strategy was involved. The import license fee scheme was designed to achieve the government-determined long-run supply price of crude oil, on average, of seven dollars per barrel.[5] The intention of the program was to gradually eliminate quotas

---

[5] This dollar price of crude oil was in real terms using 1972 as the base. Several studies, including those by the National Petroleum Council (1972) and the Ford Foundation (1974), had indicated that self-sufficiency in oil could be achieved by 1985 if the real price of crude were allowed to rise up to the seven-dollar level and remain constant. Later, the Energy Policy Project Group suggested a nine-dollar price based on assumptions adopted from the base forecasts of the NPC. Total conventional U.S. production was believed to be able to rise to between thirteen and fifteen million barrels daily, including natural gas liquids, by 1985. The real price level desired was the one that would be sufficient to maximize total domestic development of oil and gas resources while stimulat-

TABLE 31
National Security License Fee Schedule
(cents/bbl.)

	May 1 1973	Nov. 1 1973	May 1 1974	Nov. 1 1974	May 1 1975	Nov. 1 1975
Crude	10.5	13.0	15.5	18.0	21.0	21.0
Motor gasoline	52.0	54.5	57.0	59.5	63.0	63.0
Residual fuel oil, distillate products, and unfinished oils (except ethane, propane, and butanes)	15.0	20.0	30.0	42.0	53.0	63.0

Source: Department of the Treasury 1973.

while achieving a more balanced regulatory program by setting a long-term ceiling price on crude oil and adjusting tariffs to achieve this effect. The authority to regulate domestic crude prices was granted under the Economic Stabilization Act of 1974. Through the Cost of Living Council and eventually the FEO, the government was seeking to accomplish regulation under the guise of a liberal trade program.

The alternative concept for petroleum industry regulation was to achieve desired productive capacity additions, in both raw material and refining, through flexibly controlled domestic prices and import tariffs. A joint quota-tariff program would phase into a complete "equalizing" tariff scheme. This concept was one of balanced protection to assure the desired positive effect. The stimulus for balanced domestic production was clearly the energy security complications inherent in excessive reliance on Middle Eastern supplies. By 1973 OPEC was demanding accelerated participation in foreign concessions and was arbitrarily increasing export prices; late in that

---

ing sufficient investment in synthetics to balance long-term supply and demand, assuming a degree of about 80 percent self-sufficiency. The folly of such efforts to establish precision in long-term policy soon became evident. Moreover, any estimate of future supply through price increases has to be regarded as a central probability estimate with a wide dispersion around it (McKie 1972).

year the spot price of foreign crude was almost double that of domestic crude oil. With foreign supplies controlled by an effective oil export monopoly, the counterbalance for the United States was greater development of domestic crude oil and natural gas resources, expanded domestic refining capacity, the imposition of demand-reducing programs, and preparation for nationwide product allocation programs.

For the first six months of the new license fee program, several patterns were apparent. The fee-exempt ceiling on residual fuel oil for PAD Districts I–IV was over 1 million barrels per day greater than actual imports. Thus, the tariff schedule for resid was irrelevant. Based on the phasing-in schedule of allocations exempt from fees, if resid imports remained at their April-to-October average level it would be 1977 before any of the resid imports would be affected by tariff considerations. Since most of the new foreign refinery capacity in the Caribbean was designed to provide residual fuel oil to the East Coast of the United States, it appears unlikely that the attraction of U.S. sites for resid production would be stimulated by the product tariff. In contrast, distillate import levels immediately jumped more than 150,000 barrels per day over the fee-exempt level of 50,000 barrels per day, and by October, license fees were paid on almost 400,000 barrels per day of distillate. The national security fee on distillate was apparently ineffective in curtailing import demand for distillate. Fees at that time on distillate were only about one-half cent per imported gallon, compared to a New York Harbor cargo price of twenty-two cents per gallon. The tariff rate was less than 5 percent of the per-gallon value of distillate.

Imports of crude oil from countries other than Canada or Mexico tended to be consistently over the fee-exempt level. By October, 1973, imports were 180,000 barrels per day over the fee-exempt level, or about 8 percent of total crude imports. Canadian imports were some 200,000 barrels per day lower than fee-exempt levels. In PAD District V fee-exempt crude imports from origins other than Canada or Mexico were approximately equal to total fee-exempt levels. However, imports from Canada were far below the fee-exempt allowables. In summary, the short-run impacts (before the 1973 Arab-Israeli War) were that the tariff levels were inconsequential to import demand influences. Crude oil and distillate imports increased over their former quota levels, while residual fuel imports remained relatively stable.[6]

A notable effect on the new tariff program was the announcement of new refinery capacity expansions by both major and independent refiners. Many of the announced expansions were for new desulfurization capacity for residual fuel production. Thus, refiners were anticipating the period when tariff levels would have a significant negative impact on the long-run attraction of foreign refinery sites.

Ford Administration Policies

The distortion of imports following the OPEC embargo and the subsequent return to high levels of imports through 1974 prompted the Ford administration to impose additional fees on imports and reinstate customs fees. The Ford program was to increase fees on imported crude oil by $1.00 per barrel and later scale these fees up to $3.00 per barrel. Fees of $1.20 per barrel on products were also imposed.

With the average cost of crude oil landed at major U.S. ports about $11.00 per barrel in 1975, the mid-year fees of $2.00 per barrel brought the total average landed cost to $13.00 per barrel. The customs fee was refundable to product importers once the supplemental fee was collected by the Oil Import Administration (OIA). The supplemental fee arose from the Ford administration's $2.00 per barrel tariff on imported crude, effective June 1. Against this tariff, product importers received a rebate of $1.40 per barrel, resulting in a net supplemental fee of $0.60 per barrel. The license fee of $0.63 per barrel was initiated under the Nixon administration and had to be paid by all importers not holding fee-free tickets (see chapter 3). These three fees averaged about 10 percent of the total price of the product, but from indications on residual demand they had little real impact on curbing demand for residual or crude oil.

---

[6] The idea that access to the U.S. market could provide a strong enough attraction to lead to price-cutting tactics by producer countries was proposed during this period by Adelman (Cowan 1975). He suggested a quota system for access to the U.S. market, with a sealed-bid auction for quota rights.

The fee program did little to curb crude oil imports. By mid-1975 crude oil imports were 4.4 million barrels daily, up 12 percent over the comparable 1974 period. Residual fuel oil imports, however, were down largely because of depressed economic conditions in the United States. As the U.S. economy was expected to improve its level of real economic growth through 1976, imports of residual and other products were expected to continue increasing. Indeed, the softness in demand and price of residual fuel oil was also experienced by its competing substitute, coal. The shortage of products in 1973 and 1974 resulted in sharply increased demands for coal. Steam coal prices in 1973 averaged $0.40 per million British thermal units (Btu's) and moved to close to an average of $0.70 per million Btu's in 1974. However, this steam coal market is generally 75 percent long-term contract and 25 percent spot purchases. In 1973 and 1974 spot prices increased sharply to as high as $1.92 per million Btu's. However, by 1975 the lower level of economic activity resulted in substantial reduction in spot prices.

The overriding policy on domestic operations, discussed in earlier chapters, was the price control on "old" domestic oil at $5.25 per barrel. However, stripper wells and crude produced after May, 1973, along with a special released crude category, were exempt from controls, which resulted in wide dispersions in price among the major producing states relative to the normal dispersion for quality and distance.[7] The goal of eliminating artificial price differentials became a major policy goal of the Ford administration.

In addition, a concerted effort to accelerate development of the outer continental shelf was being made.[8] Under the leasing system created by the Outer Continental Shelf Act, companies, either

[7] The percentages of these oil wells that were stripper wells, that is, wells producing ten barrels daily or less, was as follows: California, 77 percent; Kansas, 96 percent; Louisiana, 45 percent; Pennsylvania, 98 percent; Texas, 51 percent. For all the United States, stripper wells accounted for over 71 percent of all oil-producing wells. However, total stripper production was about 11 percent of the U.S. total. The high percentage of stripper wells partially explains the higher per-barrel value of Kansas and Pennsylvania crude.

[8] The continental shelf of the United States includes that part of the continental margin which extends from shoreline to water depths of approximately 200 meters (656 feet). The state jurisdiction extends within three nautical miles of the coastline except for Texas and the Gulf Coast of Florida, where the state/federal boundary is three leagues (about nine miles) from the coastline.

singly or jointly, bid on tracts of 5,760 acres each selected by the Interior Department. Before the actual sale, and in accordance with the National Environmental Protection Act and the Council on Environmental Quality guidelines, the Interior Department must publish a call for nominations of areas, and later the public has the right to state its objections (environmental or others) to the sale. This process normally takes one and a half years. The high bidder at the subsequent sale would win the right to conduct exploratory drilling and produce any oil and gas found. The winning company had to pay the government a royalty on production of 16⅔ percent of the value at the wellhead.

United States development had been sporadic since the initiation of offshore lease sales in 1954 because of the varying frequency and size of sales. While the total acreage offered varied, the bonuses to the government increased significantly from 1954 to 1974. Total bonuses paid through 1974 were over $14 billion, with more than two-thirds of this amount being paid since 1970. Over nineteen million acres have been offered for lease, and over ten million acres were under lease by early 1975. By 1975 lease bonuses were expected to bring an additional $7 billion to the government plus annual government royalties on offshore production in 1974 of over $500 million. The leasing of federally controlled offshore waters was accelerated by the Nixon administration. By 1974 over five hundred million barrels, including condensate, were being produced offshore, with Louisiana federal waters accounting for almost 70 percent of the total (Table 32). Offshore production accounted for only 17 percent of U.S. production in 1974, and administration goals were for a substantial increase in this level by 1980.

In mid-1973 the Interior Department proposed lease sales of approximately three million acres per year over a five-year period. This would have been an unusual accomplishment in that in the twenty years the federal government had conducted lease sales, offerings of over one million acres had occurred only five times. The Nixon administration later increased this goal to ten million acres on the outer continental shelf, but this concerted effort was resisted by Congress. Again, the government attempted to infuse monopoly policy with its oil policy by attempting to place constraints on the joint bidding practices of major companies while

TABLE 32
U.S. Offshore Crude Petroleum Production and Value, 1974

	Production (000 bbl.)	Production Value	Federal Royalty Value
Alaska	60,178		
California, total	83,112		
Federal	16,779	$78,014,000	$13,002,000
State	66,333		
Texas, total	1,081		
Federal	504	$9,894,000	$1,613,000
State	577		
Louisiana, total	397,116		
Federal	318,423	$2,310,968,000	$379,749,000
State	78,693		
U.S. total offshore	541,487*		
U.S. total domestic	3,199,328		

SOURCE: U.S. Bureau of Mines, *Crude Petroleum, Petroleum Products, and Natural Gas Liquids*, Mineral Industry Surveys, 1974; U.S. Geological Survey, Conservation Division, *Outer Continental Shelf Statistics, Calendar Year 1974*, June, 1975.

NOTE: Natural gas production in federal waters totaled 3.5 trillion cu. ft., or about 16 percent of the U.S. total. Production value was $877.7 million, and royalty value was $141.6 million.

* Total production from offshore federal waters was 360,594,065 barrels. Production value was $2,398,776,748; royalty value was $394,365,003.

placing no limitations on independents. In general, twelve companies dominated offshore production in federal waters in the Gulf of Mexico: Standard Oil of California, Exxon, Shell, Gulf, Union, Continental, Mobil, Getty, Cities Service, Atlantic Richfield, Phillips, and Texaco. Of this group, Exxon tended to bid independently for offshore tracts, while other companies tended to bid jointly and occasionally independently. Several congressmen saw illegal collusive activity in this joint bidding. Furthermore, the belief was that huge bonuses required to win a given tract tended to restrict entry into offshore bidding to only the large firms. Public objections resulted in congressional proposals "to assume competition" by establishing a Federal Oil and Gas Corporation (FOGCO) that would have the right of first choice of acreage on the outer continental shelf. Moreover, it was proposed that no company could hold more than 20 percent of an offshore venture. Again, the government was attempting to carve a market for smaller firms while ostensibly limiting the power of the majors.

THE TAX REDUCTION ACT OF 1975 AND
WINDFALL TAX PROPOSALS

In March, 1975, the percentage depletion allowance was eliminated for all major U.S. producers of crude oil and natural gas, with certain exceptions. A special allowance of 22 percent of gross revenues was retained for very small independent producers and royalty owners, but retailers and petroleum refiners were precluded from percentage depletion. The small-producer exception itself was to be phased down to 15 percent by 1984,[9] as indicated in Table 33, with the maximum tentative depletable quantities of one thousand barrels of oil daily or six million cubic feet of gas per day. The allowable of 22 percent on this initial average daily production level was the net amount of the taxpayer's average daily secondary or tertiary production. This secondary and tertiary production was allowed to remain at 22 percent, limited to the volumes of the taxpayer's depletable oil quantity.

The depletion allowance was originally obtained to provide for the exhaustion of a natural resource. It was intended to permit the tax-free recovery of capital value that straight cost depletion could not accomplish. However, with rising capital costs required to find new oil and gas reserves, the value of percentage depletion was no longer adequate for its designed task. Its existence, nevertheless, had been a political albatross for the petroleum industry since the beginning of the energy problem of the 1970's. In the punitive mood of Congress in 1974, and with the dramatic increase in oil company profits and rising crude oil prices, the death of depletion was inevitable. Fortunately for both majors and independents, their major tax preference—charging intangible development drilling costs to expenses—was left unchanged, as was cost depletion. Nevertheless,

---

[9] Stripper well production in 1973 was 385,683,527 barrels. Of this amount, about 27 percent was secondary and tertiary production. Thus, the value of depletion was still significant for a large percentage of all U.S. oil wells (see footnote 7, this chapter).

TABLE 33
Rate of Depletion and Depletable Oil and Gas Quantities
for Independent Producers, 1975

Year	Depletion Rate (percentage)	Tentative Depletable Oil Quantity (bbl./day)	Tentative Depletable Gas Quantity (cu. ft./day)
1975	22	2,000	12,000,000
1976	22	1,800	10,800,000
1977	22	1,600	9,600,000
1978	22	1,400	8,400,000
1979	22	1,200	7,200,000
1980	22	1,000	6,000,000
1981	20	1,000	6,000,000
1982	18	1,000	6,000,000
1983	16	1,000	6,000,000
1984 and years thereafter	15	1,000	6,000,000

SOURCE: L. E. Fiske, *Federal Taxation of Oil and Gas Transactions* (New York: Mathew Bender, 1975), p. 103.

loss of depletion allowance meant loss of some two billion dollars in cash flow to the industry, and capital outlays were slightly lowered by companies. Higher oil and gas prices, however, offset the negative effect of depletion elimination.

As Congress and the administration debated the question of the gradual decontrol of "old" domestic oil prices, the policy option of imposing windfall profits taxes on oil companies was considered to be a foregone conclusion. Indeed, an "emergency windfall profits tax" had been proposed by the Nixon administration as part of its Project Independence energy goals in order to restrain "excess" industry profits derived from rising prices. The windfall profits tax was to be an excise tax levied over a period of time on the excess of the crude oil field price over an escalating base price. Although the industry actively sought to have a "plowback" provision in the windfall profits tax, no such allowable appeared to be forthcoming. The impact of the decontrol of prices that appeared likely by 1976 would only result in an income redistribution away from companies to the government and indirectly to consumers.

THE ENERGY POLICY AND CONSERVATION ACT OF 1975

The end of the regulatory phase in U.S. oil policy had been generally expected by late 1975. It was widely hoped that controls on domestic oil prices and supply would be dismantled. However, the timing was not in the petroleum industry's favor. The U.S. economy, and indeed, that of the rest of the world, was suffering through the worst economic crisis since the Great Depression of the 1930's. Because of the immense importance of oil and gas to the economic infrastructure of the United States, a wide-spread debate on the decontrol of oil prices focused on its inflationary and unemployment impact on the U.S. economy. Both major and independent refiners disagreed on whether to opt for immediate decontrol versus a phaseout of price controls over a longer time period. The final result was known on December 22, 1975, when the Energy Policy and Conservation Act (EPCA) was enacted into law, Public Law 94-163.

Before the enactment of the EPCA, old crude oil prices were controlled at about $5.25 per barrel and new and released uncontrolled crude prices were averaging about $12.46 per barrel. With about 60 percent of U.S. production defined as old crude oil and 40 percent as new oil, the weighted average price was about $8.75 per barrel. Under the EPCA the average price of crude oil was to be rolled back from the $8.75 level to a weighted average first-sale price of $7.66 per barrel, a reduction of $1.09 per barrel. All U.S. crude oil was to return to some level of price controls. To achieve the weighted average of $7.66 per barrel, the Federal Energy Administration created a two-tier program that retained controls on old oil at $5.25 and maintained a weighted average first-sale price of $11.28 for upper-tier crude oil. All new, stripper, and released crude prices were rolled back to this upper-tier level. However, in applying the $11.28 upper-tier rule, the FEA decided to use the field posted price of September 30, 1975, as the reference date and therefore subtracted $1.32 to reach the new ceiling. Posted prices were slightly higher than actual sales prices in September, 1975.

The president was given full authority over annual changes in crude oil prices, and the law specified an initial discretionary limit of up to 10 percent per year. The phaseout period of price controls was forty months. In examining the new EPCA program, the FEA could exercise substantial latitude. Moreover, the $2 per barrel import fee on crude oil was removed. Table 34 displays FEA estimates of the differences in domestic composite and new oil prices after forty months of the EPCA program based on six separate scenarios. In these cases, OPEC prices are assumed either to rise annually at the rate of inflation or to remain constant at their October, 1975, levels. The FEA estimated that with a continuation of pre-EPCA controls, new oil prices would rise to $15.58 per barrel by 1980 and old oil would rise accordingly to more than double its 1975 level. The thirty-nine-month scenario assumed that new oil would sell at controlled prices of $11.50 per barrel and be increased $0.50 per month. Old oil would remain controlled. The EPCA options in Table 34 reflect the president's authority under the law to include or exclude Alaskan oil from the averaging process. In the first option, Alaskan oil is included. It is excluded in the second option with the base price of $7.66 inflated at 10 percent annually. Option 3 excludes Alaskan oil but increases prices by 12 percent in 1976 and 15 percent annually thereafter. Under all options, and at the end of the forty-month period, new oil would still be priced at $15.58. In all cases, the difference between the domestic composite price and the new price is less than the difference for the base period January, 1976, under controls, which was about $5.34 per barrel.

It was readily apparent that the EPCA options would not arrest the level of oil imports appreciably until possibly 1980. Even then, given the expected differences in foreign and domestic crude oil prices, it was likely that some form of price controls or monitoring would characterize the U.S. petroleum industry through the 1980's. Indeed, a deepening of the fifth phase of oil regulation was imposed by the EPCA in that it created the legislation for the permanent presence of executive and congressional direction in the pricing of crude oil. Reinforcing this presence was the adoption of a strategic oil storage program that was initially designed to store 500 million barrels of crude oil and products. The FEA storage program would evolve over seven years, but in the interim several special industry/government storage goals were to be met. Thus, the prospect of direct government purchases of foreign crude oil for strategic storage was likely. Not since World War II had the government become

TABLE 34

Forecast Differences in Domestic Composite and New Oil Prices after Forty Months
(Nominal $/bbl.)

Scenario	With OPEC Increases			Without Further OPEC Increases		
	Domestic Composite Price	New Oil Price	Difference	Domestic Composite Price	New Oil Price	Difference
Current controls without fees	$11.14	$15.58	$4.44	$9.85	$13.32	$3.47
Thirty-nine-month program without fees	13.45	15.58	2.13	13.32	13.32	—
Immediate decontrol without fees	15.58	15.58	—	13.32	13.32	—
Energy policy and conservation act						
option 1	9.88	15.58	5.70	9.88	13.32	3.44
option 2	11.39	15.58	4.19	11.39	13.32	1.93
option 3	12.52	15.58	3.06	12.52	13.32	.80

SOURCE: U.S. Federal Energy Administration, Office of Data and Analysis, *Analysis of Petroleum Price Decontrols in the Energy Policy and Conservation Act of 1975*, January 12, 1976, p. 5.

so thoroughly involved in the operations of the oil business. The EPCA also amended the existing rules on cost recovery and pricing of refined products. In addition, the entitlements program was continued but adjusted for the reduced value of entitlements. A special change, however, concerned refiners with capacity of less than 100,000 barrels daily. These refiners were exempted from the entitlements program; smaller refiners with access to low-cost old oil were exempted from the cost-equalizing entitlements program.

Because of the dramatic rollback in crude oil prices and the elimination of import fees, the FEA amended its regulations on "banked" costs and ruled on the pass-through of cost decreases. These "banks" amounted to about $1.2 billion as of January, 1976. The FEA specified that not more than 10 percent of the "banks" attributable to the cost of crude oil and purchased product could be passed through in any month. Future increased costs could be passed through without limitation only within two months. Later pass-throughs would be subject to the 10 percent limitation. The EPCA, furthermore, made it mandatory for refiners to allocate increased crude oil costs proportionately to No. 2 oils and aviation jet fuel. The FEA continued its "special propane rule" which requires that a volumetric proportion of increased costs be applied to propane over a one-year period. This special rule was adopted because of the seasonal nature of propane sales. With respect to the pass-through of cost decreases, the crude price rollback was reflected in a reduction in the amount of increased costs available for pass-through in a given months. Meanwhile, the FEA set out an agenda for the price decontrol of refined products and in early 1976 eliminated residual fuel oils from controls. By late 1976 plans were to eliminate controls on distillates and gasoline. Thus, the final aspect of Phase Five was to evolve to a crude oil price control program while allowing fewer controls on refined products. This decontrol aspect of the phase made integration into refining an even more valuable asset. Indeed, the yield patterns at refineries were beginning to place more emphasis on residual fuels and distillates, with the expectation that gasoline markets could remain relatively stable through the 1980's.

6

OPEC's Rise to World Economic Power

DURING the period of OPEC's early challenge to the dominance of major international oil companies, the United States had not yet formulated a long-term national or global energy supply strategy. Indeed, the U.S. government was more preoccupied with domestic issues and with the monumental problems of the Vietnam War than it was with formulating energy policy. The primary domestic energy focus was on curbing the assumed monopoly power of the majors while assuring the survival of small independents. A real demonstration of monopoly power, however, was unfolding by the end of 1970.

The greatest resource transfer in economic history was achieved by OPEC members from 1970 through 1975 by setting monopoly prices on crude oil and demanding greater "government take" and "participation" in their own domestic oil operations. The short-run economic consequence of the OPEC cartel was a massive and immediate transfer of funds from oil consumers to oil corporations to oil producers. Huge oil payments deficits on trade accounts by the major oil-consuming countries developed. Although manageable, the burden of the oil payments transfer led to considerable short-term world monetary instability. By mid-1975 there were indications that these short-term problems would give way to effective long-term solutions developed by both producing and consuming countries. By 1975 OPEC had widely advanced its concurrent take-over strategy: (1) an initial stage of raising posted prices, taxes, and royalties (government take) on oil-company-controlled "equity" crude to the level of OPEC-country-controlled "participation" crude prices, and (2) the gradual increase of the percentage of OPEC governments' ownership and control first over their domestic oil producing operations and later over refining and transport.

The OPEC energy coup was a clear manifestation of resource nationalism which soon spread to other raw materials. OPEC's long-run growth can be viewed, however, in terms of three separate stages of resource nationalism: (1) the formative years from 1960 to 1970, (2) the government revenue maximizing stage from 1970 to 1974, and (3) the consolidation or stabilization stage from 1974 to the present. As a countervailing response, the reaction of the United States was two-fold: (1) a push for cooperation and coordination among oil consuming countries through the development of the International Energy Agency (IEA), and (2) pronounced regulation of output and price of the domestic petroleum industry as a stepping-stone to forging a domestic energy policy. The United States had finally resorted to government direction and planning on a global scale to deal with both the power of OPEC and the imbalanced economic bridge between OPEC, the multinational oil companies, and the oil consumer.

Stage One: OPEC as a Price Follower, 1960–1970

The level and structure of posted prices in the Middle East remained essentially unchanged from 1960 to 1971. Before the creation of OPEC in September, 1960, world crude oil prices demonstrated considerable "softness." Disguised indirect discounts of Persian Gulf posted prices were employed to market Middle East crude. These discounting methods included long-term financing of crude oil purchases, acceptance of soft currencies as partial payment by American suppliers, extra concessions for quality differences, "spiking" of crude with refined products, freight allowances on delivered prices, and recharter of vessels at favorable rates to f.o.b. buyers (Frank 1966). Because the budgets of Middle East governments were primarily based on revenues from their oil production, any reduction in the posted price resulted in considerable fiscal instability. In August, 1960, following the unilateral cut of fourteen cents per barrel in the posted price of its Middle East oil by

Standard of New Jersey, the oil-producing countries organized to form OPEC and demanded both a reversion of the price cut and future stable posted prices (Lubell 1963; Klebanoff 1974; Hartshorn 1967; Rouhani 1971).

Posted prices, the artificial rates upon which government tax and royalty take are computed, did remain constant from 1960 to 1970.[1] Indeed, the post-1960 percentage of profit split between producing countries and oil companies shifted in favor of the producing countries. As Table 35 shows, from 1960 to 1970 the average take by an OPEC country had risen from 57 percent to 76 percent of total profit. In 1970 Iran was earning eighty-nine cents on each barrel of crude produced, a nine-cent increase over the decade, while oil company profit had dropped to twenty-eight cents on each barrel.

Stage Two: OPEC as a Price Leader

Negotiations in 1971 by the major oil companies were actually with individual OPEC member countries, basically the Persian

TABLE 35
Posted Price, Government Take, and Profit Split
on OPEC Crude Oil, 1960-1970*
(dollars/bbl.)

Year	Posted Price	Realized Price	Govt. Tax Take (current dollars)	Indicated Co. Profit	Profit Split (percent) Co.	Govt.
1960	$1.78	$1.54	$0.80	$0.61	43	57
1965	1.79	1.44	0.83	0.48	37	63
1966	1.79	1.38	0.87	0.38	30	70
1967	1.79	1.38	0.87	0.38	30	70
1968	1.79	1.38	0.88	0.37	30	70
1969	1.79	1.28	0.89	0.26	23	77
1970	1.79	1.30	0.89	0.28	24	76

* Based on representative Iranian light crude.

[1] Posted prices were introduced into the Middle East by ARAMCO and the government of Saudi Arabia in 1950 (see Stocking 1970).

Gulf producers and Libya. At Tehran in February, 1971, the oil companies agreed with the Persian Gulf producer states on increases in posted price. They also accepted changes in taxation and a schedule of future price increases that extended to 1975. At Tripoli in April, 1971, the principles of the Tehran agreement were adapted to the case of Libya with the addition to the posted price of a low-sulfur premium, a Suez Canal closure premium, and a freight rate component. This agreement, with various adjustments, was later accepted by Nigeria, Saudi Arabia, and Iraq. Venezuela, Algeria, and Indonesia did not directly participate in the Tehran and Tripoli agreements, but they did go along with the general rise in posted prices, taxes, and royalties. Table 36 shows the record of representative posted prices up to June, 1971, after which an adjustment for inflation was imposed. Persian Gulf prices in general went up 30 percent from their 1970 levels.

Less than one month after these five-year agreements were signed, OPEC member states decided at their Vienna meeting on July 12 to press for "governmental participation" in the ownership of concession-holding companies. The demands for participation were made chiefly by the six members in the Persian Gulf, Libya, and Nigeria. Circumstances in Venezuela, Indonesia, and Algeria were different. In Venezuela, concessions were already near their end, with about 70 percent due for relinquishment by 1984. In Indonesia there were no concession agreements, as most companies operated on a production-sharing or contract-of-work basis. In Algeria, agreement had already been reached on a 51 percent interest in the concessions of Getty, Cie Francais du Petrole (CFP), and

TABLE 36
Representative Crude Price Postings, 1970–1971
(dollars/bbl.)

Crude	June 1970	Jan. 1971	June 1971
Iranian light 34°	$1.79	$1.79	$2.274
Arabian light 27°	1.47	1.56	2.059
Libya (Brega) 40°	2.21	2.55	3.423

SOURCE: *Petroleum Economist* 37, no. 6 (June, 1970); 38, no. 1 (Jan., 1971); 38, no. 6 (June, 1971).

Sonatrach (the state oil company) with Elf. As Table 37 shows, most Persian Gulf concessions made before 1971 were to expire about the year 2000. The classic concessions of the Iraq Petroleum Company and its affiliates, the Kuwait Oil Company, and ARAMCO had about thirty years to go.

As a prelude to participation negotiations, at Geneva in January, 1972, OPEC again increased posted prices by 8.49 percent to compensate for the devaluation of the U.S. dollar in terms of gold (the gold price increased from thirty-five to thirty-eight dollars an ounce). The Geneva agreement of January, 1972, was again used to justify a further increase in April (6 percent) following an additional devaluation of the dollar. Under the Geneva formula, the dollar had been tied to a group of major world currencies. Negotiations on participation continued through 1972, and on December 20,

TABLE 37

Expiration Dates on Selected OPEC Concessions before
Demands for Participation

Country	Company and Ownership	Expiration Date
Saudi Arabia	ARAMCO (Socal/Texaco/Esso/Mobil)	1999
Kuwait	Kuwait Oil Company (BP/Gulf)	2026
	Arabian Oil Company (Japan Petroleum Trading/ Kuwait govt./Saudi govt.)	2003
Iran	Iranian Consortium (BP/Shell/Socal/Esso/Mobil/ Gulf/Texaco/CFP)	1994
Iraq	Iraq Petroleum Co. (BP/Shell/CFP/Esso/Mobil/Partex)	2000
Abu Dhabi	Abu Dhabi Petroleum Co. (BP/Shell/CFP/Esso/Mobil/Partex)	2014
Libya	Occidental	2016
	BP/Hunt	2011
	Esso Standard	2011
Nigeria	Gulf Oil	1996
	Shell/BP Petroleum Dev.	1989

Source: *Petroleum Economist* 38, no. 12 (Dec., 1971): 449.

1972, a general agreement on participation was signed in Riyadh by Saudi Arabia and Abu Dhabi which provided that the government's share would be an initial 25 percent participation beginning in January, 1973, and would rise to 30 percent in 1978, 35 percent in 1974, 40 percent in 1980, 45 percent in 1981, and 51 percent in 1982 (*Middle East Economic Survey*, Jan., 1975). The foreign oil companies were allowed to buy back the volume of crude—participation crude—then under government ownership at "buy-back" prices well above their tax-paid costs on their remaining 75 percent equity, or concession, crude.[2] The total payments for their 25 percent participation by OPEC countries to oil companies, based on an updated book value formula, were as follows: Saudi Arabia to the Arabian American Oil Company (ARAMCO), $500 million; Kuwait to the Kuwait Oil Company (KOC), $150 million; Iraq to the Basrah Petroleum Company (BPC), $68 million; Qatar, $71 million ($28 million for the Qatar Petroleum Company onshore and $43 million for Shell offshore); and Abu Dhabi, $162 million ($81 million for the Abu Dhabi Petroleum Company onshore and $81 million for Abu Dhabi Marine Areas offshore). Participation was allowed to be either the undivided interest form of concession ownership or the corporate form. Saudi Arabia opted for the corporate form by purchasing a 25 percent interest in ARAMCO, a Delaware corporation.

The impact of these Tehran-Tripoli-Geneva agreements was to establish a two-tier price structure: one for equity or company-controlled crude, and the other for buy-back or participation crude. The cost of crude from the Persian Gulf came to be evaluated in terms of its weighted average cost of equity crude plus participation crude. The immediate reaction of oil companies was to raise prices by eighteen cents per barrel to their term contract customers—seven cents per barrel for escalations under the Tehran-Geneva agreements and eleven cents per barrel for the average cost of participation. As a benchmark for pricing their participation oil to customers, Saudi Arabia set their basic selling price at 93 percent of posted price. Saudi government take increased from $1.51 per barrel in January, 1973, to $1.80 per barrel in August, 1973.

[2] The terms allowed for "bridging" crude and "phase-in" crude, but these technical distinctions later became relatively unimportant.

In May, 1973, Saudi Arabia's directly marketed participation oil (68.5 million barrels) was sold at $2.55 per barrel. The Saudi strategy was to sell to nonmajor third parties and carve out a market position for its state oil company, PETROMIN. Major oil companies that applied (Mobil and Shell) were disqualified from eligibility for purchasing Saudi participation crude. Typical third-party purchasers were Tenneco, Ashland Oil, New England Petroleum, Coastal States, Shaheen Natural Resources, and numerous Japanese and European customers. These direct sales of Saudi crude, however, only amounted to about 6 percent of ARAMCO's production. The remaining percentage of Saudi participation crude was by agreement automatically bought back by the ARAMCO partners at the same third-party sales price (93 percent of posted price.)

The loss of this "cost" or equity crude available to the majors was not as great in Saudi Arabia as it was in Algeria, Iraq, and Libya, where nationalization of oil operations occurred. In Iran the situation differed in that a new agreement in 1973 was signed in which the National Iranian Oil Company (NIOC) would take over all of the operations of the Iranian consortium. Under this new agreement, the companies were entitled to buy the bulk of Iran's output under a schedule extending twenty years, with the remaining output sold directly by NIOC. The price paid by the companies was set in accordance with prevailing average prices in the Persian Gulf, that is, an average of the equity crude and participation crude prices. Interim agreements between Iraq Petroleum Company (IPC) and Iraq's government and between Libya and several independents and majors remained unsettled through most of 1973, although most independents acquiesced in Libya to 51 percent nationalization. In Nigeria the government increased its share to 35 percent. In Latin America, Venezuela announced production restrictions, and similar moves were announced by Ecuador.

THE OIL EMBARGO

Success in increasing total government take and in participation was only the beginning in the politically motivated price and production strategy of the Persian Gulf states in 1973. Stability in prices, one of the assumed goals of the Tehran-Geneva agreement, was soon shattered by the events that began with Arab-Israeli hostilities in October, 1973. In October the Arab bloc within OPEC, the Organization of Arab Petroleum Exporting Countries (OAPEC), announced a 5 percent cutback in crude oil production and threatened an embargo. On the same day they unilaterally raised the level of posted prices by about 70 percent and in effect abandoned the five-year Tehran agreement. On November 4 a further cutback of 25 percent of September, 1973, production was announced, and an embargo on oil shipments to the United States and Holland was put into effect. Iraq did not participate in the production cutbacks against the United States; however, the Iraq National Oil Company took over most of the nationalized oil operations as Iran had done earlier.

The effects of the embargo became evident in November as U.S. imports from OAPEC declined to 950,000 barrels per day from the October level of 1,175,000 barrels per day. The lowest import level was reached by January, 1974, at some 30,000 barrels daily from the OAPEC group. However, increased liftings from non-Arab OPEC member states Iran, Indonesia, Nigeria, and eventually Ecuador offset this interruption to some extent. Nonetheless, because oil tankers normally take fifty to sixty days to make the trip from the Persian Gulf to the United States, the impact of the embargo on the United States in December and January was much greater. The embargo by Arab OPEC members against the United States ended in March, 1974, and was lifted from Holland in July. (Embargoes against Portugal, South Africa, and Rhodesia, related to a show of solidarity with the African countries, continued.)

After the October hikes in posted prices and the announcement of the embargo, a worldwide scramble for oil supply developed, and spot sales prices of crude were recorded at fifteen dollars and twenty dollars per barrel. This panic buying further strengthened the power and daring of OPEC, and in January, 1974, the new posted prices of October were again doubled. Increases in official OPEC prices versus OPEC "government take" per barrel from October 1, 1973, to January 1, 1974, were startling. Government take increased from $1.87 per barrel to $7.11 per barrel during that period for Saudi crude.

FULL TAKEOVER OF CONCESSIONS AND
COORDINATED PRICING POLICY

By March, 1974, Middle East governments were demanding even greater participation in their oil operations. The new demand was for sixty-forty participation between governments and oil companies. It soon became obvious to the companies that their position of control over equity or cost crude was vanishing. The sixty-forty principle gained immediate OPEC acceptance, and in March Kuwait reached agreement with British Petroleum (BP) and Gulf Oil on sixty-forty participation with buy-back prices at 95 percent of posted prices, retroactive to January 1, 1974. Similar "understandings" were achieved by Saudi Arabia, and in April Nigeria took a 55 percent participation.

Growing evidence of the responsiveness of the quantity demanded of oil to changes in its price—the elasticity of demand for oil—influenced OPEC's subsequent revenue strategy toward narrowing the gap between tax-paid costs on equity crude and buy-back prices for participation crude. Although the Saudis were giving lip service to supporting a reduction in posted prices, they were the leaders in supporting increases in tax-paid costs. Indeed, a letter to Saudi Oil Minister Yamani from the general manager of Italy's Ente Nazionale Idrocarburi (ENI) claimed that the majors had an average cost advantage over the independents. Arguing that the majors had a profit margin of $3.72 between the tax-paid cost of $7.11 per barrel and the market price of $10.83 per barrel, ENI's manager then proposed a margin of $0.50 per barrel. This figure was to be attained either by reducing market price to $9.50 per barrel and moderately increasing taxes to $9.00 per barrel (Alternate B) or by leaving prices unchanged and increasing taxes significantly to $10.33 per barrel (Alternate A). In reply, Yamani stated, "We certainly do not agree to or see any justification for a reduction in the market price of oil. We would favor a situation more in line with Alternative A as mentioned in your letter and will see to it that it can be accomplished in the near future."[3] The ENI

---

[3] ENI, through its dynamic leader Enrico Mattei, had been an irritant to internationals in suggesting more aggressive Middle East government action against the "Seven Sisters." For example, Mattei espoused participation long

letter was incorrect with respect to its declared profit margin of $3.73 per barrel, since weighted equity/participation crude average prices were the relevant consideration in comparing the cost structure of the independents with that of the integrated majors.

It is pertinent to note here that U.S. oil policy makers persistently placed their hopes for a decline in the price of OPEC crude oil on the Saudis. The Treasury Department and the State Department continuously prophesied that oil prices would fall and implied that OPEC would collapse as a cartel if prices were not lowered. Individual trips were made to the Middle East to argue the case for a reduction in oil prices, and each time, the U.S. government officials declared that it was not a question of *whether* oil prices would fall but *when*. The treasury secretary was particularly unbending in the face of facts contrary to his impression that he had "assurances" from the Saudis that they would seek price reductions and indeed initiate this effort by a two-million-barrel-per-day crude oil auction in August, 1974. The promised Saudi auction was cancelled.

Middle East governments were committed to increasing their own government revenues, and they well knew that by increasing tax rates or royalty rates, even while allowing small reductions in posted prices, their government take would increase. Any increase in government take meant an increase in average world crude oil prices and hence a worsening payment problem for consuming countries. At their June, 1974, meeting in Quito, OPEC decided to leave posted prices unchanged. The governments nevertheless agreed to add two percentage points to their royalty rates,

---

before the now obsolete Tehran-Geneva agreements. Nonetheless, the design of OPEC's long-term strategy was clearly spelled out in 1969 by Yamani when he noted, "the majors are the only means of market stability available to us. But if they lose their power in the market, they will lose their attraction for us; they will mean nothing to us." Yamani stated that he sought participation as an "insurance premium to safeguard the security of our future income." He added, "our aim is firstly to strengthen the majors and their role whether directly or indirectly, in the world market in order to maintain prices; and secondly to enable our national companies to grow in the market." Yamani clearly intended both upstream and downstream operations. See Yamani's essay, "Participation versus Nationalization: A Better Means to Survive," in Mikdashi (1970) and also in Hartshorn (1967).

increasing them from 12.5 percent to 14.5 percent of posted prices. Venezuela, however, went its own way. It raised its "tax reference" prices (similar to posted prices) by an average of $0.35 and also threatened to increase tax rates. The Saudis declined to go along with the Quito increases. At the organization's next regular quarterly meeting in Vienna, the OPEC governments decided to increase the total government take by 3.5 percent, effective October 1, to "compensate for inflation in the industrialized countries." The increase was solely on equity crudes and had the effect of increasing the average take for OPEC governments from $9.41 to $9.74 per barrel. Saudi Arabia refused to go along with the Vienna increase as well. For the fourth quarter of 1974, posted prices were to remain unchanged.

The ostensible isolation of Saudi Arabia from other Arab states tended to give credibility to the U.S. forecast of a decline in the OPEC oil price. However, the Saudi position is explained by its ongoing negotiations for the 100 percent takeover of ARAMCO. Moreover, the Saudis appeared to be locked in a policy battle with Iran over the price leadership of OPEC, with the Iranians continuously arguing for higher posted prices. In this context, the Saudis, Abu Dhabi, and Qatar startled the major oil companies on November 1 by announcing a new pricing formula that had the effect of increasing the average weighted cost to oil companies by $0.40 per barrel. The new Saudi pricing formula consisted of four key elements: (1) crude oil posted prices were cut $0.40 per barrel across the board with no allowances for differences in quality, gravity, or location; (2) income tax rates were hiked to 85 percent from the basic 65.75 percent level that had become effective on October 1; (3) royalty rates were raised to 20 percent from the 16.66 percent that had taken effect on October 1; and (4) buy-back oil sold to the concessionary companies was to be priced at 94.85 percent (instead of 93 percent) of the new lower posted prices. Those terms were actually more stringent than those imposed at OPEC's September meeting. The Saudis announced that their new system would remain in effect for nine months, to July, 1975.

Given this price turnaround by the Saudis, the OPEC oil ministers met in Vienna in Decmber, 1974, to construct a uniform pricing system that, when imposed, would provide the same financial effect as the Saudis' system. At this 42nd Ministerial Conference of OPEC, government take on the activities of the operating companies was increased to $10.12 per barrel based on the benchmark Saudi Arabian (gravity API 34°) light crude. Although the Saudis had their own policy, Saudi crude was used as the standard on which pricing changes were based. This Vienna conference was significant in that it organized a benchmark pricing scheme that ostensibly set the framework for ending the awkward posted price and fiscal system, while individual OPEC member countries negotiated full 100 percent takeovers from their concessionnaire oil companies. The Vienna meeting also imposed a nine-month freeze on posted prices and delayed the formalizing of an inflation index to guide future crude oil price changes. Finally, the Vienna meeting imposed lower theoretical profit margins on the major oil companies and attempted to limit their capacity to expand their market shares by reselling OPEC crude oil in world markets outside the requirements of their own integrated corporations. Thus, OPEC countries were attempting to arbitrarily carve a share of the total world crude oil market for their own national oil companies. In effect, the traditional Persian Gulf–plus crude oil pricing system was formally redesigned as a Saudi Arabian light crude–plus formula.

The new tax-paid cost to oil companies of $10.12 was the weighted average of government take on equity oil (42.1 percent of oil company liftings) and on participation oil (57.9 percent of oil company liftings) made on the basis of the November Saudi decision. The $10.12 level represented an increase of $0.38 per barrel over the previous weighted average of $9.74 per barrel prevailing in October, 1974. The $0.38 was achieved by increasing government take on equity oil from $8.255 to $9.815 per barrel (up $1.56) coupled with a reduction from $10.835 to $10.463 per barrel (down $0.372) in the buy-back price of participation crude on the basis of a price equal to 93 percent of the new postings decided on by the Saudis in November. In applying this still awkward OPEC formula, individual producer states could opt to charge income taxes, royalties, or buy-back prices or develop new mechanisms to achieve the same fiscal result of $10.12 government take. For example, Kuwait opted to set the oil companies' per-barrel costs at a flat rate identical to "averaged" government take (based on a theoretical forty-sixty split of equity and participation oil). BP and Gulf Oil were to pay a "single acquisition cost" for Kuwaiti crude consisting of equity oil cost, buy-back oil cost, and a new supplemental oil cost. The three totaled $10.15 per barrel, or $0.71 over the oil companies' average October 1 cost of $9.44 per barrel. The new $10.15 cost (including $0.08 per barrel in production cost) was exactly the amount needed to achieve a government take of $10.07 per barrel, which was equivalent to OPEC's theoretical $10.12 per barrel take on Saudi marker crude.

Under these new pricing rules, the oil company profit margins were totally subject to policies the OPEC countries followed on their own direct sales of crude. On benchmark Saudi light crude, company profit margin was reduced from the October 1 level of about thirty-five cents per barrel to about twenty-two cents per barrel on January 1. (The Saudi price system of November 1 was actually more limiting than that finally decided upon at the OPEC ministerial conference, since it allowed a profit margin of only eleven cents per barrel.) The theoretical margin of $0.22 between the companies' weighted tax-paid cost ($10.12) plus lifting cost ($0.12) and the $10.46 government selling price (posted price of $11.26 per barrel × .93 = $10.46) placed a ceiling on company selling prices. If companies limited their offtake to 40 percent equity oil at a tax-paid cost of $9.92 per barrel, the $10.46 would provide a theoretical ceiling of $0.54 per barrel. As the OPEC oil minsters saw it, if the oil companies chose to compete with OPEC national oil companies, they would be forced to reduce their profit margins. Such a conclusion, however, was not warranted, as oil companies had little interest in absorbing these cost increases.

The January, 1975, OPEC price increases did not eliminate the existing structure of premium prices charged for crudes of better quality or those closer to market. Prices were adjusted upward for differences in gravity and for low sulfur content in Libya, Algeria, Nigeria, Abu Dhabi, Iran, Qatar, and the special case of Indonesia. These prices were set well above the OPEC average price, but the lower level of world demand soon placed inordinate pressure on these countries to bring their crude prices into line. This issue of premium prices for all OPEC countries was deferred to late 1975. Table 38 indicates the values of the special premiums, which were

TABLE 38

Special Price Premiums above OPEC Base Posted Price of
Key Middle East and African Crude Oils, Early 1975

Crude Oil	Gravity (API)	Marker Base	Differentials			Current Posting
			Gravity	Sulfur	Freight	
Arab light	34°	$11.251	—	—	—	$11.251
Iran light	34°	11.251	—	+0.250	−0.026	11.475
Abu Dhabi						
Murban	39°	11.251	+0.300	+0.300	−0.015	11.836
Zakum	40°	11.251	+0.360	+0.150	+0.005	11.76
Qatar (Dukhan)	40°	11.251	+0.360	+0.420	−0.017	12.014
Nigerian light	34°	11.651*	—	+1.300	+1.740	14.691
Libyan	40°	11.651	+0.360	+1.336	+2.421	15.768

SOURCE: *Petroleum Intelligence Weekly* 14, no. 9 (March 3, 1975): 4. Reproduced by written permission. Copyright 1975 by Petroleum & Energy Intelligence Weekly, Inc.

* Based on "old" pre-November 1, 1974, posting for Arab light.

nonetheless selectively trimmed through 1975. Adjustments of the overpriced crudes was a normal reaction to world market conditions.

Stage Three: Consolidation of Price Leadership

From late 1974 through 1975 a framework for what can be called the consolidation stage of OPEC evolved. Recessionary conditions were contributing to low world demand for crude oil. The oil companies reduced their liftings of participation crude while generally maintaining equity crude liftings. OPEC countries were unable to market all of their own crude oil by 1975, and some 25 percent of OPEC's production capacity was shut in. As a result, oil revenue volumes declined sharply while OPEC government spending continued to rise. These difficult conditions in 1975 forced the gradual erosion of certain OPEC oil prices that were out of line with the more appropriate average levels. This experience tended to restore in the minds of OPEC leaders their conviction that the major oil companies did have value and were an important element in maintaining stability in the oil revenue flows.

The consolidation stage was characterized through 1975 and early 1976 by the full takeover in certain OPEC countries (Venezuela and Kuwait) of oil operations while changes in the price of oil became more gradual and more cautious. Following the end of the initial nine-month price freeze, OPEC ministers meeting in Vienna in September, 1975, raised the price of the benchmark or "marker" crude, Arab light, from $10.46 per barrel to $11.51 per barrel, an increase of 10 percent. Another nine-month price freeze was imposed to June, 1976. Although the Economic Commission Board of OPEC had struggled with various formulas by which to justify alternative levels of price increases, no single formula or index could be decided upon. After extended debate, OPEC settled on the 10 percent increase, which actually increased "government take" by 10.4 percent, as shown in Table 39. As the table shows, the average government take of $10.12 per barrel increased 10.3 percent to $11.175, while average costs to oil companies of participation and equity crude increased about 10.24 percent to $11.295 per barrel. This calculation assumes the $0.12 per barrel lifting costs employed by OPEC; however, there is substantial evidence that actual lifting costs are about twice as large as that amount. In this case, the profit margin to companies would derive from the length of credit terms on oil payments and the lowered average cost to companies as the volume of participation oil bought back from the governments falls below the full 60 percent. Even then, the assumption that oil companies effectively resell crude at $10.46 or that this net return is achieved from product prices under current economic conditions was questionable. Assuming that oil companies achieved their $0.22 margin, and given current tanker freight rates at about Worldscale 57.7 and existing special fees on crude imports, the landed cost of crude oil (over API 25°) into the United States was over $14.50 per barrel. In the case of Japan, where most crude is imported from Iran, Saudi Arabia, the United Arab Republic, and Indonesia, the average landed cost of crude oil would have been $13.25 per barrel.

Venezuela nationalized the physical assets of all foreign oil operations in November, 1975; this action was followed in early December with final agreement between Kuwait and Kuwait Oil Company (Gulf Oil and BP) on the acquisition of their remaining 40 percent share of KOC. ARAMCO negotiations were expected to achieve agreement "in principle" with Saudi Arabia, and contract meetings with Iran were scheduled in 1976. In other countries, the sixty-forty relationship was continued, and in Nigeria the government took over the responsibility for marketing its full 55 percent of participation oil output beginning on January 1, 1976. Other countries, such as Indonesia, set about to gradually increase government take as a means of easing their financial burdens.

Thus, it was apparent by early 1976 that OPEC would consist of a mix of countries where oil operations were either fully nationalized as part of official policy or where nationalization was resisted, and the sixty-forty general relationship was to prevail through 1980. Nevertheless, the important role of the major oil companies in most OPEC countries was generally assured by virtue of new joint arrangements made in the refining, transportation, and marketing sectors of the business and, in some countries, in a continuation of the exploration and production role. Many of the OPEC nations still required access to the capital sources and technical expertise of the companies. The consolidation phase was to be

TABLE 39
Impact of OPEC Vienna, 1975, Price Increase on
Oil Companies and Government Take

	Government Take* Impact, Arab Light 34° (dollars/bbl.)	OPEC Price Declaration, Arab Light 34° (dollars/bbl.)
(1) Posted price	$11.251	$11.251
(2) Buy-back price (93 percent of posted)	10.460	10.460
(3) Government take on equity crude	9.790	
(4) Production cost	.120	
(5) Tax-paid cost equity crude	9.910	
(6) Average govt. take on participation and equity crude (60/40)	10.120	
(7) Vienna price increase	1.050	1.050
(8) New government take	11.170	
(9) Add (4)	.120	
(10) Average cost to oil companies	11.290	
(11) Theoretical oil company margin [(2) − (4) − (6)]	.220	
(12) Total new OPEC Arab crude price	$11.510	$11.510

* Government take based on 85 percent tax rate and 20 percent royalty rate adopted as of November, 1974.

characterized by both price leadership in OPEC and cooperative commercial ventures with the oil companies. Resource exploitation shifted to resource nationalism, and this nationalism in turn shifted to a program of collaborative economic development.

Consuming Nation Responses

The incidence of gasoline and fuel oils price increases to consumers worldwide through 1974 and 1975 set off nothing less than revolutionary responses by governments and their monetary authorities. The monetary authorities engaged in huge-scale oil revenue recycling activities while the seeds for a permanent worldwide governmental energy planning effort unfolded. In the United States a massive energy bureaucracy was established as the FEA and the State Department led in the establishment of the International Energy Agency (IEA) to seek cooperation among the major energy-consuming countries.

Throughout this period, the strategy of the major oil-consuming countries to control the pricing power of OPEC took several conflicting twists. Adopting "security of oil supply" as a justification, several countries concluded that the oil supply business was too important to be left to oil companies and proceeded to initiate direct government-to-government oil supply deals. This bilateral policy was clearly manifested by the position of the French government, which attempted to secure Saudi Arabian crude while rejecting the U.S. government's efforts to get the major oil-consuming countries coordinated in a response to OPEC. The U.S. government announced its "Project Independence" energy plan, which was initially a blueprint for total energy freedom from OPEC. An intensive monitoring of major oil company operations by the FEA also continued.

The oil companies had to continue operations under a worldwide political assault on their profit-making flexibility; the OPEC countries were weakening the resource strength of the companies by acquiring control of oil production; and the oil-consuming countries imposed punitive tax legislation and set up a massive regulatory system to control imports, the prices of domestic production of crude oil and refined products, and the allocation of supplies. Nevertheless, higher crude oil prices, higher product prices, and the resultant inventory profits provided major oil companies the greatest profits in their corporate history. These record profits in 1973 and 1974 provided the ultimate rallying points for the industry's political opponents. The industry, according to its critics, was presumably gaining at the expense of the oil consumer during a period when recession, high inflation, and high unemployment were clearly evident. OPEC obviously exploited the transparent political power of the oil companies, but more decisively it took advantage of the indecision of major OECD governments. Nevertheless, because the oil companies were identified with the monopoly powers of OPEC, the oil industry was strapped with controls by its own governments.

However, to the consumer governments it soon became apparent that the only substantive short-run weapon effective against the cartel would be involuntary energy conservation induced by the price mechanism. Indeed, changes in the inelasticity of world oil demand—one cornerstone of OPEC power—were evident by late 1974 and through 1975. For the oil companies, however, the 1973–1974 period was one in which their practical value was being seriously questioned by the cartel members.

EVIDENCE OF OIL DEMAND ELASTICITY AND THE HOPE FOR OPEC'S COLLAPSE

Through the first half of 1974 various OPEC governments attempted to market or auction their participation crude at full posted prices, but the panic buying of nonembargoed oil that had gone on from October, 1973, to January, 1974, was over. With production restrictions removed, there was an adequate world oil supply and hence greater buyer resistance to the higher asking prices on spot sales. In addition, as product prices in the various oil-consuming nations increased, consumers began to economize on the use of refined products. Governments began to impose a mix of voluntary and mandatory restraints on energy use; even for countries heavily dependent on imported oil, consumption *declined* significantly through the first six months of 1974. Table 40 shows the degree of energy and oil dependence by all OECD countries. In OECD Europe, oil accounted for 61 percent of energy requirements, and nearly 98 percent of that oil was imported. For all OECD countries, including the United States, Canada, and Japan, imports accounted for 66 percent of requirements. Table 41 shows the apparent changes in the consumption of oil in 1974. With the exception of Canada and Spain, oil consumption fell dramatically for OECD countries during the first half of 1974. This consumer reaction continued through 1974 and early 1975, but it may have been initially stimulated by the serious world recession of 1974–1975, and the price increases may have accounted only for a smaller fraction of the total decline in the

TABLE 40
Degree of Energy and Oil Dependence
by OECD Countries, 1973

Country	Net Energy and Oil Imports As Percentage of Total Primary Energy Requirements		Net Oil Imports As Percentage of Total Oil Requirements
	All Sources	Oil	
Canada	−21.2	−8.0	−15.2
United States	16.4	16.9	36.6
Japan	92.4	81.0	100.0
France	82.0	72.1	100.0
Germany	56.0	49.6	96.8
Italy	83.3	76.4	96.3
United Kingdom	46.8	46.9	98.3
Belgium	85.5	60.2	96.6
Netherlands	19.2	52.3	92.0
Denmark	100.0	90.4	100.0
Norway	47.4	44.7	89.6
Sweden	81.1	76.7	98.4
Spain	79.0	73.3	100.0
EEC	61.6	59.4	98.2
OECD Europe	64.0	61.0	97.8
OECD Total	36.9	36.2	66.0

Source: Organization for Economic Cooperation and Development, *OECD Economic Outlook* 16 (December, 1974): 110.

demand for oil. Milder weather, in addition, also accounted for lower demand.

These reductions in consumption began to show in the form of (1) unseasonably high crude oil and product inventories of major oil companies, (2) rising spare productive capacity of OPEC countries, (3) an increase in world oil tanker capacity, and (4) excess refining and chemical plant operating capacity. In spite of production cutbacks in the name of conservation, like those that occurred in Venezuela and Kuwait, substantial volumes of crude were available by mid-1974, but they had few takers. Many OPEC members took their royalties in crude and, along with their participation crude, attempted to auction these volumes at 93 percent to 94 per-

TABLE 41
Percentage of Changes in the Consumption
of Oil, 1974
(Jan.–June, 1974, over Jan.–June, 1973)

Country	All Products	Industry and Energy	Road*	Residential
Canada	5.9	7.6	4.1	6.7
United States	−4.9	−11.3	−4.7	−4.5
Japan	−0.7	−3.7	−2.5	7.6
France	−5.7	−3.9	−3.6	−12.6
Germany	−14.3	−20.3	−6.4	−19.3
Italy	−3.7	−5.3	−2.5	6.1
United Kingdom	−9.5	−12.2	−4.7	−14.0
Belgium	−19.4	−30.1	−10.3	−13.2
Luxembourg	−15.8	−24.6	7.1	−17.6
Netherlands	−14.2	−32.7	−11.3	−55.8
Austria	−12.2	−16.3	−8.1	—
Denmark	−18.6	−21.4	−8.5	−18.7
Norway	−10.6	11.5	6.2	−23.4
Sweden	−12.3	−2.7	−12.8	−23.4
Switzerland	−9.2	−12.1	−7.7	−9.9
Spain	11.7	21.8	3.1	−13.3

SOURCE: Organization for Economic Cooperation and Development, *OECD Economic Outlook*, 16 (December, 1974): 110.
* Road includes gasoline and diesel oil. The breakdown does not add up to the total due to other uses of oil not reported here.

cent of the high posted price. With product prices falling on European markets, there were few buyers for crude at the asking price.

Another reflection of world oil industry conditions was the dramatic decline in oil tanker freight rates as measured by the World-scale (WS) index. WS 100 is the normal freight rate for oil commodities from all origins and destinations, and supply and demand for tankers can lower or increase the base rate. The virtual collapse of these competitive rates in 1974 was the combined result of a reduced demand for oil tanker services plus an excess tanker supply caused by the introduction of new tanker capacity. When the oil embargo against the United States was lifted in March, 1974, the impact of unfixed tonnage—available ships not under either spot or term charter—in the Persian Gulf caused rates to continue to fall.

Very large crude carriers (VLCCs) could only bring WS 50 in May, 1974, down from WS 85 at the beginning of the year. By late August, VLCCs were taken at WS 35 or less for cargoes from the Persian Gulf to Europe. At that rate, few VLCCs could even recover their fixed costs.[4] A world tanker surplus emerged and was expected to persist until 1980. By the end of 1974, the world operating oil fleet was 264.6 million deadweight tons, with 5.3 million deadweight tons laid up in spite of the fact that 7.0 million deadweight tons of capacity in combined carriers had left the oil fleet.[5]

By the first quarter of 1975, 8.3 million deadweight tons of tanker tonnage had been delivered, 1.6 million deadweight tons had been scrapped, and idled tonnage had increased to 19.3 million deadweight tons, or some 7 percent of the world fleet.[6] As one consequence of these declining Worldscale rates, crude oils from the Persian Gulf became more competitive over wider distances and hence could compete effectively against the crudes demanding premium rates. Consequently, special freight premium values were all but eliminated. A realignment of the special gravity, freight, and sulfur quality premium differentials built into the sales prices of crude oils was formally approved by the OPEC ministers at the March, 1975, meeting.

Abu Dhabi was the first Arab country in the Persian Gulf to lower its premiums in order to compensate for lower government oil sales. Premiums were lowered some $0.60 per barrel, and sixty-day credit terms on payment were granted. However, these cuts still left this crude some $0.55 per barrel more expensive than Arab light crude delivered to Europe. Algerian, Libyan, and Nigerian crudes were about $1.00 per barrel more expensive than Arab light in

---

[4] The break-even cost for tankers has shifted through the years, reflecting technical advances in size. The average tanker was about 18,000 deadweight tons in 1958 and 57,300 deadweight tons in 1973, with the average size along the most important oil routes increasing from 32,000 deadweight tons in 1958 to 79,000 deadweight tons in 1973. The break-even tanker rates in the Worldscale index in mid-1974 were 50,000 d.w.t., WS 47.5; 70,000 d.w.t., WS 41; 90,000 d.w.t., WS 37.5; 120,000 d.w.t., WS 34; 160,000 d.w.t., WS 31.5; 200,000 d.w.t., WS 30; 300,000 d.w.t., WS 27. A VLCC is generally considered to be a vessel over 160,000 deadweight tons (see Nelson 1974).

[5] See *Petroleum Times*, May 2, 1975.

[6] Ibid. Cancellations of new tankers were also seen as necessary. See *Petroleum Times*, November, 1974.

Europe. Through early 1975 Algeria lowered its average sales price to $11.75 per barrel with thirty days' credit, Libya lowered producers' offtake costs to $11.20, and Nigeria reduced its direct sale price to $11.40. Before the September, 1975, OPEC meeting, the only Arab country to lower its prices below the Arab light market crude was a non-OPEC country, Oman, which reduced its average offtake cost to $10.17 per barrel, $0.07 per barrel cheaper than comparable Saudi crude.

These short-run OPEC price adjustments were taken as evidence by many governments of the imminent collapse in world oil prices and eventually of OPEC itself. Indeed, oil production by OPEC countries was far below its capacity levels through 1975. Table 42 shows the level of OPEC output through the first half of 1975 compared to pre-embargo levels and the total level of usable productive capacity. The table indicates that in spite of substantial reductions in oil output since the pre-embargo level, the cartel was able to maintain its price structure. Only countries whose price was above the OPEC average were forced to reduce price, and these countries tended to suffer the greatest loss of output. The country suffering the greatest percentage of loss of output was Ecuador, where higher government price levels affected the level of exportable sales. By mid-year Ecuador finally reduced tax-paid costs to $10.41 per barrel for its producers, Texaco and Gulf Oil.[7]

Nevertheless, the obvious persistent market strength of OPEC led to gradual acceptance of the need for some emergency energy planning among the major OECD countries. Led by the U.S. State Department, the IEA was formally established with eighteen members in November, 1974. The long-term goal of the IEA was to reduce dependence on imported oil through conservation and joint efforts to develop energy alternatives. Its short-term goal was to coordinate plans for the eventuality of a renewed oil boycott. On the financial side, through 1974 and 1975 fears of the adverse monetary implications of long-term rising world crude oil prices, plus fear of a renewed Arab-Israeli conflict during the continuing period of worldwide recession, led to a sequence of new efforts by the IEA countries and the International Monetary Fund (IMF) to minimize the economic burden of high oil payments. For, as the *Middle East*

[7] Net of royalty to a Canadian firm.

TABLE 42
OPEC Oil Production, First Half of 1975 versus
Pre-Embargo Levels, 1974, and Levels of Operable Capacity
(000 bbl./day)

Countries	Jan.–June, 1975, Average	Percentage of Change, 1974	1974 Average	Pre-Embargo Average*	Productive Capacity
Middle East					
Saudi Arabia	6,819	−18.2	8,479	8,569	10,300
Iran	5,432	−11.3	6,021	5,786	6,500
Kuwait	2,133	−25.1	2,547	3,526	3,800
Iraq	2,173	+17.2	1,870	2,097	2,600
Abu Dhabi	1,200	−18.4	1,414	1,378	1,920
Dubai	251	+ 8.6	242	273	317
Sharjah	40	0.0	23	0	45
Qatar	460	−11.3	519	609	650
Middle East total	18,508	−13.5	21,115	22,238	26,132
Other OPEC					
Venezuela	2,524	−19.0	2,976	3,387	3,300
Nigeria	1,712	−24.8	2,256	2,138	2,500
Indonesia	1,225	−16.3	1,393	1,338	1,600
Libya	1,120	−22.1	1,521	2,286	3,000
Algeria	851	−22.1	1,005	1,128	1,100
Gabon	205	+22.8	202	161	210
Ecuador	139	−40.3	177	244	255
OPEC total	26,284	−16.7	30,645	32,920	38,097

SOURCE: *Petroleum Intelligence Weekly* 14, no. 30 (July 28, 1975): 7. Reproduced by written permission. Copyright 1975 by Petroleum & Energy Intelligence Weekly, Inc.
* September 1973. Post-embargo peak production was 32.2 million barrels daily, May, 1974.

Economic Digest (December, 1974) warned, "The danger is that for the first time in modern history, economic power has fallen into the hands of those who do not have the military ability to protect it and as the Middle East, a traditionally volatile as well as strategic area is involved, the risk of a military flareup which could drag in the United States on one side and the Soviet Union on the other cannot be underestimated."

The Magnitude of Oil Revenues and
the Petrodollar Problem

The economic history of the previous section has shown clearly that incremental resource cost—that is, marginal resource cost—had very little significance in the price of crude oil. Supply and demand had little effect on price, particularly after 1971. Because real marginal costs of Persian Gulf crude were less than fifteen cents per barrel, it was in the interest of both oil companies and OPEC governments to avoid open price competition. However, since 1960 the share of the rents from petroleum resources has been shifted from the companies to OPEC governments even though the companies have earned good returns on their investments. It appears, though, that by 1975 companies were earning little more than the supply price of developmental capital; OPEC's announced policy was to reduce the net earnings of the companies to a level no higher than that necessary to attract private capital and to arbitrarily set a ceiling on the level of these earnings. Beyond 1975 the key question for the OPEC nations was how to maintain or increase the real value of their shares of the total economic rents accruing from rising oil prices.

The problem of "petrodollars" was another of the issues that irreversibly attracted greater government involvement in the oil business. In early 1974 preliminary estimates forecast total OPEC revenues at over one trillion dollars by 1985. Armed with such estimates, responsible OECD officials publicly feared the collapse of the world monetary system. The problem of "recycling" oil revenues back to consuming countries was viewed as a hopeless task. Even greater fears of a massive real resource transfer from consuming to producing countries were voiced. By the end of 1974 and through 1975 these fears faded as the large declines in the demand for crude oil became translated into lower oil revenues and smaller "surplus" or excess revenues available for non–Middle East investment.

There has been considerable variation since the initial estimates of total oil revenues and the "surplus revenues" or petrodollars. In early 1974 the IMF estimated that surplus revenues for *all* oil exporting countries, both OPEC and non-OPEC, would total $65 billion. That figure was considered quite large at the time it was published. For example, the OECD started with a smaller surplus estimate but later revised its figures upward, approaching the IMF estimate. A European Economic Community (EEC) report estimated that 1974 surplus revenues would be more than $61 billion but that within four years the surplus would *decline* to less than $60 billion annually as a result of increased foreign exchange requirements. Hence, the EEC concluded that in spite of total annual oil payments to OPEC of more than $143 billion by 1978, rising foreign exchange requirements would cause the OPEC oil revenue surplus to decline. The U.S. Commerce Department estimated oil revenues in 1975 of $90 billion; based on EEC assumptions, this estimate would have led to 1975 surplus revenues of $55 billion. Estimates of the EEC and the *Middle East Economic Survey* (*MEES*), are provided in Tables 43 and 44, respectively. As shown in Table 43, according to the EEC oil revenues of OPEC member governments would rise from $22.9 billion in 1973 to $85.7 billion in 1974. However, the imports of these countries would grow from $18.1 billion in 1973 to $24.2 billion in 1974, thus leaving an annual surplus of $61.5 billion in 1974.[8] EEC added that Venezuela, Iraq, Iran, and Algeria were capable of absorbing most of their oil revenues, whereas Kuwait, Saudi Arabia, Libya, and the United Arab Emirates would have increasing capital surpluses. Only moderate absorptive capability was concluded for Nigeria and Indonesia.

In the *MEES* study, Table 44, cols. (1)–(3), oil revenues are defined as government revenue from taxes and royalties plus additional profits gained by state oil companies from sales of participation crude. The assumptions behind these estimates are that participation crude income is 93 percent of current postings and that equity crude income is calculated on present government "take" (royalty plus tax). A production split of 60 percent participation and 40 percent equity crude is assumed for all Middle East producers. For all other countries, net government income from oil is calculated on the basis of arrangements then in force (including in Nigeria's case the new fifty-five–forty-five participation deals with

---

[8] OPEC members prefer the term *forced savings* in the sense that since oil is a depletable asset, the accumulation of funds is saving for the day when these resources are exhausted. This is, of course, a distortion of the economic concept of saving.

TABLE 43
EEC Estimates of OPEC Oil Revenues, Import Foreign Exchange Requirements, and Oil Revenue Surpluses
(millions of current dollars)

	1973			1974			1978		
	(1)	(2)	(3)	(1)	(2)	(3)	(1)	(2)	(3)
Gulf countries	13,830	7,280	6,550	55,020	10,360	44,660	98,880	44,250	54,630
Iran	3,880	3,470	410	14,970	5,925	9,925	25,250	21,960	3,290
Arab countries (Saudi Arabia, Iraq, Kuwait, Emirates)	9,950	3,810	6,140	40,050	5,315	34,735	73,630	22,290	51,340
Other Arab oil-producing countries (Algeria and Libya)	3,280	3,830	−550	11,660	4,680	6,980	16,880	10,000	6,880
Other oil-producing countries (Indonesia, Nigeria, Venezuela, Ecuador)	5,790	6,960	−1,170	19,030	9,200	9,830	27,560	28,900	−1,340
Total	22,900	18,070	4,830	85,710	24,240	61,470	143,320	83,150	60,170

(1) Government oil revenues
(2) Total imports
(3) 1 minus 2, or the surplus revenues available for external investments, donations and loans.

SOURCE: European Economic Community, "The Absorptive Capacities," cited in *Arab Oil and Gas* 3, no. 69 (Aug. 1, 1974): 21.

agreed-upon buy-back provisions.) Based on these estimated oil revenues, oil revenue surpluses are obtained by assuming the import foreign exchange estimates of the EEC and applying them to the *MEES* income estimates. Final figures are shown in Table 44, columns (4) and (5). These calculations show that based on total OPEC oil revenues of $114.996 billion for 1974, some $90.7 billion is available as investable capital surplus. Some $66.4 billion, or almost 75 percent of total surplus revenues, will come from the Middle East. The differences in EEC and *MEES* estimates of oil revenues in available surplus revenues is on the order of $30 billion. The EEC study is dated July, 1974; the *MEES* study is dated May, 1974.

Later, the FEA adopted estimates from the *Petroleum Intelligence Weekly* (*PIW*), as shown in Table 45. Unfortunately, production volumes in these estimates were dated from September, 1973. Their Case I estimate is revenue from equity revenues and taxes alone. Case II is revenues assuming a sixty-forty participation with the oil companies buying back 50 percent of the host government's 60 percent share. Comparing the EEC, *MEES*, and FEA/ *PIW* estimates of oil revenues, it is apparent that *MEES* and FEA/ *PIW* tend to agree on Middle East total oil revenues but diverge on revenues from other OPEC members. Differences are related to price and output assumptions. Estimates of total oil revenues for 1974 and 1975 are overly inflated because of the apparent failure to incorporate more realistic assumptions regarding the price elasticity of demand. Differences on *surplus* revenue estimates are greater. None of these estimates are strictly comparable, and they do not accurately reflect funds available for investment abroad. In particular, in the *MEES* and EEC estimates of surplus revenues the annual OPEC foreign exchange requirements are assumed to be proportional to the level of annual OPEC import demand. Hence, by simple subtraction of import values from oil revenues, surplus reserves are estimated. This proportionality assumption seems unwarranted because (1) the requirement for disposable revenues is not determined solely by import demand and (2) it ignores the liquid foreign exchange balances accumulated by OPEC members over previous time periods.

Aside from these limitations, the fundamental underestimation

TABLE 44

MEES Estimates of Oil Production, Income, Import Requirements, and Oil Revenue Surpluses for OPEC Countries

Producing Area	(1) 1974 Production (bbl./day)	(2) Estimated Net Oil Income (millions of dollars)	(3) Average Income per Barrel (dollars)	(4) Total Imports* (millions of dollars)	(5) Oil Revenue Surplus (millions of dollars)
Middle East					
Saudi Arabia	8,574†	28,945	9.25	—	—
Iran	6,160	20,911	9.30	5,925	14,986
Kuwait	2,880†	9,381	8.93	—	—
Iraq	2,000	7,645	10.47	—	—
Abu Dhabi	1,600	5,733	9.82	—	—
Qatar	570	2,080	10.00	—	—
Oman	300	1,052	9.60	—	—
Dubai	240	803	9.17	—	—
Bahrain	70	232	9.08	—	—
Subtotal, Middle East	22,394	76,782	9.39	10,360	66,422
North Africa					
Libya	2,000	8,954	12.27	—	—
Algeria	1,100	4,922	12.26	—	—
Subtotal, North Africa	3,100	13,876	12.26	4,680	9,196
Total Middle East and North Africa	25,494	90,658	9.74	15,040	75,618
Other OPEC					
Venezuela	3,060	10,602	9.50	—	—
Nigeria	2,360	9,232	10.71	—	—
Indonesia	1,500	4,988	9.10	—	—
Ecuador	250	800	8.77	—	—
Subtotal, other OPEC	7,170	25,622	9.79	9,200	16,422
Total OPEC‡	32,294	114,996	9.76	24,240	90,756

SOURCE: *Middle East Economic Survey* 16; 17, nos. 1–15.

* Based on EEE import estimates.

† Including Neutral Zone output of 274,000 bbl./day for each of Saudi Arabia and Kuwait.

‡ Excluding Oman and Bahrain, which are not members of OPEC. Otherwise, production rises to 32,664,000 bbl./day and revenues to $116,280 million.

TABLE 45
Estimated 1974 Revenues for Major Oil-Exporting Areas
(adopted by FEA)

		Case I		Case II	
Producing Area	Volume (million bbl./day)	Govt. Take per Barrel	Total Revenues (billions of dollars)	Govt. Take per Barrel	Total Revenues (billions of dollars)
Middle East					
Saudi Arabia	8.7	$ 7.00	$ 22.23	$ 8.57	$ 27.22
Iran	6.2	7.00	15.84	8.57	19.39
Kuwait	3.0	7.00	7.67	8.57	9.38
Iraq	2.3	7.00	5.88	8.57	7.19
Other	3.7	7.00	9.45	8.57	11.58
Total Middle East	23.9	$ 7.00	$ 61.07	$ 8.57	$ 74.76
Africa					
Nigeria	2.6	$ 8.61	$ 8.17	$12.77	$ 12.12
Libya	2.7	9.34	9.20	13.76	13.56
Algeria	1.3	14.25	6.76	14.25	6.76
Total Africa	6.6	$10.02	$ 24.13	$13.47	$ 32.44
Southeast Asia	2.5	$ 6.18	$ 5.64	$ 6.18	$ 5.64
South America	5.4	$ 8.49	$ 16.73	$ 8.49	$ 16.73
Other	1.5	$ 7.00	$ 3.83	$ 8.57	$ 4.69
	39.9	$ 7.65	$111.40	$ 9.22	$134.26

SOURCE: Cited in *Arab Oil and Gas* 3 (1974).

of the capability of OPEC countries to spend their revenues and the failure to account for the massive decline in oil demand in 1974 and 1975 resulted in lower surplus revenues than were forecast. Indeed, the only significant surpluses accrued to Saudi Arabia, Kuwait, and the United Arab Emirates. Other OPEC members—especially Indonesia and Iran—remained borrowers of foreign capital. These generous estimates of surplus revenues were later trimmed as world demand for crude lowered through 1974 and 1975. Also, as OPEC demonstrated an unparalleled ability to increase imports it became evident that earlier forecasts were obsolete.

Revised opinions about the future of OPEC surpluses are indicated in Table 46. The three bank estimates and those by petroleum economist Walter Levy differed substantially on the future level of OPEC revenues and surpluses. This difference is as expected because of differing assumptions. Levy assumed OPEC per-barrel revenues of $14.65 in 1980, while the banks tended to be more optimistic regarding a fall in future oil prices.

It is evident that the primary variables in any model designed to estimate oil surplus revenues would include:

(1) OPEC crude oil production over time.

(2) OPEC average crude price over time.

(3) Absorptive capacity of OPEC countries for merchandise imports over time.

(4) The magnitude of payments for invisibles on balance-of-payments current account. Invisibles include difficult-to-trace payments such as military expenditures, special loans and grants, insurance, travel, and the like, over time.

(5) The legal currency cover.

(6) OPEC earnings on foreign investment over previous time periods; that is, the yield on previous surplus oil revenue investments.

TABLE 46
Revised Alternative Projections of OPEC Petrodollar Surpluses
(billions of dollars)

	1975	1977	1980
OPEC Total Revenues			
Citibank	$107	$114	$103
Irving A	119	116	141
Morgan Guaranty	110	125	143
Levy	93	138	168
OPEC Current Surplus			
Citibank	36	30	−7
Irving A	64	34	−17
Morgan Guaranty	57	40	−56
Levy	47	73	47

SOURCE: *Petroleum Economist* 42, no. 8 (August, 1975).

(7) Foreign exchange earned from exports of OPEC countries other than oil and oil products.

Estimates of total OPEC oil revenues can still vary substantially at given output levels because of the varying discount from posted prices for the participation and third-party-sale crude. In this case we define revenues as oil revenues minus foreign exchange requirements for invisibles, foreign exchange requirements for merchandise imports (the visibles), foreign exchange requirements as currency cover, and investment income. Forecasting these disposable surpluses to 1985 is extremely complicated. A major component of surplus revenue estimates is the demand for foreign exchange for imports. There is considerable variation in forecasts of the absorptive capacity of the major Middle East producers. So much depends on political considerations.

Case examples of Saudi Arabia and Kuwait emphasize this point. The Saudi budget for fiscal year 1974–1975 was about $23 billion, of which 99 percent was oil revenues. Government expenditure was set at $12.8 billion, including $4.5 billion for completion of existing projects, $3 billion for new projects, and $1.3 billion in the form of aid and loans for development projects in friendly states. Military expenditures were about $2.5 billion. The remaining $15 billion were to be set aside for industrial and agricultural development projects vested on a short- and medium-term basis. These estimates would be slightly reduced by subtracting foreign exchange for invisibles such as freight and insurance, transport and travel (approximately $356 million in 1974 and assumed to increase 15 percent annually). Saudi Arabia is the key country that will demonstrate significant magnitudes of surplus revenue. Its visible absorptive capacity is much less than its potential absorptive capacity, and as the "needs" of the country are converted into "demands," the productive employment of these resources will increase (Wells 1974). Kuwait anticipated oil revenues for the fiscal year beginning April 1, 1975, of over $10 billion. Only $3 billion was allocated to the 1974–1975 budget. Domestic investment would be about $2 billion, with about $1.5 billion set aside for aid to Arab and other friendly nations and $1.7 billion for the Kuwait Fund for Arab Economic Development. Other invisibles included $115 million for defense (this amount, however, excludes a major portion of defense expenditures that could exceed $1 billion) and freight, insurance, and travel of $360 million. This left surplus revenues of some $5 billion.

REVISED ESTIMATE OF OPEC REVENUE AND SURPLUSES

To simplify the problem of estimating surpluses for all OPEC nations, the assumptions about absorptive capacity developed in a recent study by the International Bank for Reconstruction and Development (IBRD) are adopted with adjustment for invisible foreign exchange requirements. Currency requirements are ignored in these estimates, as these monies are kept in liquid instruments and are effectively part of surpluses although technically they should be subtracted. Earnings from sectors other than oil (including natural gas) are not considered. OPEC countries are combined into three divergent absorptive capacity groups as shown in Table 47. In the table, Groups II and III have larger domestic investment opportunities. In Group I, limited investment opportunities compared to oil revenues suggest that increased government consumption and transfer expenditures would be necessary to raise disposable incomes in these countries. In the IBRD study the investment rate was assumed to rise in Group I countries from 16 percent of GNP in 1973 to only 19 percent of GNP in 1985, whereas in Group II it rises from 30 percent to 33 percent and in Group III from 18 percent to 24 percent. Indeed, for countries in Groups I and II the large increase in financial resources cannot be immediately absorbed, and the investment rate will actually fall in 1975 relative to 1973. Of course, since oil revenues flow directly to government agencies and become part of disposable incomes only to the extent that they are spent domestically, government decisions will be the major influence on consumption expenditures over the next ten years in these countries. Hence, discretionary decisions by governments will largely determine the growth of consumption in Group I countries. Indeed, because accumulated revenues go into the coffers of the state and not into private hands, the demand by Middle Eastern private institutions for funds may still be greater in Eurodollar markets until a Middle East money market is developed.

TABLE 47
OPEC Countries Grouped By Absorptive Capacity Limitations,
Proven Reserves, and Reserve Life Index, 1975

	Proven Reserves (billions of bbl.)	Years Life at 1975 Rate
Group I: Countries with limited absorptive capacity		
Abu Dhabi	29.5	56.7
Kuwait	68.0	97.1
Libya	26.1	51.0
Qatar	5.9	39.5
Saudi Arabia	148.6	58.1
Subtotal	278.1	60.5
Group II: Countries with larger absorptive capacity, higher income group		
Algeria	7.4	21.6
Iran	64.5	32.2
Iraq	34.3	39.4
Venezuela	17.7	20.2
Ecuador	2.5	40.8
Subtotal	126.4	30.8
Group III: Countries with larger absorptive capacity, lower income group		
Indonesia	14.0	29.5
Nigeria	20.2	29.9
Subtotal	34.2	29.7
Total OPEC	438.7	40.3

SOURCE: "Worldwide Report," *Oil and Gas Journal* 73, no. 52 (Dec. 29, 1975).

To arrive at estimates of surplus revenues from 1974 to 1985, the following basic assumptions were adopted:

1. Production is programmed by OPEC countries to equal world demand and is assumed to grow at an annual rate of 3.5 percent to 1985.

2. There will be no interruptions of oil supply; in other words, there will be peace in the Middle East.

3. All OPEC members will control 100 percent of domestic crude oil operations.

4. The average crude oil price will increase annually 5 percent to 1980 and then slow to 1 percent annual increases to 1985. The 1975 average price is $10.48 per barrel.

5. Demand for foreign exchange for invisibles (imports) is assumed to grow at 15 percent annually, while demand for merchandise imports by OPEC countries (visibles) is assumed to vary based on the absorptive capacity groupings developed by the IBRD. This growth averages between 15 percent and 30 percent annually for different countries.

Figure 14 shows the cumulative total oil revenues and net surplus revenues for all OPEC countries to 1985. Based on these assumptions, the cumulative surplus revenue position of all OPEC countries will reach between $300 billion and $375 billion by 1980, but because of the substantial demands for foreign exchange, the surplus position is expected to decline by 1985. These figures do not include any revenue derived from future liquified natural gas sales, petrochemical sales, or any non-oil revenues, all of which could be increased considerably between 1980 and 1985. These other revenues could offset the cumulative decline, as could greater price increases in the early 1980's. This estimate of the cumulative OPEC position is in general agreement with the revised Levy estimate. Although most OPEC countries will be in a deficit position beyond 1980, others will continue in substantial surplus beyond that year.

Adapting to the Oil Payments Burden

The impact of the actual oil payments burden from 1973 to 1975 on the trade balance of member countries of the OECD, the major oil-consuming countries, was significant. The trade balance turned from a surplus of about $5 billion in the second half of 1973 to a deficit of some $25 billion in the first half of 1974. The trade balance with OPEC (on an f.o.b. basis) increased by roughly $40–$45 billion against an increase of exports of about $6 billion. The overall balance of international payments from 1973 through the first quarter of 1975 indicated that the collective deficit of the in-

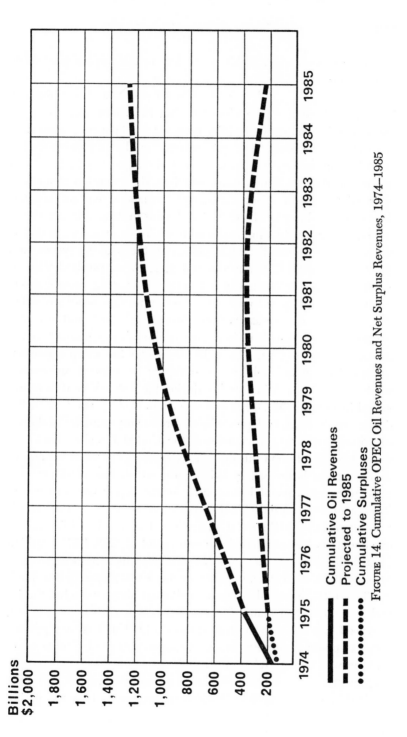

Billions $2,000

FIGURE 14. Cumulative OPEC Oil Revenues and Net Surplus Revenues, 1974–1985

Cumulative Oil Revenues
Projected to 1985
Cumulative Surpluses

dustrial countries was roughly equivalent to the surplus position of OPEC countries.

Following the sudden increase in oil prices, a new pattern of international payments developed during 1974. Essentially, this expansion of international liquidity reflected the financing of oil deficits through the creation of international credit and the fact that OPEC countries kept the bulk of their claims on the financial system of the West in liquid forms. In effect, the extension of massive international credit offset the sharply expanded current account deficits. Capital outflow by OPEC and gains in their official reserves were quite impressive. International liquidity increased since OPEC reserves were essentially liquid claims on the banking system and governments of OECD countries and these claims resulted from an extension of credit instead of a transfer of existing reserve assets (OECD 1975). Figure 15 indicates the composition and distribution of total official reserve assets from 1965 to early 1975 and indicates the tremendous growth in international liquidity beginning in the second quarter of 1974. Figure 15 also shows the sharp expansion of OPEC countries' holdings of currency reserves. A substantial portion of the growth in liquidity during the first half of 1974 represented investment by OPEC and other non-OECD countries in the Eurocurrency market; deposits by oil-producing countries in dollars and other nonsterling currencies in the United Kingdom banks increased by $7.2 billion during that six months. International liquidity during the latter half of 1974 improved because of direct government-to-government loans (such as the one from Germany to Italy) and because individual countries drew on their IMF credit *tranche* and the IMF special oil facility. Through late 1974, thirty-two countries had purchased the equivalent of SDR 1,571.4 million ($1.9 billion) under the fund's oil facility, which began operation in June, 1974. At that time Italy was the leading user of that facility. The initial financial surpluses indicated above reflected the inability of OPEC to match increased revenues with corresponding increased imports from the rest of the world. This less-than-proportional response of import demand to a percentage of change in oil revenue was not entirely catastrophic, as alternative financing arrangements were secured. Effective recycling, however, was dependent upon the degree of liquidity preference and the risk-taking

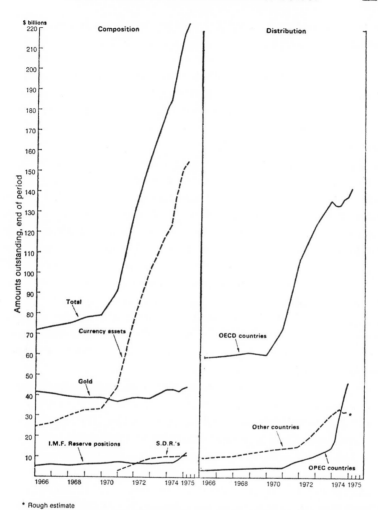

FIGURE 15. Total World Official Reserve Assets (Reprinted, with permission, from *OECD Economic Outlook* 17 [July, 1975])

behavior of the major surplus countries. Through early 1975 key surplus countries preferred minimum-risk, short-term investments; the return flow of funds to deficit oil-importing countries has been left to intermediaries.

This constraint of credit risk and bank capitalization alone on private money markets created the demand for new public arrangements to maintain the mobility of payments flows to needy deficit countries. Although changes in the interest rate structure attracted some funds to long-term investments, they did not solve the problem of the maldistribution of deposits. Most of the return capital flows accrued to the United States and the United Kingdom, although the bulk of the payments deficits occurred with other OECD countries. The IMF's first and second oil facilities provided help, but other necessary oil financing arrangements took the form of direct government-to-government transactions. Financing, even under "soft" loan bases, was still considered to have a costly limitation: the burden of cumulative debt maintenance on top of current account deficits. This debt-servicing limitation on oil deficit financing suggested that the balance of payments of a borrowing country would worsen beyond its current deficit unless the rate of growth of total lending was at least equal to the rate of interest on outstanding loans. Nevertheless, what should be compared is not new lending with old interest, but new lending with new imports for capital investment and old interest with the increase in exports and decrease in imports resulting from the productivity of former investments. To ease the real problem of the declining credit of nations, accelerated real resource transfers to OPEC countries for oil imports as opposed to exports for consumption may become inevitable. It was nonetheless clear that improving the absorptive capacity and hence the import demand of OPEC countries by 1980 was a key ingredient to the long-term international payments problem.

The effects of OPEC price increases on OECD economies were then basically fivefold: (1) price effects, (2) income effects, (3) exchange rate effects, (4) substitution effects, and (5) redistribution effects. The 1974 reduction in the consumption of refined petroleum products in Europe and the United States was an indicator of the negative price effect. The income effect was revealed by the increased proportion of income necessary to obtain the same quantity of oil-based products. Although some of these other goods and services were available for export to OPEC countries, the limited absorptive capacities would only offset a fraction of the outflow payments to OPEC. Hence, the rise in OPEC surpluses, in the absence of any alternative financing, was associated with lower demand for domestic output and an associated fall in income and employment. Stated another way, the combination of limited OPEC absorptive capacity and high liquidity preferences reinforced the recessionary conditions already occurring in OECD countries. Under such conditions, some countries sought to rely on flexible exchange rate movements to restore payments equilibrium. Indeed, there had been significant exchange rate movements (for example, that of the Italian lira) since oil prices increased fivefold.[9] The substitution effect was limited in the case of oil. Aside from voluntary conservation efforts or self-imposed life-style changes, the substitution effect had little short-run impact. In summary, because of the uncertain value of retaliatory options in the absence of workable oil revenue recycling, the role of governments in future oil payments arrangements would inevitably increase, which meant even greater future government monitoring of the international oil trade.

The Changing Role of Petroleum Companies and U.S. Policy

U.S. petroleum investments abroad provided significant contributions to the U.S. balance of payments before the 1970's. The trade deficit on petroleum account was generally offset by receipts on capital, income, and service account. The pivotal year was apparently 1964. In 1964 the U.S. trade and transport deficit in oil and petrochemicals was $1.2 billion; the oil sector's contribution to the balance of payments was $467 million. Of course the decade of the 1960's was the period when U.S. imports were from foreign affiliates of U.S. firms before the "participation era." The effects of U.S. company control of foreign producing properties was that only about two-thirds of the total import price for oil was actually transferred abroad (Hudson Institute 1974). The balance, about one-third, was retained in this country in the form of parent company earnings, various forms of service fees for management and engineering, international shipping charges by transport affiliates of U.S. firms, payments to American oil engineers working abroad, and imports by foreign affiliates of U.S. oil-producing equipment. This balance

[9] G. Pollack, in a paper delivered at the Council on Foreign Relations, 1974, suggests that the adjustment mechanism may lead to further exchange rate adjustments.

was combined with remittances of substantial earnings by affiliates on their exports to third countries. Such affiliated companies included Creole Petroleum (Exxon), Mene Grande (Gulf), Caltex (Texaco and Standard of California), Kuwait Oil Company (BP and Gulf) and, of course, the ARAMCO partners (Exxon, Texaco, Mobil, and Standard of California) and numerous Canadian affiliates.

The favorable balance declined after 1964, however, with increased company taxation and the transferral of ownership of oil properties. With loss of control over these foreign resources, the United States faced not only higher oil import prices but also diminishing portions of this price retained directly by U.S. oil-importing companies in the United States in the form of earnings, managerial and engineering fees, and related credits. Given the rising capital requirements of the petroleum industry over the next decades and the decline in foreign-origin earnings, it is increasingly likely that major oil companies will become more aggressive in seeking capital in external markets, including possibly capital from OPEC sources.

The rise of OPEC power was associated with the spectacular improvement of earnings in 1974 by the major oil companies. Governmental intervention was in part designed to attempt to sever and destroy this perceived price and output bridge between the major oil companies and OPEC. In the United States, congressional response was to reduce some of the foreign tax credit advantage accruing to oil companies, to eliminate percentage depletion, and later to transfer pricing controls on the foreign affiliates of U.S. firms. Government policy attempted to regulate indirectly the future magnitude of oil-related capital flows to the United States. The mood of Congress was to make the oil companies—both majors and independents—the scapegoats for the oil supply problems in this country. As long as OPEC remained strong, the policy response seemed to be to act aggressively against the oil companies and thereby indirectly against OPEC. In addition, the United States appeared to view OPEC as a monolithically controlled cartel and hence tended to rely on Saudi Arabia to keep the lid on further OPEC price increases. More than one thousand bills in Congress dealt with legislation designed to somewhat control or restrict the perceived economic power of the companies in the oil, gas, and coal businesses. Many of these proposed restrictions were levied against the major importers and the major and independent refiners in the United States.

A governmental role in the U.S. oil business was likely to remain permanent as long as OPEC remained a strong cartel. In spite of a general world recession in 1974 and 1975, the gradual improvement of world economic conditions thereafter suggested that OPEC would become even stronger in the future. A formal governmental energy planning function appeared to be the latest element in the post–World War II evolution of government involvement in the U.S. oil industry.

Epilogue: Past and Future Energy Policies

THE case against previous energy policies must begin with the mutually constraining goals of national security and monopoly policy. The contribution to national security was subverted by the misallocating effort to regulate petroleum industry structure and the associated effort to provide special exemptions to smaller-sized firms. Moreover, with the rise in OPEC's economic power, federal policy aimed at increased regulation of oil companies of all classes. In part this regulation was an effort to respond indirectly to OPEC by controlling the pricing flexibility of domestic oil companies and monitoring the margins on refined petroleum products. In doing so the government again followed its past policies of granting exemptions to special classes of refiners. In any regulatory scheme, it is generally impossible to balance all the conflicting preferences of firms so that no one will perceive itself to be worse off than it would be under an unregulated format. Nevertheless, the trial-and-error pattern of rules that characterized the early phase of the allocation program was more or less resolved by the market in terms of reduced quantities demanded for the higher-priced petroleum products. During that hectic period the crude oil program provided the very small refiners with access to enough crude oil to raise their operating capacity from 56 percent to 77 percent. Smaller refiners increased their capacity position during the allocation period relatively more than in any post–World War II period. The other side of the coin is that what may have been the normal market process of forcing the exit of least efficient firms was thwarted by government policy.

The power of OPEC to manipulate price became associated with the power of the major oil companies. This view became reinforced when most oil companies reported record 1974 profits, with some reporting increases of over 100 percent. Higher prices for OPEC crude oil also meant higher inventory profits along with improved profits in the 1974 world market for crude oil, chemicals, and products. Profits were also aided by the related increases in coal prices and by exchange rate profits on foreign operation. Even though inventory profits were a one-shot affair, the mood of Congress became punitive. Elimination of the depletion allowance and threats of crude oil price rollbacks were part of the political response to the petroleum refiner. Throughout this period there was little sympathy for the concern that the rising costs of petroleum development and processing required a substantial improvement in petroleum company earnings without endangering the financial quality of the companies and the process of capital formation in productive energy facilities in the United States. The folly of government policy in regulating price had already been demonstrated with respect to natural gas. In response to the OPEC supply interruption, a temporary and hastily drawn set of "crisis" regulations was simply extended far beyond its economic usefulness. However, the misallocating propensity was not restricted to the crisis of the 1970's.

The earlier evidence to support this misallocating effect was the voluntary and mandatory oil import quota programs. An effective quota program should have provided the domestic price support for oil that in turn would have stimulated the search for new petroleum reserves. These new reserves would have provided the excess capacity available for emergencies like the one the United States experienced in the early 1970's. By diffusing the value of import licenses between small and large firms, the government encouraged the wasteful continuance of uneconomical refining operations. By granting liberal exceptions to import restrictions on oil and products, the domestic oil price stabilizing effect was eliminated. Firms had little incentive to invest heavily in higher-cost domestic resources when potential competition from less expensive foreign supply was imminent. In the process of granting these quota exceptions, the government actually compromised its monopoly policy by reinforcing the permanent component of the market shares of major refiners. Many smaller firms were forced to exit the refining industry through merger or acquisition with other smaller firms. With oil import exceptions being granted, and with increasing uncertainty over future oil policy, refiners were hesitant to invest in major new increments to capacity. The attempt to maintain a cushion of refining capacity above market requirements failed.

In short, under the mandatory quota program and the new modified license fee program, federal petroleum policy had been tailored to accommodate both the major and the independent firms in refining as well as in production and marketing. However, the market power balance was decidedly in favor of major refiners although there was a definite reinforcement for increasing the market share of independents at the expense of the majors. A net effect of the energy policy from 1948 to 1972 was nevertheless beneficial for the market power of the majors while creating an economic climate that encouraged energy consumption and while restraining incentives for resource expansion. By 1972 the attempt to ensure survival of independents by the sliding-scale quota scheme had failed; the value of import quota licenses was reduced to nothing, and domestic crude oil inputs to refiners were in a substantial decline.

The modified program was designed to restore the health of the oil industry. As Secretary of the Treasury Simon stated in the announcement of the new program:

Implementation of license fees on May 1, 1973, would help to give value to unused 1973 import tickets, providing landlocked independent refiners with some leverage to bargain for domestic sweet crude oil. The current worldwide shortage of sweet crudes, coupled with rising foreign prices, has wiped out the value of the independent refiner's tickets and has led to many small refiners cutting back production for lack of refinery feedstock. Import licenses, in general, now have no exchange value because the landed price of foreign crudes is roughly equivalent or above domestic crude prices. Raising the value of independents' unused licenses should help the independents to bargain for additional sweet crude supplies. Moreover, the ability of the independent refiner to obtain additional fee-exempt licenses from the [Oil Import Appeals Board] would, hopefully, enable him to obtain an adequate number of tickets necessary to arrange exchanges with the majors under present-day price relationships. [Department of the Treasury 1973]

However, the national security license fee program continued the price leadership of the majors and hence their relatively nontransitory component of market power. Unlike the standard conclusion when tariffs replace quotas under monopoly conditions, the market power of the majors was not significantly curbed by the entry of new firms and the expansion of domestic output. Instead, quasi-cartel powers were virtually implied by the provision for fee-exempt imports to former quota holders. As established firms, the majors could be expected to extend their normal maximizing behavior and directly or indirectly seek to establish (or obtain through acquired regulations) price structures that are competitive yet that indirectly reinforce their market position. New entry could be restrained. It is likely that future potential entrants will decide to compete in the provision of substitute or synthetic crude oil and natural gas supplies as opposed to entering the barrier-prone segment. Financing of these substitutes, however, may limit their entry.

The failure of oil policy was reinforced by a second underlying flaw: the failure of government to establish policies as if all petroleum commodities were independent; in particular, the failure of government to consider the joint supply characteristics of crude oil, natural gas, and natural gas liquids. Policies ostensibly designed for crude oil and oil products only had an impact on gas and gas liquids, and vice versa. The most glaring example of an inept policy was the FPC's regulation of the field price of natural gas below market clearing levels. By controlling natural gas prices below competitive levels, a clear economic deterrent was created toward investment in petroleum resource development. The combined effect of a weakened quota policy with artificially low natural gas prices reduced the incentive to explore for oil and gas. The national security goal of a cushion of spare productive petroleum capacity failed. State prorationing policies designed to stabilize crude oil prices were also ineffectual because of the numerous exemptions granted to stripper wells and pressure maintenance projects.

Moreover, the government explicitly assumed that foreign supplies of crude oil, natural gas, and crude products would always be available at less than domestic prices. Foreign supply was economically (and politically) perfectly elastic, so no real contingency plans were developed to protect the economy in the event of a supply interruption. This vulnerability became most apparent as OPEC unilaterally took over oil production facilities through demands for "participation" and began threatening to use oil as a political weapon. Furthermore, government failed to understand the unique geologic characteristics of resource regions. By viewing the United States as a homogeneous plain, policy makers failed to tailor specific incentives for specific regions to maximize resource development. A regionalized energy policy was never entertained. In addition, the air pollution control policy imposed on refiners only managed to worsen the energy crisis by stimulating demands for scarce low-sulfur crude oil, natural gas, and low-sulfur products.

By 1973 the United States had little or no spare crude oil capacity, it had no spare refining capacity, existing major oil fields were on a decline, natural gas shortages were growing, and greater reliance on imports was inevitable. From 1973 on, the government's response to these problems was primarily to reallocate the burden of shortages while attempting to design a strategy toward the oil companies, OPEC, and the long-term role of government in domestic energy planning. A grudging appreciation of the inevitable short-term reliance on OPEC imports prompted the government to begin the design of its own long-term energy planning function, particularly with respect to the security of future energy supply. The low level of real economic growth in 1974 and 1975 provided the government a necessary breathing spell to cope with the economic power of OPEC. Indeed, low oil demand forced periods of price stability upon OPEC, and a situation of excess production, refining, and tanker capacity persisted into the post-1975 period.

The concentration of federal planning efforts was placed on the price of crude oil and its relationship to other energy commodities. As Figure 16 shows, the real price of crude oil in the United States by 1975 had increased to levels that approached the perceived long-term supply price of $7.00 per barrel, the price considered by the government to be that necessary to attract resources to develop alternative supplies of energy. However, it became apparent that because of rising capital costs and the technical unknowns of synthetic fuel development, the true long-run supply price (or range of prices) was much higher in real terms. Indeed, in terms of Btu's the price structure of refined products, gas, and crude oil by mid-1975 was narrowing. It is evident, for example, from Table 48 that the government-controlled natural gas and old oil prices were far below unregulated levels on a Btu basis. Indeed, the price per Btu for intrastate natural gas had reached parity with the weighted average refiner acquisition cost of $1.47 per million Btu's. Government regulation again provided explanation for the seemingly perverse relationship between price-exempt crude and gasoline. Since refiners could not recoup their high crude costs immediately according to FEA rules, these distortions could persist over several quarters. From Table 48 it would appear that with price controls lifted on crude oil and natural gas, the price of these fuels would rise up to the level of $2.00 per million Btu's. Indeed, with the expectation that OPEC crude prices would rise, and with increasing scarcities of natural gas, there was every likelihood that prices could rise well above that level through 1980. With this rising price, there would appear to be favorable incentives to invest substantially in the development of synthetic fuels. However, whether government would avoid the misallocation policy prescriptions and formulas of earlier periods was problematical. In particular, the failure to develop policies for one energy resource that would not be counterproductive for others persisted through 1975, as did the notion that government planning could supplant the market mechanism.

A more appropriate policy would be one that is mutually reinforcing between industry and government, with the focus on capital formation in petroleum resources. Notably, this emphasis should be in the areas of research and development to provide the key breakthrough necessary to find the remaining U.S. oil and gas resources, which will require, in turn, detailed analyses of the range of resource price elasticities by geologic areas for alternative technologies.

This study has indicated several limited proposals as the basis for insuring a sound national energy policy. None of them seem superior to increased domestic resource development. However, two basic benchmarks have been suggested: that the government should assure through tax or other incentives that a minimum of normal

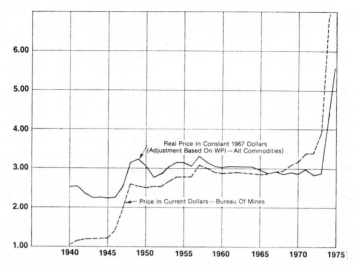

FIGURE 16. Average Nominal and Real Prices of Crude Oil, 1940–1975 (Reprinted, with permission, from Shofner Smith, "The Effect of Economic and Technological Factors on Estimates of Proved Reserves and Productive Capacity," Seminar on Reserves and Productive Capacity, American Petroleum Institute, Washington, D.C., April 1, 1975)

operable refining capacity be required for national emergency use, and that the government seek to provide insurance against a minimum level of 10 percent of U.S. petroleum demand. Such emergency capacity could be developed in combination with demand-reducing programs. Special subsidies could be granted to private industry to develop this excess capacity, but this emergency capacity might easily work more effectively as part of the working inventory of oil companies. The difficulties of such a proposal, of course, are manifest, including the problem of foreign supply and the price of crude oil for such a venture.

Another major policy goal should be the deregulation of natural gas prices. The maximum price flexibility should be available to producers of both oil and gas. In allowing such price flexibility, the government should consider a program of extra incentives to develop resources from the more promising geologic provinces. For example, firms developing continental shelf resources might be granted special tax incentives with respect to the expensing of lease bonuses. Furthermore, firms investing in major secondary and ter-

TABLE 48

Comparison of Prices of Petroleum Products, Gas, and Coal
per Million Btu's, Mid-1975

	Price	Price/Million Btu
Domestic price-exempt crude	$11.70/bbl.	$2.08
Domestic price-controlled crude	5.25/bbl.	0.94
Imported crude	13.11/bbl.	2.34
Domestic average	8.22/bbl.	1.47
Average refiner acquisition cost	9.76/bbl.	1.74
Regular motor gasoline	0.2655/gal.	1.99
No. 2 fuel	0.2355/gal.	1.76
Residual fuel oil	0.1177/bbl.	2.10
Interstate natural gas	0.5298/thousand cu. ft.	0.52
Intrastate natural gas (avg.)	1.50/thousand cu. ft.	1.48

tiary oil recovery programs should be allowed special development tax benefits. To achieve the cushion of spare capacity, the government could subsidize research and development in tertiary recovery.

Because the economy will need to rely on oil and gas for the bulk of its energy requirements, the following series of oil and gas demand-reducing and import-limiting projects could also be considered:

1. Projected consumption of oil and gas could be reduced by increasing use of coal and nuclear energy for electric power generation.

2. Coal or nuclear power could be substituted for oil and gas as boiler fuel and process heat for industrial use.

3. Use of motor gasoline could be reduced by mandatory development of lighter cars and more efficient engines.

4. Tax incentives could be offered to stimulate investment in improved thermal insulation in homes and buildings.

5. Synthetic liquid fuels could be developed from nonconventional sources such as shale and coal.

6. A massive research and development effort could be organized to resolve the technical secondary and tertiary oil recovery problems.

7. Sulfur content standards in fuel oils could be eased to allow time for more efficient substitution away from natural gas.

8. A special task force in government could be established to deal with the problem of bureaucratic bottlenecks in obtaining permits for the development of alternate supply sources.

9. A joint industry/government effort could be made to overcome the immobility of capital resources to the new and risky projects for resource development.

10. Auto emission standards could be more gradually phased in to allow more time for industry to adjust to the new clean air laws.

11. A more sensible "Project Independence" evaluation could be made to outline the role for all fuel sources, both imported and domestic.

Assuredly, the Energy Policy and Conservation Act of 1975 has dealt with some of these issues. However, the missing link has too often been the lack of interaction between industry and government in an atmosphere other than legislative confrontation. Indeed, point 11 above is an appropriate starting point for cooperation. A recent Project Independence update forecasts no slowdown in oil imports from 1975 levels and indicates a pessimistic outlook for the growth of nuclear power. Apparently, the FEA estimated that only coal among other fuels would achieve its forecast annual production level, over one billion tons, by 1985. According to the FEA, oil, gas and nuclear reactors were expected to fail to achieve their targeted goals.

These energy development goals are important to both industry and government, especially since there has recently been a growing concern for the real limitations involved in developing synthetic fuels. The current predicted cost of synthetics is large, and the commercial success of the new plants is uncertain. More and more, major companies feel a need to allocate relatively greater corporate resources to secondary and tertiary oil recovery, to coal development, and also to refinery and petrochemical plant technology to gain improved value from the basic refinery inputs.

The players in the oil drama, as always, are the companies, the consuming governments, and OPEC. The regulation of competition in oil as a response to company market power or OPEC market power has consistently failed. However, regulation is not new to the petroleum industry; it has characterized the industry since its evolution and has always fallen far short of the type of regulation that is common among public utilities. For the foreseeable future a joint relationship of consuming governments with the companies may be the ultimate deterrent to OPEC's use of oil as a political weapon. Particularly, with the control of foreign supply and price by OPEC through the 1980's, the policy error of infusing monopoly policy with energy policy will continue to weaken the U.S. position. Indeed, the recent clamor for divestiture of the top eight oil companies must surely be comforting to OPEC. With no apparent gain in efficiency in production or refining, divestiture would only worsen the investment climate for companies of all sizes—majors and independents. A further involvement of government would not bring about faster discovery of oil or better refinery operations. Indeed, few companies could even afford to buy the massive refining and transportation facilities owned by the majors. Divestiture, as a method of regulating competition in oil, would only divert attention from the long-run energy development problems of the United States. Indeed, there is every indication that the failure to develop our resources in the next ten years could lead to an even greater U.S. energy deficit position by the late 1980's.

Finally, the posture of dealing with OPEC through punitive regulatory measures against the U.S. oil industry is self-defeating. One of the greatest of OPEC's strengths, besides the condition of relatively inelastic demand for crude oil worldwide, has been the weakness of the consuming governments in dealing internally with their own domestic resource policies. Fundamentally, domestic governments need to come to grips with the increasing-cost nature of all non-OPEC oil supply and of all synthetic forms of energy yet considered commercial. If the recessionary conditions of the mid-1970's give way to a gradual long-term improvement in the consuming world's economies, the only excess productive capacity available to provide for this demand is OPEC—(primarily Saudi Arabia, Iraq, and Iran). Non-OPEC supplies and synthetics will only provide for a fraction of normal demand growth. Canadian and Soviet oil will not be available for significant export, and oil exports from the People's Republic of China, so far, have been tied to that nation's need for foreign exchange. Hence, a turning point in industry/government relations in the United States is inevitable: either regulated competition in oil will be deemphasized, or even greater long-run control over the petroleum industry will be imposed. The final choice will have a substantial impact on the rate of resource development in the United States and on its efforts to restrain the cartel pricing power of OPEC.

The overriding theme in these chapters has been that the allocation of government resources and power in conjunction with the major and independent segments of the petroleum industry has quite often been to the detriment of one or both of those classes. Indeed, the industry has occasionally sought to acquire certain forms of favorable regulation. This history led to an effective suspicion of industry guidance in the difficult days of 1973–1975. With Congress continuing to press for a formal government energy planning role, the industry will be working within the environment of regulation in every aspect of the petroleum business. Whether such a relationship will flourish without encouraging a formal government corporation in production, refining, and marketing will be a key political question through the 1970's and 1980's.

Increased government involvement in the petroleum business nonetheless seems inevitable, as the issues of energy supply and demand have largely gone beyond the capability of corporate resolution. How painful this intervention will be to the majors and independents will depend in the short run on industry's behavior. Since the government is slowly developing its expertise in resolving major energy problems, the requirement for the industry to develop its own initiative on policy matters is apparent. Industry too often in the past placed itself in a position of reacting to policy issues instead of identifying these questions in advance and working to resolve them, both in its dealings with OPEC and with the U.S. government. Failure to dissolve this pattern will only be to the future detriment of both majors and independents.

Appendix

Economic Analysis of the
National Security Fee System

THE new post-1972 energy policy on crude oil and products involves both tariffs and quotas on imports. Moreover, the tariff is an "equalizing" type in that the government is attempting to stabilize a long-run target supply price of about seven dollars per barrel on domestic crude oil. Advance deposits are required on import volumes, and fee revenues are used to subsidize producers in their research and development of increased supplies of crude oil and natural gas. The problem involves an initial condition of a quota on the input, crude oil and unfinished oils, and also a quota on the output, either gasoline, distillate, or residual products. These quotas are part of a complete tariff scheme that is reinforced by governmental controls on the long-term ceiling price of crude oil and natural gas. Foreign supplies are dominated by a cartel, OPEC. Therefore, these supplies are not characterized by infinite elasticity. To deal with these issues of energy policy, a general equilibrium approach is more desirable, but such an exhaustive approach would extend beyond the scope of this study. Although the more restrictive partial equilibrium approach is adopted, the main analytical conclusions can be reached. A key problem, however, is that in this partial approach relative prices must remain unchanged as a condition of deriving the graphic functions displayed in the figures in this appendix.

To deal wth these characteristics in a partial equilibrium approach, several simplifying assumptions are necessary: (1) the analysis is comparative-static, (2) the economy is fully employed,

(3) the ability to substitute between imported goods and similar domestic goods is unlimited, (4) the conditions of domestic supply are such that there would be domestic production of the goods even if a tariff or quota were eliminated, (5) the supply of imports has a positive elasticity, (6) there is a fixed physical input coefficient in domestic production of crude oil into crude oil products, and the coefficient is the same for all firms, and (7) there is an initial cartel of domestic importers that has been created by a government quota policy.

The assumption of a fixed coefficient is not overly restrictive. Consider an imported refined product (for example, gasoline) which is produced by two factors of production; crude oil and another factor to be called the *value-added product*. The latter is the value added by the refining industry—the product of the activity of refining. The value-added product is the "product" of primary factors of production, that is, of various kinds of labor, capital, and other resources. It can also be considered as a "bundle" of primary factors. One unit of value-added product is simply the value of those factors used to produce one unit of crude. This assumption of a fixed coefficient does not mean that there must be fixed coefficients in the production of the value-added products; the proportions in which labor, capital, and so on, are employed can vary. For initial simplicity, refined products are combined into a homogeneous output—refined British thermal units (Btu's). Thus, crude oil can be considered in terms of unrefined Btu's, and the value-added product is the value added to those Btu's by refining. Domestic production of crude oil (unrefined Btu's) is vertically integrated.

In summary, the production function for refined Btu's can be described as functionally related to crude oil, labor, capital, and other inputs, where the inputs other than crude oil can be described as value-added product. As indicated, outlays spent on value-added product always yield the same bundle of inputs. For every outlay there is a corresponding output. In deriving the refined Btu marginal cost curves, the quadrant graph, Figure A-1, is adopted. Quadrant I describes the economic region of production for the production function $R = R(V,O)$ where V is value-added product, O is crude oil input, and R indicates maximum output of refined

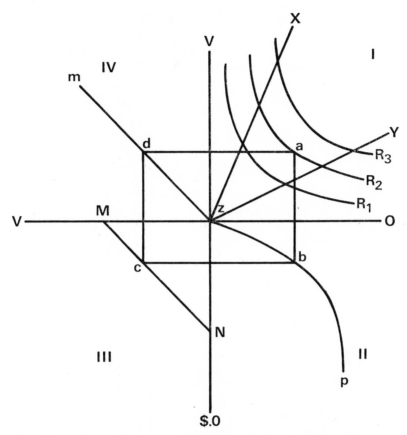

FIGURE A-1. Derivation of the Refined Btu Marginal Cost Curve

Btu's. The economic region is enclosed by the rays from the origin (Z) of Zx and Zy. Quadrant IV indicates the assumption of constant value-added product (ZZ) and quadrant III, the assumption of fixed factor prices (MN). Quadrant II indicates the cost value of the oil product. Shifts in curve ZP by virtue of changed factor prices could give substantially different results. For purposes of this analysis, these prices are assumed to remain unchanged. By connecting points a, b, c, and d, we can obtain the total cost curve for refined Btu's. To obtain the graph of the marginal cost, we can differentiate the total cost curve to yield the marginal cost curve of refined Btu's indicated in Figure A-2.

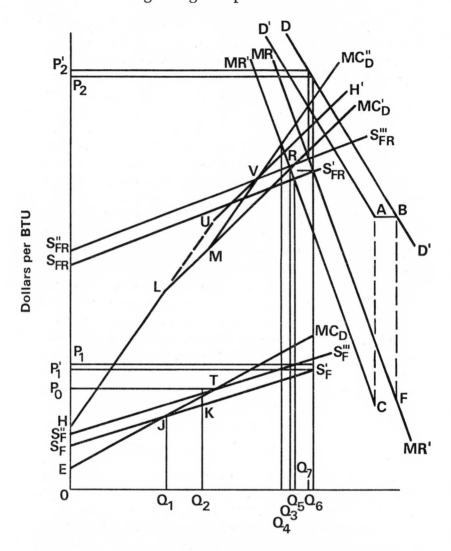

Quantities of Refined & Unrefined BTU's

FIGURE A-2. Partial Equilibrium of the Vertically Integrated Refined and Unrefined Btu Industry under Joint Quota and Tariff Policies

In Figure A-2, quantities of both crude oil and refined product measured in Btu equivalents are shown along the horizontal axis. The units are so chosen that one Btu equivalent unit of crude oil is required by domestic refiners to make one unit of refined product, also in Btu equivalent, as indicated by the fixed input coefficient derived from their production function.

The foreign supply curve of crude oil is $S_F S_F'$. This supply curve is drawn for a given exchange rate. It is defined here as the price of imports at the frontiers of the United States and thus includes cost of transporting crude oil to our frontiers. It is the c.i.f. (cost, insurance, and freight) price.

The foreign supply curve of refined product is $S_{FR} S_{FR}'$. The demand curve for refined product is DD', and the marginal revenue associated with this curve is $MRFMR'$. The supply curve of refined product requires special derivation. It is the vertical addition of the supply curve of crude oil and the supply curve of the refined Btu value added product. The domestic supply curve of crude oil is the marginal cost of producing crude oil and is EMC_D. Both domestic and foreign supply curves assume increasing costs of production. The foreign supply curve starts from a higher point on the vertical axis to reflect the tariff and costs of transportation from foreign areas. In the short run, with a fixed supply of tankers, an increase in imports would tend to raise freight costs.

In the absence of any tariff or quota, any extra crude oil beyond OQ_1 demanded by product refiners will be obtained by imports. Therefore, the crude oil supply curve facing refiners is EJS_F' with a kink at J. The supply curve of the refined Btu value added product is then added vertically to the curve EJS_F' to yield the supply curve of refined product $HLMC_D'$. Under nonrestrictive trade, domestic production of refined Btu's would be OQ_3, and total output would be OQ_6 (output at which marginal revenue equals marginal cost). Refined Btu imports would be $Q_3 Q_6$.

The actual policy imposed on the industry is that of two quotas, one on crude oil and the other on refined products. A quota on refined product shifts the demand curve facing domestic refined Btu producers. Assume that the quota is AB and that $D''A$ is parallel to DD'. Then the quota-distorted demand curve facing refined Btu producers is $D''ABD'$, and the quota-distorted marginal revenue curve is $MR''CABFMR'$. With no quota on crude oil, total output would be OQ_5 with crude oil imports of Q_1Q_5.

Now introduce a quota on crude oil of $JK = Q_1Q_2$. This quota will shift the crude oil supply curve facing refiners. To purchase more crude oil, refiners must pay a higher price than the import price to attract additional domestic supplies. With imports constrained to quota levels, the quota-distorted crude oil supply curve becomes $EJKIMC_D$. By adding it to the supply curve of the value added product, we obtain $HLM\ MC_D''$, the quota-distorted refined Btu supply curve. The intersection of this curve with the quota-distorted marginal revenue curve yields total output of OQ_4, resulting from both quotas combined. Note that these two quotas provide a lower total output of refined Btu's, but that with both quotas domestic output of crude oil *increases* from Q_1 to Q_4, minus Q_1Q_2. Output of refined Btu's under both quotas, however, *decreases*. This effect depends upon the size of the quota and the elasticity of the quota-distorted supply and demand curves. Under this system, the domestic producers reap the monopoly quota profits on both crude oil and refined Btu's.

Assume now that the government chooses to impose a lump-sum import fee, independent of import volume, on both crude oil and refined Btu's. The fees are to increase gradually to higher levels during a fixed period. Exemptions from fees, however, are allowed for preexisting quota volumes on both crude oil and refined Btu's. In turn, revenues from the fees are to be returned to the producers of both crude oil and refined Btu's in the form of energy research subsidies. Quota profits are to be phased out, and as previously noted, advance deposits of import fees are required prior to importing.

Recall that in the absence of quotas or tariffs, total output of refined Btu's is OQ_6, with OQ_3 as total domestic production of refined Btu's and Q_3Q_6 as imports of refined Btu's. The domestic output of refined Btu's also yields the demand for crude oil or unrefined Btu's. With no protectionism, imports of crude oil are equal to Q_1Q_3, and domestic crude oil production is OQ_1. Under these conditions, OP_1 and OP_2 are the nondistorted prices of crude oil and refined Btu's, respectively. The price that will be charged for a unit of value added by the refining industry, that is, for the value-added product, is P_1P_2. This price can be considered the effective price of refined Btu's as distinct from OP_2, the normal price.

Assume that a tariff on refined product only is imposed and that there are no quotas on crude oil. The tariff is reflected by the curve $S_{FR}''S_{FR}'''$. The imposition of a tariff causes an adjustment to the supply curve of refined Btu's equivalent to $HLMRS_{FR}'''$. This results in an increase in price to OP_2' and reduces consumption to OQ_7. The effective price of refined Btu's rises from P_1P_2 to P_1P_2'. The proportional increase in the effective price yields the effective protective rate of P_2P_2'/P_1P_1'. Now, in the absence of quotas, assume instead that the tariff is placed on crude oil imports as indicated by $S_F''S_F'''$. This has the effect of shifting the supply curve of crude oil facing refiners upwards from EJS_F' to ETS_F'''. From the viewpoint of refiners, a tariff on crude oil constitutes a tax on their input, and this tax raises their costs of production. The new supply curve of refined Btu's is then $HLUH'$.

If we simultaneously impose a nominal tariff on both crude oil and refined Btu's, the supply curve of refined Btu's is $HLUVS_{FR}'''$. This results in the same price for refined Btu's P_2P_2'. However, if the tariff on crude oil had been greater, the price differential would have been greater. The effective price changes from P_1P_2 to $P_1'P_2'$ and the effective protective rate of the tariffs would have been $P_2P_2' - P_1P_1'/P_1P_2$. The net positive or negative protective rate would hence depend upon whether P_2P_2' is greater or less than P_1P_1'.

Consider the situation in which a fixed volume of imports of both crude oil and products is exempt from tariffs. Beyond this fee-exempt volume, imports are subject to tariffs. The relevant refined Btu demand and marginal revenue again becomes DD' and $MRMR'$, as there are no volume constraints on imports. However, the former quota levels help determine the adjusted shapes of crude oil and refined Btu supply curves. Elimination of the quota does not completely eliminate the importer's cartel in that the total import volume of this government cartel is provided fee-exempt imports. Thus, we would expect that the demand curve would become more elastic over time as the number of effective potential entrants increases and as license fees become equalized for all firms. It is likely that to prevent this from occurring the former cartel members will set a price OP_0 without attracting new entry. This problem is analogous to that discussed in chapter 1. The entry-barring price may be set at levels lower than OP_1' and OP_2'. This was, in essence, the foundation of major oil industry support for a "rollback" of high crude and product prices in late 1973. The mutually agreed upon rollbacks tended to reduce the threat of potential entry while ensuring long-run dominance of the major member of the importers' cartel.

Ignoring these entry-forestalling price adjustments, the new fee-exempt crude oil supply curve is now given by $EJKITS_F'''$. With the size of the fee-exempt imports declining over time, the point J can be viewed as moving along the domestic marginal cost of the crude oil production curve to point T, where this curve intersects with the $S_F''S_F'''$ curve. In turn, as fee-exempt volumes decline the curve $S_F''S_F'''$ will shift upward to its permanent long-run level desired by the federal government. Because advance deposits are required, there is an implicit tariff on imports, and thus the curve $S_F''S_F'''$ shifts upward even more by an amount equivalent to the product of the import volumes, the license fee, and the rate of interest.

This change in the crude oil supply curve also changes the refined Btu supply curve. The supply curve of refined Btu's distorted by the new national security license fee becomes HLM-UVS_{FR}'''. Thus, the initial impact of imposing a joint system of fee-exempt and nonexempt imports to replace a joint quota system is to increase the effective price of refined Btu's and to increase imports of both crude oil and products. Depending on the increase in the level of the tariff and the elasticity of foreign supply, domestic production of crude oil could either increase, decrease, or remain unchanged. In the case illustrated here, domestic output decreases from its quota-program level. Only as fee-exempt quota level imports phase out and fees increase does domestic crude oil output begin to dominate the crude supply situation. Imports of refined Btu's will increase, depending on the level of the product tariff, the elasticity of product demand, and the elasticity of total domestic and foreign supply. In this case, the imports of refined Btu's actually *increase* along with increasing the price of refined products.

In the longer term, the revenues obtained from the national

security license fee program will be used to develop new resources of crude oil and natural gas. If these fees are provided directly to producers of crude oil, this plan will reduce the cost of production and result in a shift toward the right in the domestic marginal cost curves. This shift would result in a major substitution of domestic for foreign crude oil and products and would result in lower prices on both crude oil and its products.

However, the allocation of fees could become discriminatory. For example, if all fees are given only to domestic refiners, they could reduce the price of the value-added product and thereby reduce the total prices of refined products. Such a policy would reduce imports of refined Btu's while increasing the demand for both domestic and foreign crude oil. However, a superior advantage of this discriminatory policy toward refiners would be that it would create a relative advantage for domestic expansion of refining capacity over expansion in foreign locations. The allocation of research and development subsidies to refiners or producers would depend upon the productivity at the margin of these expenditures and hence the relative magnitudes of the shifts in marginal costs of refined Btu's over crude production.

So far in this appendix I have not mentioned the joint-product impact on natural gas marginal costs of the new fee system or the possibility of eliminating the intrastate advantage for natural gas. The interactions on natural gas marginal costs for movements along the crude oil cost curve, and for shifts in this curve as stimulated by quotas and/or tariffs, are analogous to that discussed in chapter 4. Reconstituting shifts in these curves on Figure A-2 would tend to greatly complicate the graph. However, we can consider the imposition of flexible federal price controls on crude oil. In this situation, we assume that the FEA exerts national pricing authority over all crude oil and sets domestic prices at a "target" level that is generally *below* the price of foreign imports of crude. Such a price is at OP_0 in Figure A-2, which approximates the point at which the foreign price is equal to the domestic price. With a domestic crude oil ceiling price, an increase in the tariff on imports will shift the foreign supply curve upward and induce the consumption of relatively more expensive imports. Thus, a ceiling crude oil price, for given demand conditions, can only act as an inducement to create a short-run price differential that increases profits of foreign suppliers and reduces incentive to expand domestic output.

If, however, the government decides to use national security import license revenues to subsidize domestic production, it can cause a shift toward the right in the marginal cost of domestic production (and hence a rightward shift in the marginal cost of natural gas). If compensating subsidies are made continuously as import tariffs rise, the government can reduce the potential negative impact of forced reliance on higher-cost imports. In the real world, adjustments are not as instantaneous as they are presumed to be here. Tariffs can be adjusted rapidly upward, but the only program of equivalent speed would be an outright cash subsidy to producers (or refiners). If the subsidy was earmarked for exploration research, the returns to this expenditure might take several years to influence the marginal cost of production. In the interim, import prices would increase and domestic output would remain static. Therefore, a federal program to impose ceiling prices at levels below the foreign price would have a negative short-run effect in the absence of any compensatory subsidy policy. If the domestic crude oil supply curve is inelastic and the foreign supply relatively elastic, it would require substantially greater compensating subsidies to reduce the cost burden of imports.

Glossary of Refining Terms

ALKYLATE. A synthetic gasoline of high octane number used in aviation and motor gasoline and produced from an olefin and an iso-paraffin.

ALKYLATION. A refinery process for chemically combining an iso-paraffin and an olefin in the presence of a catalyst. Sulfuric acid and hydro-fluoric acid are the most commonly used catalysts.

API GRAVITY. American Petroleum Institute gravity is an expression of the density or the weight of a unit volume of material when measured at a temperature of 60° Fahrenheit.

AROMATIC HYDROCARBONS. Hydrocarbons characterized by the presence of a six-membered, unsaturated ring of carbon atoms. Examples include benzene, toluene, and the xylenes.

BENZENE. A clear, colorless, extremely flammable liquid with a molecular weight of 78.11 found as a high-octane component of catalytic reformate. Used in organic synthesis and as a solvent.

BUTANE. A hydrocarbon of the paraffin series, consisting of four carbon atoms and ten hydrogen atoms. A naturally occurring component of crude oil and natural gas as produced at the well, it is a gas at room temperature and atmospheric pressure. Used in motor fuel, as petrochemical feedstocks, and as LPG (bottled gas).

BUTYLENE. A hydrocarbon of the olefin series, consisting of four carbon atoms and eight hydrogen atoms. It is a product of a cracking operation and a gas at ambient temperature and atmospheric pressure and may be used as a component of motor fuel, as feed to an alkylation unit, or in petrochemical operations.

CATALYST. A substance capable of changing the rate of a reaction without itself undergoing any net change.

CATALYTIC CRACKING UNIT. A refinery process unit that converts a fraction of petroleum with a high boiling range (gas oil) to gasoline, olefin feed for alkylation, distillate, fuel oil, and fuel gas by use of a catalyst and high temperature.

CATALYTIC REFORMING. A catalytic process used to improve the antiknock quality of low-octane gasoline by converting naphthenes (such as cyclohexane) and paraffins into higher-octane aromatics such as benzene, toluene, and the xylenes.

CETANE INDEX or CETANE NUMBER. A term indicating a quality of diesel fuel just as octane number indicates a quality of gasoline.

CONVERSION. The chemical change of one material into another through chemical processes such as cracking, polymerization, alkylation, hydrogenation, and isomerization.

CRUDE UNIT. The first processing equipment which crude oil reaches after it enters a refinery. The unit separates the crude oil into at least four different boiling range fractions: gasoline, distillate, gas oil, and topped crude.

CYCLONE SEPARATOR. A mechanical device for separating liquid or solid particles from a gas stream by use of centrifugal force.

DESULFURIZATION. The process of removing undesirable sulfur or sulfur compounds from petroleum products, usually by chemical or catalytic processes.

DISTILLATE. That portion of a liquid which is removed as a vapor and condensed during a distillation process. As fuel, distillates are generally within the 400° to 650° boiling range and include No. 1 and No. 2 fuel oil, diesel oil, and kerosine.

DISTILLATION. The general process of vaporizing liquids, such as crude oil or one of its fractions, in a closed vessel and collecting and condensing the vapors into liquids.

DOWNTIME. Time during which a machine, department, or refinery is inactive during normal operating hours.

EFFLUENT. Material discharged or emerging from a process or from a specific piece of equipment.

ELECTROSTATIC PRECIPITATOR. A device used to separate particulate materials from a vaporous stream. Separation is made by electrically charging the solid particles, which are then attracted to an electrode of the opposite charge while the vapors pass through without change. This device is commonly used to remove particulates from catalytic cracking unit flue gases.

FLUE GAS. The products of combustion consisting principally of nitrogen, steam, and carbon dioxide, with small amounts of other components such as oxygen and carbon monoxide.

FRACTIONS. Refiners' term for the portions of oils containing a number of hydrocarbon compounds within certain boiling ranges that are separated from other portions in fractional distillation. Fractions are distinguished from pure compounds, which have specific boiling temperatures, not a range.

FUEL OILS. Any liquid or liquefiable petroleum product burned for the generation of heat in a furnace or firebox or for the generation of power in an engine. Typical fuels include clean distillate fuel for home heating and higher-viscosity residual fuels for industrial furnaces.

GAS OIL. A petroleum product produced either from the distillation of crude oil or synthetically by a cracking process. Its boiling range may vary from 500° F to 1,100° F.

HEATING OILS. Trade term for the group of distillate fuel oils used in heating homes and buildings as distinguished from residual fuel oils which are used in fueling power installations.

HEAVY ENDS. The highest boiling portion of a gasoline or other petroleum oil.

HYDROCARBON. Any of a large class of organic compounds containing only carbon and hydrogen, including paraffins, olefins, acetylenes, alicyclics, and aromatic hydrocarbons. Crude oil, natural gas, coal, and bitumens are primarily hydrocarbons.

HYDROCRACKING. The cracking of a distillate or gas oil in the presence of a catalyst and hydrogen to form high-octane gasoline blending stocks.

HYDRODESULFURIZATION. The removal of sulfur from hydrocarbons by reaction with hydrogen in the presence of a catalyst.

HYDROFLUORIC ACID. A colorless compound of hydrogen and fluorine boiling at 67° F and soluble in all proportions in water. The water mixture is extremely corrosive to metals. Adequate safety precautions must be used when working with either liquid or vapor hydrofluoric acid. Its use in the oil industry is as a catalyst in alkylation units and in acidizing oil wells.

HYDROGEN SULFIDE. A poisonous, colorless, flammable gas which may be prepared by the direct combination of hydrogen and sulfur. Hydrogen sulfide can be reacted with caustic to form sodium sulfide or charged to a sulfur plant to produce sulfur. It is a component of sour crude oils.

HYDROTREATING. A treating process for the removal of sulfur or nitrogen from feedstocks by replacement with hydrogen.

INTERMEDIATE CRUDE OIL. A crude oil containing both naphthenes and paraffins. It is usually of moderate sulfur content and in the medium gravity range.

ISOBUTANE. A hydrocarbon containing four carbon atoms and ten hydrogen atoms like normal butane, but with a different arrangement of the molecular structure which results in different physical properties. Isobutane with olefins is the feed to an alkylation unit to produce high-octane gasoline.

ISOMERIZATION. A refining process which alters the fundamental arrangement of atoms in the molecule. It is used to convert normal butane into isobutane, an alkylation process feedstock, and normal pentane and hexane into isopentane and isohexane, high-octane gasoline components.

ISOOCTANE. A hydrocarbon composed of eight carbon atoms and eighteen hydrogen atoms, a liquid at normal temperatures, and a highly desirable component of gasoline. Although found in crude oil, its principal source is from synthetic processes such as alkylation.

LIQUEFIED NATURAL GAS (LNG). Natural gas which has been liquefied at a temperature of −258° F for ease of storage and transportation.

LIQUEFIED PETROLEUM GAS (LPG). As a rule, a mixture of natural and/or refinery gases compressed until it is a liquid and contained under pressure in steel cylinders. It is used as fuel for tractors, buses, trucks, and stationary engines; for domestic and industrial purposes; and for power generation where commercial natural gas is not available. New uses are constantly being found. A recently developed use of LPG as a direct quick-freezing agent in the frozen foods industry. It is also known and marketed as butane, propane, or bottled gas.

NAPHTHA. Liquid hydrocarbon fractions, generally boiling within the gasoline range, recovered by the distillation of crude petroleum. They are used as solvents, dry cleaning agents, and charge stocks to reforming units to make high-octane gasoline.

NAPHTHENIC CRUDE OIL. A crude oil that contains a large amount of naphtha compounds. It is a source of naphthenic lubricating oils. Its characteristics vary widely among the different producing fields.

NATURAL GAS LIQUIDS (NGL). A mixture of liquid hydrocarbons naturally occurring in suspension in natural gas and extracted by various means to yield a liquid product suitable for refinery and petrochemical feedstock.

OCTANE NUMBER. A term numerically indicating the relative antiknock value of a gasoline. It is based upon a comparison with the reference fuels isooctane (100 octane number) and normal heptane (0 octane number). The octane number of an unknown fuel is the percentage of volume of isooctane with normal heptane which matches the unknown fuel in knocking tendencies under a specified set of conditions.

OLEFINS. A class of unsaturated (hydrogen deficient) open-chain hydrocarbons of which butylene, ethylene, and propylene are examples. Propylenes and butylene olefins with isobutane are used in an alkylation unit to produce high-octane gasoline. Ethylene is the feedstock used by chemical plants to produce polyethylene plastic.

PARAFFIN. A white, tasteless, odorless, waxy substance obtained from some petroleum oils.

PARAFFINIC CRUDE OIL. A crude oil containing predominantly paraffinic hydrocarbons. Some types of this crude oil are used to produce high-quality motor oils.

PETROCHEMICAL FEEDSTOCK. A fraction of crude oil or hydrocarbons which is used as a charge to process units in the production of petroleum-based chemicals.

POUR POINT. The temperature at which an oil commences to flow under stated conditions; the lowest temperature at which an oil can be poured. It is reported in increments of 5° F.

PROPANE. A saturated hydrocarbon containing three carbon atoms and eight hydrogen atoms, gaseous at normal temperature and pressure but generally stored and transported as a liquid under pressure. It is used for domestic heating and cooking and for certain industrial purposes.

REFINERY POOL. The mixture obtained if all blending stocks for a given type of product were blended together in production ratio. The term is usually used in reference to motor gasoline octane rating.

RESEARCH OCTANE NUMBER (RON). An expression of the antiknock rating of a motor gasoline. It is accepted as the guide to the antiknock qualities of fuels when vehicles are operated under conditions associated with low engine speed.

RESIDUAL FUEL OILS. Topped crude petroleum or viscous residuums obtained in refinery operations. Commercial grades of burner fuel oils Nos. 5 and 6 are residual oils and include bunker fuels.

ROAD OCTANE. A numerical value based upon the relative antiknock performance in an automobile of a test gasoline as compared with specified reference fuels. Road octanes are determined by operating a car over a stretch of level road or on a chassis dynamometer under conditions simulating those encountered on the highway.

SOUR CRUDE. Crude oil which (1) is corrosive when heated, (2) evolves significant amounts of hydrogen sulfide upon distillation, or (3) produces light fractions which require sweetening. Sour crudes usually, but not necessarily, have high sulfur content. Most West Texas and Middle East crudes are sour crudes.

STRAIGHT-RUN DISTILLATE. The fraction of crude oil which boils between 400° F and 650° F, it is primarily sold as kerosine, heating oil (No. 1 and No. 2 fuel oil), and diesel fuel.

STRAIGHT-RUN GASOLINE. A low-boiling fraction of crude which, after further processing, is used as a finished motor gasoline blending stock.

SUBSTITUTE NATURAL GAS (SNG). A gas having chemical properties and uses similar to those of natural gas. It is manufacturable from petroleum liquids, coal, and other hydrocarbons.

SULFURIC ACID. A heavy, corrosive, oily strong acid that is colorless when pure and is a vigorous oxidizing and dehydrating agent. Composed of sulfur, oxygen, and hydrogen, it is used in the chemical refining of petroleum products as one of the two commonly used catalysts for alkylation units.

SWEET CRUDE OIL. A crude oil having so little sulfur that it requires no special treatment for the removal of sulfur compounds.

TETRAETHYL LEAD (TEL). An organic lead compound which usually is added in concentrations up to three grams per gallon to motor and aviation gasoline to increase the antiknock properties of the fuel.

TOLUENE. An aromatic solvent having a specific gravity ranging between 0.8690 and 0.8730. It has many chemical uses and may be a component of aviation gasoline or motor gasoline.

TOPPED (REDUCED) CRUDE. A residual product remaining after the removal, by distillation or other processing means, of an appreciable quantity of the more volatile components of crude petroleum.

TOTAL OXYGEN DEMAND (TOD). For aqueous effluents, the sum of chemical and biological oxygen demand.

VACUUM UNIT. A unit operated below atmospheric pressure which allows vaporization of more of the heavier gas oil molecules from the crude residue without thermal disintegration of the molecules.

VAPOR RECOVERY SYSTEM. A system for controlling hydrocarbon vapor losses from a refinery.

VISBREAKING. Lowering or breaking the viscosity of residuum by cracking at relatively low temperatures.

VOLATILITY. That property of a liquid which denotes its tendency to vaporize.

Bibliography

Adams, F. G., and Griffin, J. M. 1969. "An Economic Model of the U.S. Petroleum Refining Industry." In *Essays in Industrial Economics*, ed. L. R. Klein, Philadelphia: Economic Research Unit, University of Pennsylvania.

Adelman, M. A. 1962. *The Supply and Price of Natural Gas.* Oxford: Basil Blackwell.

―――. 1964a. "Efficiency of Resource Use in Crude Petroleum." *Southern Economic Journal* 31: 300–310.

―――. 1964b. "Oil Prices in the Long Run, 1963–1975." *Journal of Business* 37 (April): 143–161.

―――. 1964c. "The World Oil Outlook." In *Natural Resources and International Development*, ed. Marion Clawson. Baltimore: The Johns Hopkins Press.

―――. 1966. "American Coal in Western Europe." *Journal of Industrial Economics* 19:199–211.

―――. 1969. "Comment on the 'H' Concentration Measure as a Numbers Equivalent." *Review of Economics and Statistics* 51:199–201.

―――. 1970. "World Oil and the Theory of Industrial Organization." *Industrial Organization and Economic Development*, ed. J. N. Markham and Gustav F. Paparek. New York: Houghton Mifflin Co.

―――. 1972. *The World Petroleum Market.* Baltimore: The Johns Hopkins Press.

―――. 1973. "Is Oil Shortage Real?" *Foreign Policy* 9 (Winter).

Allvine, F. C., and Patterson, J. M. 1972. *Competition Ltd.: The Marketing of Gasoline.* Bloomington: Indiana University Press.

American Petroleum Institute. Annual, 1959–1975. *Reserves of Crude Oil, Natural Gas Liquids and Natural Gas in the United States and Canada and United States Productive Capacity.* Vols. 13–29. Washington, D.C.: The Institute, Division of Statistics.

————. 1970. *Petroleum Facts and Figures.* Washington, D.C.: The Institute, Division of Statistics.

Areskoug, K. 1971. "U.S. Oil Import Quotas and Natural Income." *Southern Economic Journal* 37:307–317.

Avramides, A., and Cross, J. 1973. "NPC Analysis of Oil and Gas Supply." *Energy Modeling*, ed. Milton F. Searl. Washington, D.C.: Resources for the Future.

Bain, J. S. 1956. *Barriers to New Competition.* Cambridge, Mass.: Harvard University Press.

Baldwin, R. E. 1970. *Nontariff Distortions of International Trade.* Washington, D.C.: The Brookings Institution.

Balestra, P. 1967. *The Demand for Natural Gas in the United States.* Amsterdam: North-Holland, Inc.

Basevi, G. 1966. "The U.S. Tariff Structure: Estimates of Effective Rates of Protection of U.S. Industries and Industrial Labor." *Review of Economics and Statistics* 48:147–160.

Bhagwati, J. 1969. *Trade, Tariffs and Growth.* Cambridge, Mass.: The M.I.T. Press.

Biesiot, P. G., Jr. 1970. "Concentration and Trends in the California Petroleum Industry." Ph.D. diss., University of Southern California (Ann Arbor: University Microfilms).

Boatwright, J. B. 1971. "An Evaluation of the Mandatory Oil Import Program and Its Effects on the American Petroleum Industry. Ph.D. diss., American University (Ann Arbor: University Microfilms).

Boulding, K. E. 1966. *Economic Analysis.* 4th ed. New York: Harper and Row.

Bradley, P. G. 1967. *The Economics of Crude Petroleum Production.* Amsterdam: North-Holland Co.

Brown, K., ed. 1972. *Regulation of the Natural Gas Producing Industry.* Baltimore: The Johns Hopkins Press.

Burns, A. R. 1958. *The Decline of Competition.* New York: Fordham University Press.

Burrows, T., and Domencich, T. A. 1970. *An Analysis of the U.S. Oil Import Quota.* Lexington, Mass.: Lexington Books.

Carlson, S. 1965. *A Study in the Pure Theory of Production.* New York: Agustus Kelley, Inc.

Chamberlin, E. H. 1951. *The Theory of Monopolistic Competition.* 6th ed. Cambridge, Mass.: Harvard University Press.

Comanor, W. S. 1966. "Competition and the Performance of the Midwestern Coal Industry." *Journal of Industrial Economics* 19:212–225.

Cookenboo, L. 1955. *Crude Oil Pipelines and Competition in the Oil Industry.* Cambridge, Mass.: Harvard University Press.

Copp, E. A. 1974*a*. "Technical Change and Petroleum Drilling Costs." *Land Economics,* May.

————. 1974*b*. "Government Regulation and Industry Structure in Petroleum Refining: An Anatomy of Policy Failure." Ph.D. diss., Texas A&M University (Ann Arbor: University Microfilms).

———. 1975. "Petroleum Economics under OPEC Dominated Supply and Price." Seminar, April 17. Salomon Brothers, New York.

———. 1976. "Technical Change and Petroleum Drilling Costs: Reply." *Land Economics*, May.

———, and Garrett, J. 1975. "World Petroleum Reserves versus World Petroleum Supply." Paper presented at Ninth World Petroleum Congress, May, 1975, Tokyo.

———, and McRae, E. 1974. "A Linear Programming Model of Emergency Oil Storage Alternatives." In *Energy Policy Evaluation*, ed. Dilipe Limaye. Lexington, Mass.: Lexington Books.

———, and Miloy, J. 1970. *Economic Impact Analysis of Texas Marine Resources and Industries*. College Station: Texas A&M University, National Science Foundation Sea Grant Program.

Corden, W. M. 1971. *The Theory of Protection*. Oxford: Clarendon Press.

Cowan, E. 1975. "U.S. Strategy to Tempt OPEC Members to Cut Oil Prices is Urged by Professor," *New York Times*, Sept. 15, p. L-27.

Cram, I. H., ed. 1971. *Future Petroleum Provinces of the United States*, American Association of Petroleum Geologists Memoir 15, vol. 1. Tulsa, Okla.

Dam, K. W. 1971. "Implementation of Import Quotas: The Case for Oil." *Journal of Law and Economics* 14:1–60.

de Chazeau, M. G., and Kahn, A. E. 1959. *Integration and Competition in the Petroleum Industry*. New Haven: Yale University Press.

Dixon, O. F. 1964. "Gasoline Marketing in the United States: The First Fifty Years." *Journal of Industrial Economics* 13:23–42.

Edwards, C. 1974. "Exchangeable Coupon Gas Rationing." *Agricultural Economic Research* 26, no. 3 (July).

Enos, J. L. 1962. *Petroleum Progress and Profits: A History of Process Innovation*. Cambridge, Mass.: The M.I.T. Press.

Erickson, E. W. 1968. "Economic Incentives, Industrial Structure and the Supply of Crude Oil Discoveries in the U.S., 1946–58–59." Ph.D. diss., Vanderbilt University.

———, and Spann, R. M. 1971. "Supply Response in a Regulated Industry: The Case of Natural Gas." *Bell Journal of Economics and Management Science* 2:94–121.

———, and ———. 1973. "Joint Costs and Separability in Oil and Gas Exploration." In *Energy Modeling*, ed. Milton F. Searl, Washington, D.C.: Resources for the Future.

Fama, F. 1972. "The Number of Firms and Competition." *American Economic Review* 62:670–674.

Fellner, W. 1958. "The Influences of Market Structure on Technological Progress." In *Readings in Industrial Organization and Public Policy*, ed. R. B. Heflebower and G. W. Stocking. Homewood, Ill.: Richard D. Irwin.

Fisher, F. 1964. *Supply and Costs in the U.S. Petroleum Industry: Two Econometric Studies.* Baltimore: Johns Hopkins Press.

Ford Foundation. 1974. *Exploring Energy Choices.* Washington, D.C.: Ford Foundation Energy Policy Project.

Frank, H. J. 1966. *Crude Oil Prices in the Middle East: A Study in Oligopolistic Behavior.* Washington, D.C.: Frederick A. Praeger.

Frankel, P. H. 1946. *Essentials of Petroleum,* London: Chapman and Hall.

————, and Newton, W. L. 1963. "Recent Development in the Economics of Petroleum Refining." In *Proceedings of the Fifth Petroleum Congress,* June, pp. 23–26.

Friedman, M., and Kuznets, S. 1954. *Income from Independent Professional Practice.* New York: National Bureau of Economic Research.

Galal, M. B. 1970. "An Equilibrium Analysis of the American Crude Oil Industry." Ph.D. diss., Rutgers University (Ann Arbor: University Microfilms).

Gonzalez, R. J. 1968. "Interfuel Competition for Future Energy Markets." *Journal of the Institute of Petroleum* 154:177–181.

Gordon, R. L. 1970. *The Evaluation of Energy Policy in Western Europe.* Washington, D.C.: Praeger Publishers.

Gort, M. 1963. "Analysis of Stability and Change in Market Shares." *Journal of Political Economy,* February, pp. 51–63.

Greenhut, M. L. 1970. *The Theory of the Firm in Economic Space.* New York: Meredith Corporation.

Griffin, J. M. 1971. *Capacity Measurement in Petroleum Refining.* Lexington, Mass.: Lexington Books.

————. 1972. "An Economic Measure of Capacity in a Joint Product, Multi-Process Industry." *Journal of Political Economy,* July/August.

Grossack, I. M. 1972. "The Concept and Measurement of Permanent Industrial Concentration." *Journal of Political Economy,* July/August, pp. 745–760.

Grubel, H. G. 1971. *Effective Tariff Protection.* Geneva: Graduate Institute of International Studies.

Hahn, F. H. 1955. "Excess Capacity and Imperfect Competition." *Oxford Economic Papers* 7:230–240.

Hamilton, D. C. 1958. *Competition in Oil: The Gulf Coast Refinery Market, 1925–1950.* Cambridge, Mass.: Harvard University Press.

Harrod, R. F. 1952. *Economic Essays.* New York: Harcourt Brace.

Hart, P. E. 1971. "Entropy and Other Measures of Concentration." *Journal of the Royal Statistical Society,* series A, 134:100–109.

Hartshorn, J. E. 1967. *Politics and World Oil Economics.* Washington, D.C.: Frederick A. Praeger.

Hawkins, C. A. 1969. *The Field Price Regulation of Natural Gas.* Tallahassee: Florida State University Press.

Hay, G. 1971. "Import Controls on Foreign Oil: Tariff or Quota?" *American Economic Review*, September, pp. 688–691.

Henderson, J. M., and Quandt, R. E. 1958. *Microeconomic Theory*. New York: McGraw-Hill Book Co.

Herfindahl, O. C. 1950. "Concentration in the Steel Industry." Ph.D. diss., Columbia University.

Heuser, H. 1938. *Control of International Trade*. Philadelphia: P. Blackiston's & Sons.

Hicks, J. R. 1954. "The Process of Imperfect Competition." *Oxford Economic Papers* 6:41–54.

Horvath, J. 1970. "Suggestion for a Comprehensive Measure of Concentration." *Southern Economic Journal* 36:446–452.

Houthakker, H. S. 1970. *Consumer Demand in the United States*. Cambridge: The University Press.

———, and Verleger, P. 1973. "The Demand for Gasoline: A Mixed Crossectional and Time Series Analysis." Manuscript in Ford Foundation Energy Policy Project, Washington, D.C.

Hudson Institute. 1974. *Policy Analysis for Coal Development at a Wartime Urgency Level, to Meet the Goals of Project Independence*. Washington, D.C.: Department of the Interior, Office of Coal Research.

Irving, R. H., Jr., and Draper, V. R. 1958. *Accounting Practices in the Petroleum Industry*. New York: The Ronald Press Co.

Isard, Walter. 1972. *Location and the Space Economy*. Cambridge, Mass.: The M.I.T. Press.

Kaldor, N. 1952. "Market Imperfection and Excess Capacity." In *Readings in Price Theory*, ed. G. J. Stigler and K. E. Boulding. Homewood, Ill.: Richard D. Irwin.

Kamien, M. I., and Swartz, N. L. 1972. "Uncertain Entry and Excess Capacity." *American Economic Review* 62:918–927.

Karg, R. L. 1970. "A Theory of Crude Oil Prices: A Study of Vertical Integration and Percentage Depletion Allowance." Ph.D. diss., Stanford University (Ann Arbor: University Microfilms).

Kemnitzer, W. J. 1938. *Rebirth of Monopoly: A Critical Analysis of Economic Conduct in the Petroleum Industry of the United States*. New York: The Oxford Company.

Khazzoom, D. J. 1971. "The FPC's Staff's Econometric Model of Natural Gas Supply in the United States." *Bell Journal of Economics and Management Science* 2:51–93.

Kindleberger, C. P. 1969. *International Economics*. Homewood, Ill.: Richard D. Irwin.

Klebanoff, S. 1974. *Middle East Oil and U.S. Foreign Policy*. New York: Praeger Publishers.

Lanzillotti, R. F. 1957. "Competitive Price Leadership: A Critique of

Price Leadership Models." *Review of Economics and Statistics* 39:24–39.

Larson, G. E., ed. 1967. *Natural Gas, Coal, and Ground Water.* Western Resource Papers. Boulder, Colo.: Western Resources Press.

Leeston, A. M.; Crichton, J. A.; and Jacobs, J. C. 1963. *The Dynamic Natural Gas Industry.* Norman: University of Oklahoma Press.

Lichthblau, J. 1964. *The Economics and Politics of the U.S. Oil Imports.* New York: Petroleum Industry Research Foundation.

Longrigg, S. H. 1968. *Oil in the Middle East.* London: Oxford University Press.

Lovejoy, W. F., and Homan, P. T. 1967. *Economic Aspects of Oil Conservation Regulation.* Baltimore: The Johns Hopkins Press.

Lubell, H. 1963. *Middle East Oil Crisis and Western Europe's Energy Supplies.* Baltimore: The Johns Hopkins Press.

Lundberg Survey, Inc. 1975. *Lundberg Letter* 2, no. 17 (Feb. 28); no. 28 (May 16); no. 32 (June 13); no. 34 (June 27).

Lydall, H. F. 1955. Conditions of New Entry and the Theory of Price." *Oxford Economic Papers* 7:300–311.

MacAvoy, P. W. 1971. "The Regulation-Induced Shortage of Natural Gas." *Journal of Law and Economics* 14:167–199.

———, and Pindyck, R. S. 1973. "Alternative Regulatory Policies for Dealing with the Natural Gas Shortage." *Bell Journal of Economics and Management Science* 4:454–498.

McClean, J. G., and Haigh, R. W. 1954. *The Growth of Integrated Oil Companies.* Boston: The Plimpton Press.

McDonald, S. 1963. *Federal Tax Treatment of Income from Oil and Gas.* Baltimore: The Johns Hopkins Press.

———. 1971. *Petroleum Conservation in the United States: An Economic Analysis.* Baltimore: The Johns Hopkins Press.

Machlup, F. 1952. *The Economics of Sellers Competition.* Baltimore: The Johns Hopkins Press.

McKie, J. 1960. "Market Structure and Uncertainty in Oil and Gas Exploration." *Quarterly Journal of Economics* 74:543–570.

———. 1972. "Balancing Supply and Demand of Oil." In *Proceedings of the Rocky Mountain Petroleum Economics Institute.* Denver: University of Denver.

Manes, R. P. 1961. "The Effects of United States Oil Import Policy on the Petroleum Industry." Ph.D. diss., Purdue University (Ann Arbor: University Microfilms).

———. 1963. "Import Quotas, Prices and Profits in the Oil Industry." *Southern Economic Journal* 30:13–24.

Manne, A. 1951. "Oil Refining: Cross Elasticities of Supply." *Quarterly Journal of Economics* 65:214–236.

———. 1956. *Scheduling of Petroleum Refinery Operations.* Cambridge, Mass.: Harvard University Press.

————. 1958. "A Linear Programming Model of the U.S. Petroleum Refining Industry." *Econometrica* 26:67–106.

Markham, J. N. 1951. "The Nature and Significance of Price Leadership." *American Economic Review* 41:891–905.

Marshall, A. 1920. *Principles of Economics.* 8th ed. Cambridge: The University Press.

Mead, W. J., and Sorensen, P. 1971. "A National Defense Petroleum Reserve Alternative to Oil Import Quotas." *Land Economics* 68:211–224.

Megill, R. E. 1971. *An Introduction to Exploration Economics.* Tulsa: The Petroleum Publishing Co.

Meloe, T. 1966. "United States Control of Petroleum Imports." Ph.D. diss., Columbia University (Ann Arbor: University Microfilms).

Middle East Economic Digest Ltd. 1975. "Vast Spending is Rapidly Reducing OPEC Surpluses." *Middle East Economic Digest* 19, no. 46 (Nov. 14).

Middle East Research and Publishing Center. 1973–1974. *Middle East Economic Survey* 16, nos. 1–52; 17, nos. 1–52.

Mikdashi, Z. M.; Cleland, S.; and Seymour, I., eds. 1970. *Continuity and Change in the World Oil Industry.* Beirut: Middle East Research and Publishing Center.

Miller, R. A. 1967. Marginal Concentration and Industrial Profit Rates." *Southern Economic Journal* 4:254–268.

National Academy of Sciences, National Research Council. 1975. *Mineral Resources and the Environment.* Washington, D.C.

National Petroleum Council. 1949. *A National Oil Policy for the United States.* Washington, D.C.

————. 1967. *Impact of New Technology on U.S. Petroleum Industry, 1945–1965.* Washington, D.C.

————. 1970. *Future Petroleum Provinces of the United States.* Washington, D.C.

————. 1972. *United States Energy Outlook: A Summary Report.* Washington, D.C.

————. 1973*a*. *Factors Affecting U.S. Petroleum Refining.* Washington, D.C.

————. 1973*b*. *U.S. Energy Outlook, Oil and Gas Availability.* Washington, D.C.

National Petroleum Refiners Association. 1973. *U.S. Domestic Petroleum Refining Industry's Capability to Process Sweet/Sour Crude.* Special Report No. 3. Washington, D.C.

Neisser, H. P. 1943. "Theoretical Aspects of Rationing." *Quarterly Journal of Economics* 57:378–397.

Nelson, W. L. 1941. *Petroleum Refinery Engineering.* New York: Clarendon Press.

———. 1974. "Tanker Transportation Costs Decline." *Oil and Gas Journal*, June 17, pp. 67–68.

Neuner, E. J. 1960. *The Natural Gas Industry*. Norman: University of Oklahoma Press.

Ophir, T. 1969. "The Interaction of Tariffs and Quotas." *American Economic Review*, December, pp. 1002–1005.

Organization for Economic Cooperation and Development (OECD). 1966. *Energy Policy*. Paris.

———. 1975. *Economic Outlook* 17 (July).

Peterson, W. H. 1959. *The Question of Governmental Oil Import Regulations*. Washington, D.C.: American Enterprise Association.

Petroleum Times. 1975. "Further Gloom for Tanker Owners." London, May 7.

Phlips, L. 1972. "A Dynamic Version of the Linear Expenditure Model." *Review of Economics and Statistics* 54:450–488.

Pollack, G. A. 1974. "Economy and Politics of Oil: Impact on the World Monetary System." Paper presented to Council on Foreign Relations, November 14, New York.

Pollack, R. A. 1970. "Habit Formation and Dynamic Demand Functions." *Journal of Political Economy* 78:745–763.

Potential Gas Committee. 1973. *Potential Supply of Natural Gas in the United States*. Golden: Colorado School of Mines.

Preston, Ross. 1973. *The Warton Long Term and Industry Model of the U.S. Economy*. Philadelphia: University of Pennsylvania Press.

Raciti, Sebastian. 1958. *The Oil Import Problem*. New York: Fordham University Press.

Ramsey, J., et al. 1974. "An Analysis of the Private and Commercial Demand for Gasoline." Manuscript, Department of Economics, Michigan State University.

Rooney, R. F. 1970. "Taxation and Regulation of the Domestic Crude Oil Industry." Ph.D. diss. (Ann Arbor: University Microfilms).

Rosenbluth, G., ed. 1955. *Business Concentration and Price Policy*. Princeton: Princeton University Press.

Rouhani, F. 1971. *A History of OPEC*. Washington, D.C.: Praeger Publishers.

Ruffin, R. J. 1969. "Tariffs, Intermediate Goods and Domestic Protection." *American Economic Review* 59:261–269.

Salter, W. E. G. 1969. *Productivity and Technical Change*. Cambridge: The University Press.

Saving, T. R. 1961. "Estimation of the Optimal Size of Plant by the Survivor Technique." *Quarterly Journal of Economics*, November, pp. 200–231.

Schurr, S. H. 1971. *Middle Eastern Oil and the Western World: Prospects and Problems*. New York: American Elsevier.

Searl, M., ed. 1973. *Energy Modeling*. Washington, D.C.: Resources for the Future.

Shaffer, E. H. 1968. *The Oil Import Program of the United States*. New York: Frederick Praeger.

Stigler, G. J. 1947. *The Theory of Price*. New York: MacMillan Co.

―――. 1968. *The Organization of Industry*. Homewood, Ill.: Richard D. Irwin, Inc.

―――. 1971. "The Theory of Regulation." *Bell Journal of Economics and Management Science* 2:3–21.

Stocking, G. 1970. *Middle East Oil*. Nashville, Tenn.: Vanderbilt University Press.

Swan, P. L. 1970. "Market Structure and Technological Progress: The Influence of Monopoly on Product Innovation." *Quarterly Journal of Economics*, November, pp. 627–637.

Sylos-Labini, P. 1962. *Oligopoly and Technical Progress*. Cambridge, Mass.: Harvard University Press.

Tanzer, M. 1964. *The Political Economy of International Oil and the Underdeveloped Countries*. Boston: Beacon Press.

Taylor, L. D. 1972. "On the Estimation of Dynamic Demand Functions." *Review of Economics and Statistics* 54:459–465.

Thorp, W. L. 1960. "Trade Barriers and National Security." *American Economic Review* 50:433–442.

Tobin, J. 1952. "A Survey on the Theory of Rationing." *Econometrica* 20:521–553.

U.S. Bureau of Mines. Annual, 1948–1961. *Petroleum Refineries, Including Cracking Plants, in the United States, January 1*. Information Circulars 7483, 7537, 7578, 7613, 7646, 7667, 7693, 7724, 7761, 7815, 7867, 7937, 8009, 8062.

―――. Annual, 1962–1975. *Petroleum Refineries in the United States and Puerto Rico*. Mineral Industry Surveys.

U.S. Congress, House. 1953. *Statement Relative to an Agreement between United States and Venezuela. Message from the President of the United States*. 83d Cong., 1st sess., House Doc. No. 43.

―――, Select Committee on Small Business, Subcommittee on Oil Imports. 1950. *Effects of Foreign Oil Imports on Independent Domestic Producers*. 81st Cong., 2d sess., House Report No. 2344.

―――, ―――, Subcommittee on Special Small Business Problems. 1970. *The Impact of the Energy and Fuel Crisis on Small Business*. 91st Cong., 2d sess., Oct. 6–8.

―――, ―――, ―――. 1971. *Concentration by Competing Raw Fuel Industries in the Energy Market and Its Impact on Small Business*. 92d Cong., 1st sess., July 12–22.

U.S. Congress, Senate, Special Committee Investigating Petroleum Resources. 1945. *American Petroleum Interests in Foreign Countries:*

Hearings Pursuant to S. Res. 36. Testimony of Charles Rayner. 79th Cong., 1st sess.

U.S. Council on Environmental Quality. 1973. *Coal Surface Mining and Reclamation: An Environmental and Economic Assessment of Alternatives.* Washington, D.C.: Government Printing Office.

U.S. Department of the Interior. 1961. Oil Import Regulation 1 (Revision 2), Amendment 6, March 8.

———. 1966. Oil Import Regulation (Revision 4), Amendment 8, March 28.

———. 1967. *Increased Petroleum Product Shipments for Puerto Rico Approved.* December.

———. 1968. News release, Feb. 14.

U.S. Department of State. 1950. *A Statement of Principles for Economic Cooperation.* Washington, D.C.: Government Printing Office.

U.S. Department of the Treasury. 1973. "Statement by William E. Simon on the Oil Import Program," *U.S. Department of the Treasury News,* April 18.

U.S. Federal Energy Administration. 1974. *Project Independence: A Summary.* Washington, D.C.: Government Printing Office.

U.S. Federal Power Commission. 1971. *The 1970 National Power Survey.* Washington, D.C.: Government Printing Office.

———. 1972. *Statistics of Publicly Owned Electric Utilities in the United States.* Washington, D.C.: Government Printing Office.

———. 1973. *FPC News,* May.

———. 1974. "Just and Reasonable Rates for Sales of Natural Gas from Wells Commenced On or After January 1, 1973, and New Dedications of Natural Gas to Interstate Commerce On or After January 1, 1973." Docket No. R-389-B, Opinion No. 699-H, December 4.

———. 1975a. "Advance Payment Status Survey Data as of August 31, 1974." *FPC News* 8, no. 29 (July 18).

———. 1975b. "Order Issuing Staff Rate Recommendations and Prescribing Further Procedures." Docket No. RM 75-14, Opinion No. 749, December 31.

U.S. Federal Trade Commission. 1952. *The International Petroleum Cartel: Staff Report.* Washington, D.C.: Government Printing Office.

U.S. Geological Survey. 1975. *Geological Estimates of Undiscovered Recoverable Oil and Gas Resources in the United States.* Circular 725.

U.S. Office of Defense Mobilization. 1955. Press release, Aug. 8.

———. 1956. Staff memorandum on oil imports.

U.S. Office of Oil and Gas. 1965. *An Appraisal of the Petroleum Industry of the United States.* Washington, D.C.: Government Printing Office.

U.S. Office of the President. 1959. *Mandatory Oil Import Program.* Presidential Proclamation 3279.

———. 1962. Presidential Proclamation 3509.

————. 1967*a*. *Adjusting Imports of Petroleum and Petroleum Products.* Modifying Proclamation 3279.

————. 1967*b*. Presidential Proclamation 3794.

————. 1967*c*. Presidential Proclamation 3820.

————. 1973. "New License Fee Program." Presidential release to U.S. Treasury, April 18.

————, Cabinet Task Force on Oil Import Control. 1971. *The Oil Import Question: A Report on the Relationship of Oil Imports to the National Security.* Washington, D.C.: Government Printing Office.

————, Presidential Advisory Committee on Energy Supplies and Resources Policy, Special Committee to Investigate Crude Oil Imports. 1957. *Petroleum Imports: Report to the President of the United States.* Washington, D.C.: Government Printing Office.

————, President's Materials Policy Commission. 1952. *Resources for Freedom*, vol. 1, *Foundations for Growth and Security: Report to the President.* Washington, D.C.: Government Printing Office.

Van Meurs, A. P. H. 1971. *Petroleum Economics and Offshore Mining Legislation.* Amsterdam: Elsevier Publishing Co.

Verleger, P. 1973. "An Econometric Analysis of the Relationships between Macroeconomic Activity and United States Energy Consumption." In *Energy Modeling*, ed. Milton F. Searl. Washington, D.C.: Resources for the Future.

Weiss, L. W. 1964. "The Survival Technique and the Extent of Suboptimal Capacity." *Southern Economic Journal*, July, pp. 246–261.

Wells, D. A. 1974. *Saudi Arabian Revenues and Expenditures.* Washington, D.C.: Resources for the Future.

Wellisz, S. H. 1963. "Regulation of Natural Gas Pipeline Companies." *Journal of Political Economy* 71:28–43.

Williamson, O. E. 1969. "Economies as an Antitrust Defense: Reply." *American Economic Review* 59:954–959.

Zannetos, Z. S. 1966. *The Theory of Oil Tankship Rates.* Cambridge, Mass.: The M.I.T. Press.

Zimmerman, E. W. 1957. *Conservation in the Production of Petroleum.* New Haven: Yale University Press.

Index